JANE AUSTEN & CHARLES DARWIN

For K

Jane Austen & Charles Darwin
Naturalists and Novelists

PETER W. GRAHAM
Virginia Polytechnic Institute and State University, USA

LONDON AND NEW YORK

First published 2008 by Ashgate Publishing

2 Park Square, Milton Park, Abingdon, Oxon OX14 4RN
711 Third Avenue, New York, NY 10017, USA

Routledge is an imprint of the Taylor & Francis Group, an informa business

First issued in paperback 2016

Copyright © Peter W. Graham 2008

Peter W. Graham has asserted his moral right under the Copyright, Designs and Patents Act, 1988, to be identified as the author of this work.

All rights reserved. No part of this book may be reprinted or reproduced or utilised in any form or by any electronic, mechanical, or other means, now known or hereafter invented, including photocopying and recording, or in any information storage or retrieval system, without permission in writing from the publishers.

Notice:
Product or corporate names may be trademarks or registered trademarks, and are used only for identification and explanation without intent to infringe.

British Library Cataloguing in Publication Data
Graham, Peter W., 1951–
   Jane Austen & Charles Darwin: naturalists and novelists. – (The nineteenth century series)
   1. Austen, Jane, 1775–1817 2. Darwin, Charles, 1809–1882
   3. Empiricism in literature
   I. Title
   823.7

Library of Congress Cataloging-in-Publication Data
Graham, Peter W., 1951–
   Jane Austen & Charles Darwin: naturalists and novelists / Peter W. Graham.
       p. cm. — (The nineteenth century series)
   Includes bibliographical references.
   ISBN 978-0-7546-5851-1 (alk. paper)
   1. Austen, Jane, 1775–1817. 2. Darwin, Charles, 1809–1882. 3. Empiricism in literature.
I. Title. II. Title: Jane Austen and Charles Darwin.

PR4036.G73 2008
823'.7—dc22
                                                                                    2007020236

ISBN 13: 978-0-7546-5851-1 (hbk)
ISBN 13: 978-1-138-26535-6 (pbk)

Contents

List of Tables and Abbreviations		*vii*
General Editors' Preface		*ix*
Introduction and Acknowledgments		xi
1	"3 or 4 Families in a Country Village," or Naturalists, Novelists, Empiricists, and Serendipidists	1
2	"An Entangled Bank," or Sibling Development in a Family Ecosystem	47
3	"Marry—Mary—Marry"	87
4	Variations on Variation	133
Select Bibliography		*183*
Index		*191*

List of Tables and Abbreviations

Tables

2.1   Sibling Groups in Jane Austen's Six Novels   59

2.2   A Taxonomy of Austenworld Sibling Configurations   60

Abbreviations

A   *The Autobiography of Charles Darwin*
CCD   *The Correspondence of Charles Darwin*
CDPP *Charles Darwin: The Power of Place*
CDV   *Charles Darwin: Voyaging*
DM   *The Descent of Man*
E   *Emma*
ED   *Erasmus Darwin*
EE   *The Expression of the Emotions in Man and Animals*
FO   *The Fertilization of Orchids by Insects*
JAL   *Jane Austen's Letters*
JR   *Journal of Researches*
MP   *Mansfield Park*
MW   *Minor Works*
NA   *Northanger Abbey*
OS   *On the Origin of Species*
P   *Persuasion*
PP   *Pride and Prejudice*
SS   *Sense and Sensibility*

The Nineteenth Century Series
General Editors' Preface

The aim of the series is to reflect, develop and extend the great burgeoning of interest in the nineteenth century that has been an inevitable feature of recent years, as that former epoch has come more sharply into focus as a locus for our understanding not only of the past but of the contours of our modernity. It centres primarily upon major authors and subjects within Romantic and Victorian literature. It also includes studies of other British writers and issues, where these are matters of current debate: for example, biography and autobiography, journalism, periodical literature, travel writing, book production, gender, non-canonical writing. We are dedicated principally to publishing original monographs and symposia; our policy is to embrace a broad scope in chronology, approach and range of concern, and both to recognize and cut innovatively across such parameters as those suggested by the designations 'Romantic' and 'Victorian'. We welcome new ideas and theories, while valuing traditional scholarship. It is hoped that the world which predates yet so forcibly predicts and engages our own will emerge in parts, in the wider sweep, and in the lively streams of disputation and change that are so manifest an aspect of its intellectual, artistic and social landscape.

Vincent Newey
Joanne Shattock
University of Leicester

Introduction and Acknowledgments

Four interconnected essays: the collective consequence of two long-cherished, initially distinct interests that eventually converged. I have loved the sharp, subtle novels of Austen for many years—an expanse of time sufficient to take Colonel Brandon of *Sense and Sensibility* from swaddling clothes to his arguably premature flannel waistcoats—and my volumes of the *Oxford Illustrated Jane Austen*, a graduation gift inscribed by my grandparents, are now broken-backed after repeated readings. I became fascinated with the patient, particular observations and the world-changing ideas of Charles Darwin while on a Lilly post-doctoral fellowship at the University of Florida's Center for Programs in the Humanities, where David Locke opened my eyes to how Darwin can be read through a literary lens. Darwin and his works became even more intriguing when I became friends with Duncan Porter, a colleague at Virginia Tech with wide-ranging expertise in botanical, historical, and editorial aspects of Darwin studies. Over time, it seemed increasingly evident that this pair of interests wasn't exactly random, that some talents and sensibilities Austen and Darwin share played a part in the similarly enduring but apparently distinct fascinations. What might those shared qualities of mind be? How might they be accounted for? Having posed these questions, I felt inclined to attempt a comparison and generate an intellectual conversation that might produce some answers. The eventual result was the quartet of essays comprising *Jane Austen & Charles Darwin: Naturalists and Novelists*.

A convention from the contemporary cyberworld of fan fiction, the ampersand in this book's title is meant to signal that I am 'shipping (as fan fiction would put it) Jane Austen and Charles Darwin. That is to say, through juxtaposition I'm creating a relationship that did not actually exist. The title's seven words and one symbol—two Christian names, two surnames, two nouns, and two ways of specifying the same coordinating conjunction—indicate the book's main subjects and its eclectic, comparative method. Although one of the juxtaposed thinkers and writers is generically termed a naturalist and the other a novelist, the characterizations seem at least partially interchangeable. When I set out on a comparative consideration of the two, Austen was very widely read—but often, it seemed, without having her ideas considered as seriously as they deserve to be or respected in the forms that they actually take. Darwin's ideas were much invoked, sometimes vaguely and sometimes accurately; but the words in which he framed his thoughts seemed too often left unread by those alluding to and building upon his discoveries and theories. And thus—so my 1990s thinking ran—the ideas and the words alike of Austen and Darwin would be worth attending to in concert, for both Austen and Darwin are highly skilled in observing, thinking, and writing. In certain senses, both Austen and Darwin are naturalists who look with a clear, cold eye at the concrete particulars of the world around them. In certain senses, both Austen and Darwin are novelists who rely on storytelling and the verbal strategies that it entails (selective and artful manipulation of detail, pace, chronology, diction, and narrative voice, among others) to convey their personal observations to a wider circle of readers. Taken seriously and read carefully, the works of both Austen and Darwin encourage their readers to train their own minds along the lines of those the two writers use to such fine effect in their writings. Attuned to reading the world by reading Austen or Darwin, we learn to look closely at the social and natural phenomena around us, to form opinions based on attentive individual judgment rather than on transmitted opinion, and to act or write in accordance with what we have perceived and understood.

Soon after I seriously embarked on the juxtaposition that seemed so desirable, it became obvious that my project wouldn't and shouldn't achieve a perfectly symmetrical treatment of its subjects. The authors' respective piled-up publications make two heaps of very different sizes. Austen's stack consists of six published novels, some juvenilia and fragments, and a volume of letters. Darwin's lifetime labors resulted in 17 books, monographs, or portions of books, and more than 170 papers, some of them very hefty indeed and most existing in more than one state thanks to Darwin's habitual revision of his works when they were republished. On top of this mountain of works he himself published, Charles Darwin's multi-voluminous correspondence is still being edited and published by the Cambridge Darwin Correspondence Project. I have read all of Austen's published works repeatedly, but there are several—actually, many—of Darwin's works I've not read in full or not even tackled. Furthermore, trained as a literary scholar, I am likelier to find that a Darwinian idea illuminates an Austen text than to see how one of Austen's insights sheds light on a passage from Darwin—though, that being said, my approach is not limited to viewing Austen's novels through a Darwinian lens: interested in understanding more about both authors, I didn't want to make one of them a mere means for explaining the other. It also struck me that Austen's and Darwin's lives themselves dovetail and diverge in fascinating ways—and, further, that there are remarkable things to see when one views certain episodes of Austen's life in terms of Darwinian theory, or when one compares an aspect of Darwin's life to an episode from an Austen novel. Further still, I came to realize that "naturalist" and "novelist" were not the sole categories to be productively counterpoised in a joint consideration. Comparably observant and rooted in local particulars, Austen and Darwin are perhaps the great English empiricists of the nineteenth century. Each, too, is a past master of that felicitous quality Horace Walpole named serendipity; and it became evident that my study of Austen and Darwin should take account of their empirical, serendipitous ways of proceeding. As I eventually realized, empiricism and serendipity were guiding principles for my own method as well.

Readers who follow this frequently empirical duograph's serendipitously twisting path will find themselves passing back and forth not just from the naturalist's sphere to the novelist's realm, but also from art to life and from theory to practice. But there's at least one fascinating issue lying in the space where art, life, theory, and practice overlap that I won't consider in a sustained way: an issue important to acknowledge even though it will not be systematically explored. Whatever the affinities of their minds and the resemblances of their achievements, can't it be argued that there's a significant moral tension between the vision of Jane Austen, termed by Alasdair MacIntyre "the last great effective imaginative voice of the tradition of thought about, and practice of, the virtues"[1] and that of Charles Darwin, whose principle of natural selection has been widely invoked as evidence that the practice of virtues is neither here nor there in a competitive world where the strongest (or most selfish) survive and the weakest (or most altruistic) go to the wall? Put simply, don't Austen's works cultivate moral choice while Darwin's works undermine it? Well, the question is important, intriguing, difficult, perhaps answerable and perhaps not. Attempting to formulate a detailed and convincing answer is not one of my purposes here, though it's worth noting that Darwin, like Austen, recognized the value of ethical, unselfish human behavior. For him, unselfishness and a moral sense offer the members of a communal species an adaptive advantage in the struggle for existence. It's also worth noting that individual humans, even remarkable specimens such as Darwin and Austen, often display notable inconsistencies between their theories and their practice. Charles Darwin's meticulous observations and laboriously attained conclusions can be seen as subverting many of his culture's most cherished assumptions—but as married man, paterfamilias, and squire of Downe, he walked the conventional walk of a righteous, prosperous, philanthropic Victorian gentleman. In a similarly paradoxical way, Jane Austen's novels affirm marriage as the ordering dance that makes, mends, or enlarges the societies she depicts and as the commitment by which individual women and men implicitly declare their deepest values—but Austen did not choose to accept a partner in that dance or to define herself through that commitment.

So what does lie ahead in the four essays? The first, "'3 or 4 Families in a Country Village,' or Naturalists, Novelists, Empiricists, and Serendipitists," sets out to show how the famous phrase by which Jane Austen identified the subject matter for novels as she wrote them serves to characterize the environment that proved ideal for both Austen and Darwin in their creative lives as empirical, serendipitous novelists and naturalists. Among other things, this essay explores the surprising similarities and acknowledges the significant contrasts between the two great nineteenth-century observers and interpreters. There's little chronological overlap in their lives. The differences in gender, marital status, wealth, and both range and type of intellectual interests are obvious. Nonetheless, Austen and Darwin were alike in several ways. Both sprang from the class Austen described in her novels, the English gentry. Both grew up as younger children in large families. Both were keen observers of the world before them who excelled in noticing microcosmic particulars and in understanding the cosmic significance of those small details. Both were happiest and most productive when rooted in the tranquil security of village life. As the second part of the essay's title suggests, Austen's and Darwin's distinctive sensibilities both combined talents and characteristics associated with naturalists, novelists, empiricists, and serendipitists; so I begin with etymological and historical overviews of the qualities associated with each term. Then, after ranging selectively through Darwin's *Autobiography* and Austen's letters to hear what the two writers say about their own characters and vocations, the essay comes to rest on the notion of what Raymond Williams calls

---

1   Alasdair MacIntyre, *After Virtue: A Study in Moral Theory* (Notre Dame, IN: University of Notre Dame Press, 1984), 240.

"knowable communities," the strategically limited fields that proved congenial for the exercise of both Darwin's and Austen's talents. Examples of such communities discussed here include the finches and mockingbirds Darwin observed and collected on the Galápagos Islands, the polymorphous creatures known as barnacles that were for years his taxonomic obsession, and the fictional village of Highbury, locale of Austen's most densely particular and most powerfully empirical novel, *Emma*.

If many smaller topics comprise the first essay, the second tackles one big subject: the psychological and personal evolution of siblings. "'An Entangled Bank,' or Sibling Development in a Family Ecosystem," the title of this essay, alludes to the famous concluding paragraph of *Origin of Species*. Here, I look at the parallels between Darwin's ideas on adaptive variation (how species diverge to fill unoccupied niches in a particular environment) and the ways siblings, especially sisters, develop in relation to one another and to their parents in Austen's novels. The science historian Frank Sulloway's Darwinian theory of sibling differentiation serves as template for an assessment of personality development in sibling groups from all six Austen novels. The Dashwoods, Ferrarses, Steeles, Darcys, Bertrams, Prices, Woodhouses, Knightleys, Thorpes, Morlands, Tilneys, and Elliots all come under consideration; but the most detailed assessment involves the Bennet sisters of *Pride and Prejudice*, five scantily-provided-for sisters of marriageable age all competing for suitors at the same time. Besides examining Austen's and Darwin's writings, I look at their own situations among their siblings. Austen and Darwin developed along the lines set forth by Sulloway's theory of sibling personality formation. As younger children in large families, the two of them grew up markedly different from their older siblings (especially from Cassandra Austen and Erasmus Darwin, their respective older same-sex siblings) and from their parents.

Like the second essay, the third views an expansive topic from various perspectives. That topic is clearly evident from the title, "'Marry—Mary—Marry.'" This repetition (the second "marry" short one "r") concludes Charles Darwin's weighing of the pros and cons of matrimony in a semi-serious list he created shortly before proposing to, and being accepted by, his first cousin Emma Wedgwood. This essay begins with a close reading of Darwin's list and with a look at the pattern of intermarriage discernible in the Darwin and Wedgwood families over generations (Darwin's mother was Susannah Wedgwood, and his older sister Caroline married their cousin, Emma's older brother Josiah) in light of what Austen implies about intermarriage in her novels. In nineteenth-century England's landed class, there were economic, practical, and social advantages to marriage between cousins or between neighbors who had grown up together. Among these advantages were the greater good of the extended family, the enhancement of the country neighborhood, or both. This theme is played out in Austen's *Mansfield Park* through the union of Edmund Bertram and Fanny Price—first cousins, like Charles and Emma Darwin. In *Emma*, the marriage of Emma Woodhouse and George Knightley joins neighboring estates and further connects families allied by the previous union of her sister and his brother. In *Sense and Sensibility*, the Dashwood sisters' matrimonial choices show how families can consolidate power and comfort through complementary marriages. Marianne's husband the squire can further the career of Elinor's husband the parson— an arrangement that proves equally pragmatic if less than felicitous in *Mansfield*

Park with the Ward sisters, Lady Bertram and Mrs Norris. But intermarriage isn't always desirable. Austen's notable countercases are Elizabeth Bennet's rejection of her cousin Collins, and, without exactly having the offer made, Anne Elliot's rebuff of her cousin William Elliot. In light of the matches these cousin-refusers come to make, marriages that might from a biological perspective be called "salubrious outcrossings," the essay also considers Darwin's biological reservations about marriage of cousins as a potential source of physical weakness in offspring and looks at some of the various civilized and "savage" mating patterns Darwin noticed or compiled from correspondents and recorded in *The Descent of Man* as compared with what Austen discerned among the Regency gentry and reflected in her novels.

"Variations on Variation," the last essay, reverts to the multi-topical approach of the first essay and considers many different instances of how for both Austen and Darwin minute distinctions and gradual, constant change are the way of the world, whether the microcosm under consideration is geological, biological, social, or literary. The discussion begins by focusing on Darwinian instances of variation under artificial selection (fanciers' development of the widely varying morphologies of breeds of domestic pigeons) and natural selection (the intricate adaptive developments of wild orchids). Then comes a more panoramic view of change that grapples with the question of uniformitarianism vs. catastrophism—competing explanations for changes in the earth and its life forms in Austen's and Darwin's days—and an argument that for both empiricists the uniformitarian model of continual variation prevailed. Passages testifying to this natural effect can be found in Darwin's geological publications and in his monograph on coral reefs and atolls. Like Darwin the uniformitarian geologist but working on the much shorter scale of human time, Austen seems to see her world as proceeding along lines it has always followed rather than rent asunder by sudden catastrophe. For Austen, it seems that individual character and personality evolve rather than radically altering. Families rise and subside like uplifted and eroded land masses, or perhaps even more like the organisms that live or die on account of uplift and subsidence.

A form of natural variation constantly at work and easily observed is the essay's next main topic: the flushing or going pale of the human face, a phenomenon both Austen and Darwin intently scrutinized. The central question: what are the social and psychological significances of the blush in Austen's works as compared to those in Darwin's *The Expression of the Emotions in Man and Animals*? To move towards an answer, I compare Darwin's ethological explanation of blushing—the physiological response that he sees as most peculiarly human—to instances of flushing and going pale in Austen's novels, where it is interesting to notice that coloring, an index of sensibility stereotypically considered a gauge of female refinement in both Austen's and Darwin's times, is a response displayed by women and men alike. The fourth essay's final concerns are how large political and economic events change the fortunes of families—even in works as famously devoid of explicit political and historical content as Austen's novels are—and how small, repeated acts have great consequences in both the social world described by Austen and the natural world observed by Darwin. The south coastal town of Lyme Regis, surrounded by cliffs of fossil-bearing chalk and sandstone where naturalists hunted for specimens in the early nineteenth century, seems a particularly apt destination in Austen's last novel

Persuasion. This novel, in which Austen turns her back on the country-house class and finds her hero in the naval meritocracy, displays specimens destined for extinction (those social dinosaurs the landed Elliots) and other beings on the ascent because better equipped in the struggle for existence (naval officers along the lines of Admiral Croft and Captain Wentworth and the women wise enough to value and marry them). The variations on variation end in the south counties of England with a juxtaposition of *Sanditon*, Austen's final fragment of a novel, and Darwin's last published monograph *The Formation of Vegetable Mould through the Action of Worms*, a patient study of the incremental effects the actions of earthworms have had on the English landscape. Darwin's accounts of Roman villas and Druid monuments slowly buried by worms offer a striking analogy to the forces of social change facing Austen's hereditary country-house class at the end of the eighteenth and start of the nineteenth centuries.

If I am any sort of "-ist" in the ensuing paragraphs and pages, it's an essayist in the way that Michel de Montaigne meant that word when he coined it—a person who's trying out ideas in a highly personal thought experiment. I've chosen to write the four interconnected pieces in essay style because this informal conversational genre best serves my goal of establishing and moderating an intellectual conversation between Jane Austen and Charles Darwin. But this generic choice has its disadvantage: foregrounding Austen, Darwin, and their words means backgrounding the lively, learned, extensive, and intensive discourses about them and their works. There are many scholars contributing to these discourses—enough to constitute an Austen Industry and a Darwin Industry. In the years that have passed since I first began thinking about Jane Austen and Darwin in relation to one another, connecting the novelist and the naturalist has ceased to seem idiosyncratic and perhaps appears downright trendy. A consciously defined cross-disciplinary approach called literary darwinism now applies Darwin's theories to literary texts; and much recent scholarship has been inclined to take Jane Austen seriously as a writer grounded in the ideas of her time. The books and essays mentioned below are only a few of the many texts to which readers interested in individual or comparative study of Darwin and Austen, or more broadly of Darwinian science and literature, might turn for further information or for other ways of looking at matters examined here.

Gillian Beer's *Darwin's Plots: Evolutionary Narrative in Darwin, George Eliot, and Nineteenth-Century Fiction* (London and Boston: Routledge & Kegan Paul, 1983; second edition, Cambridge: Cambridge University Press, 2000) is the *locus classicum* for comparative work relating Darwin and literature. Beer's book considers Darwin's language and his plots alike—anthropomorphism, analogy, metaphor, and myths in his narratives—and then discusses literary responses to his evolutionary ideas, particularly in George Eliot's fiction but also in Thomas Hardy's. The sort of literary darwinism Beer pioneered has lately cohered as a critical school. *The Literary Animal*, edited by Jonathan Gottschall and David Sloan Wilson (Evanston, IL: Northwestern University Press, 2005), collects a diverse array of disciplinary perspectives on literary darwinism, including those of the sociobiologist Edward O. Wilson, who offers a "Foreword from the Scientific Side," the literary metacritic Frederick Crews, providing a comparable "Foreword from the Literary Side," and the novelist Ian McEwan, who writes on "Literature, Science, and Human Nature." Some of the other individual pieces in this ambitious and suggestive book consider the big questions of the relationship between science and literature or assess the shortcomings of postmodern critical theories that ignore the biological roots of behavior. Other contributions blend conceptualizing with practical applications. Notable among them for readers interested in Austen and Darwin is Joseph Carroll's "Human Nature and Literary Meaning: A Theoretical Model Illustrated with a Critique of *Pride and Prejudice*." Still others argue for, and deploy, scientific or empirical methods far more rigorous than my own eclectic approach and bring quantitative research methods of the hard sciences to bear on literary texts, from fairy tales to Romantic literature (the term "Romantic" here being used in its period-defining rather than genre-characterizing sense) to erotica. A much looser and breezier way of reading literature through a Darwinian lens characterizes *Madame Bovary's Ovaries: A Darwinian Look at Literature* (New York: Delacorte Press, 2005) by psychologist David P. Barash and Nanelle R. Barash. This father–daughter team's self-described "bio-lit-crit" ranges widely from the title character Emma Bovary to Othello, Rhett Butler, Cinderella, Alexander Portnoy, and others, with one chapter devoted to "The Key to Jane Austen's Heart: What Women Want and Why."

Darwin may have been self-deprecating about his writerly skills, but they were considerable—and they are taken seriously in an increasing number of books treating his life and works, among them Janet Browne's magisterial two-volume biography *Charles Darwin: Voyaging* (Princeton, NJ: Princeton University Press, 1995) and *Charles Darwin: The Power of Place* (Princeton, NJ: Princeton University Press, 2002), and Rebecca Stott's narrowly focused but broadly suggestive and beautifully written *Darwin and the Barnacle* (London: Faber and Faber, 2003). Twin towers of eminence in biological studies, James Watson and Edward O. Wilson have recently brought out collections of Darwin's works, respectively titled *The Indelible Stamp: The Evolution of an Idea* (Philadelphia, PA: Running Press, 2005) and *From So Simple a Beginning: The Four Great Books of Darwin* (New York: Norton, 2006). Studies explicitly centering on Darwinian rhetoric include Misia Landau's *Narratives of Human Evolution* (New Haven, CT: Yale University Press, 1991), which considers Darwin's works among others, and *The Literary Structure of Scientific Argument: Historical Studies*, a collection edited by Peter Dear (Philadelphia, PA: University of Pennsylvania Press, 1991) that contains essays featuring or touching on Darwin. Some of the most compelling work on Darwin as rhetorician has been done by John A. Campbell, presently at work on a rhetorical biography of Darwin. Campbell's publications on this subject include "The Invisible Rhetorician: Charles Darwin's 'Third Party' Strategy," *Rhetorica* VII (1989), 70–74; "Scientific Revolution and the Grammar of Culture: The Case of Darwin's Origin," *Quarterly Journal of Speech* LXXII, 4 (1986), 351–76; and "Charles Darwin: Rhetorician of Science", in *Rhetoric of the Human Sciences*, ed. John S. Nelson *et al.* (Madison, WI: University of Wisconsin Press, 1989). In *Darwin Loves You: Natural Selection and the Re-enchantment of the World* (Princeton, NJ: Princeton University Press, 2006), literary scholar George Levine blends widely contextual reflection and close reading to show how Darwin the naturalist and writer reveals sublimity in a material world.

Marilyn Butler's *Jane Austen and the War of Ideas* (London and New York: Oxford University Press, 1975) was arguably the groundbreaking text for taking Jane Austen's ideas seriously. The Austen Butler presents is a woman looking backwards: a Tory reactionary at odds with her age of revolutionary and evolutionary change. Subsequent accounts of Austen as a woman of ideas sometimes build on the foundation of Butler's Anti-Jacobin Austen, sometimes modify it, and sometimes differ with it. Particularly notable contributions to our present understanding of Jane Austen's relations to the ideas of her time include Claudia L. Johnson's *Jane Austen: Women, Politics, and the Novel* (Chicago, IL: University of Chicago Press, 1988), Janet Todd's edited collection *Jane Austen: New Perspectives* (New York: Holmes and Meier, 1983), and two recent publications, Peter Knox-Shaw's *Jane Austen and the Enlightenment* (Cambridge: Cambridge University Press, 2004) and Sarah Emsley's *Jane Austen's Philosophy of the Virtues* (New York: Palgrave Macmillan, 2005). Knox-Shaw's book situates Austen in the context of the Enlightenment philosophy, psychology, and science and thereby shows how intensely Austen engaged with the ideas of her time. Emsley's book, similarly meticulous and convincing, emphasizes the religious and philosophical contexts of Austen's novels and explains how a comprehensive understanding of the classical and Christian traditions of the virtues undergirds the ethical principles evident in her novels.

My thinking about Jane Austen, Charles Darwin, their works, and their times is clearer and stronger because of the works mentioned above and others acknowledged in the essays and their notes. I've also profited by the generosity of many individuals and institutions, the most important of whom I'd like to acknowledge and thank here.

To begin with the institutions whose support I deeply appreciate: one of the essays was written during a semester's research leave granted by the Department of English at Virginia Polytechnic Institute and State University. My research was also expedited by a Humanities Summer Research Stipend from Virginia Tech, by a grant from the Earhart Foundation, and by an agreeable and productive week spent at the Goucher College Library as an Alberta Clarke Scholar in Residence. For permission to republish material that first appeared in two essays, "Why Lyme Regis?" and "Born to Diverge," I am grateful to *Persuasions*, the journal of the Jane Austen Society of North America.

As I've pursued work on this project, I've also been fortunate in having the support and advice of family, friends, and colleagues. Many people have discussed Jane Austen, Charles Darwin, and their works with me; quite a few have read extracts or entire essays and have generously offered their opinions. I truly value all the advice received, whether taken or not—and it has been a real pleasure exchanging ideas about Austen and Darwin. I'd especially like to acknowledge Bernard Beatty, Mary Margaret Benson, Inger Sigrun Brodey, Christopher Clausen, John Clubbe, Richard Cooper, Ann Donahue, Michael Edson, Sarah Emsley, Lilian Furst, Jonathan Gross, Pamela Gurney, Laurie Kaplan, Malcolm Kelsall, Katherine Kernberger, Sheila Johnson Kindred, Nancy Magnuson, J. Clinton McCann, Jerome McGann, Fritz Oehlschlaeger, Duncan Porter, David Radcliffe, Linda Relias, Sydney Roby, Brian Southam, Patrick Stokes, Frank Sulloway, and Stephen Wilkerson. In seminars on Darwin and on Austen, graduate and undergraduate students at Virginia Tech have enriched my understanding with keen insights of their own. Over the years, I've been fortunate to have so many fruitful conversations with friends, colleagues, and students. My family has been continually inspiring and sustaining. A thousand thanks aren't nearly enough for Austin, James, and especially Kaye.

Chapter 1

"3 or 4 Families in a Country Village," or Naturalists, Novelists, Empiricists, and Serendipidists

"3 or 4 families in a country village"[1]: this phrase by which Jane Austen identifies the most congenial subject matter for novels as she chose to write them can also serve to characterize the environment that proved ideal for Charles Darwin's naturalist observations. He found nothing so repaying as to watch the sometimes cooperative, sometimes competitive inhabitants of a microenvironment, whether his version of Austen's "country village" happened to be a volcanic Galápagos island, a nitrogen-deficient bog hospitable to insectivorous plants, or the herbaceous border at Down House. But besides offering a fertile field of study, the "country village" provided both Austen and Darwin with the best place to thrive and to pursue their chosen projects. Both flourished in the tranquil stability of country life in the south of England. Hypothetically, the world was all before independently wealthy Darwin; but with adequate means to live where he would after returning to British terra firma from the five years' Beagle voyage, marrying his first cousin Emma Wedgwood, and starting a family, he chose neither academic Cambridge nor metropolitan London as his permanent base. Instead Darwin retired from the hubbub of London to Downe, a secluded village in Kent, to cultivate his lifelong naturalist investigations. Austen, an unmarried, unpropertied woman dependent on others for a roof over her head, never had the luxury of choice but was obliged to live wherever her parents' or a brother's resources provided a home. She passed her life in several places—the Hampshire villages of Steventon and Chawton, the spa city Bath, the busy naval port of Southampton—and paid long visits to other households, notably her brothers'. But Austen found the settled peace crucial to pursuing her art only in village houses: Steventon Rectory in her early adulthood and Chawton Cottage from 1811 until the end of her life. Austen's mature creative life contains a gap that coincides with her period of rootless migrations; and her six completed novels principally derive from two fertile periods of composition, 1796–99 and 1811–16. The first period ended when her father retired and left the parish of Steventon with his wife and two uprooted daughters. The second began when the Austen women settled at Chawton, thanks to the generosity of the third Austen brother, Edward Austen Knight.

---

1 Jane Austen, *Jane Austen's Letters*, ed. Deirdre Le Faye (Oxford and New York: Oxford University Press, 1995), 275. Subsequent citations will refer to this edition, abbreviated *JAL*, and will appear parenthetically.

Finding sustenance in rural seclusion and being fascinated by the intricate workings of a small community are only two of a number of ways Austen and Darwin might be seen as alike. The ensuing pages will explore some of the surprising similarities and significant contrasts between their lives, works, and ideas. First, though, it's worth briefly stating the main differences. There's little chronological overlap: Darwin (1809–82) was a child when Austen (1775–1817) died. There are the obvious differences of sex (a matter much considered by Darwin in various papers and books) and gender (a phenomenon explored throughout Austen's novels). There's Darwin's wealthy, married paterfamilias status as opposed to Austen's financially constrained spinsterhood. Darwin's range of intellectual interests was global, both geographically and figuratively, whereas Austen focused her attention on an unusually narrow segment of the human world: the lower reaches of the English ruling class in the late eighteenth and early nineteenth centuries.

But despite these significant differences, Austen and Darwin were alike in several ways—ways crucially formative to their particular talents. Both sprang from the provincial English gentry, the social class Austen described in her novels. Both grew up as younger children in large families, Austen as second daughter and seventh child in a sibling group of eight, Darwin as second son and fifth child in a sibling group of six. More important, Austen and Darwin possessed congenial temperaments and analogous talents worth examining in light of one another. Intriguing blends of conformity and independence, both were superficially conventional people who remained, at heart, uncompromisingly determined to keep faith with their respective vocations as novelist and naturalist—vocations that themselves share a number of attributes. Both Austen and Darwin were keen observers of the world before them, observers who excelled both in noticing microcosmic particulars and, because they observed with trained eyes, in discerning the cosmic significance of those small details.

If human beings and their societies are understood to be part of nature, then it can be said that both Austen and Darwin are naturalists, for they look with scrupulous, penetrating, and relatively unbiased attention at the rich and messy details of the world around them. In a somewhat less literal sense, both Austen and Darwin can be called novelists. Each relies on storytelling and the verbal skills that it entails to convey personal observations of new things noticed in specific detail to a wider world of readers. Each presents character (for Darwin's purposes, character is not only human but also zoological, botanical, or geological) modified by contingencies and incrementally changed over time. In making their observations and drawing their conclusions as naturalist or novelist, Austen and Darwin were part of the strong and flourishing tradition of British empiricism—indeed, they might be seen as the two great British empiricists of the nineteenth century. But mere empiricism—and "mere" is an adjective often found explicitly or implicitly preceding the nouns "empiricism" and "empiricist" in English—doesn't suffice to explain Austen's and Darwin's triumphs as novelist and naturalist. Trained sagacity prepared their minds to profit by the accidental details that observation and chance brought before them. This blend of strengths makes their respective careers ideal embodiments of serendipity, a coinage and concept Horace Walpole introduced to English a few decades before Austen's birth—and nearly a century before the word "scientist" appeared in print.

Novelists—naturalists—empiricists—serendipitists: with all these terms in play, it would be best to begin with definitions and distinctions. Before turning to Austen's and Darwin's minds and sensibilities, the circumstances in which their mental powers flourished and the subjects with which they fruitfully engaged, let's think about what "naturalist," "novelist," "empiricist," and "serendipitist" mean. More precisely, let's consider how the meanings of these terms have morphed over time—for words, like the species naturalists observe and the characters novelists chronicle, evolve if they endure.

Empiricists

Empiricism, at root, was medical practice based upon first-hand experience and observation as opposed as opposed to esoteric doctrine. Tradition has it that Greek medicine was first practiced by the Asclepiadiae, a clan of doctors supposedly descending from the mythic Asclepius and professing knowledge of medical secrets handed down from their legendary ancestor and transmitted by Hippocrates. The doctors of the Asclepian school of medicine, established in the fourth century BCE by Thesalus the son and Polybus the son-in-law of Hippocrates, were known as the Dogmatici or the Hippocratici. The Empirici, a rival school, arose in the third century. Founded by Serapion of Alexandria and Philinus of Rhodes, the Empirici consciously distinguished themselves from the dogmatic proprietors of hereditary knowledge by basing their practice on experience only. In the first century BCE, Themison founded the Methodici, a school of medical practice blending the approaches of the Dogmatici and the Empirici.[2]

It is interesting to notice that because the positions of the Dogmatici and the Empirici were absolutist when practical common sense might suggest a variable blending of the schools' approaches—exactly what the Methodici eventually did—the terms derived from each school's name, "dogmatism" and "empiricism" (but especially the former) have come to carry pejorative connotations. Because of early association with the exclusion of theory and the rejection of transmitted knowledge, the words "empiricist" and "empiricism" as used in later times often connote unscientific practice, ignorance, and quackery—all possible or likely consequences of experience uninformed by theory or principles. More neutrally, "empirical" can signify induction without deduction—and thus in math might refer to a formula arrived at by the accretion of specifics; in chemistry to enumerating a compound's elements without theorizing on how they are combined; and in psychology to a practice based on specific observation and experiment instead of general principle. Thus in nineteenth-century usage "empirical" in its various forms typically exists in direct or implied contrast with the terms "scientific" or "rational." The *OED* specifically cites James Mill, "Mere observation and empiricism, not even the commencement of science"—and likewise Sir John Herschel, "If the knowledge be merely accumulated

---

[2] Thomas Henry Huxley, "The Connection of the Biological Sciences with Medicine," *Nature: A Weekly Illustrated Journal of Science* DCXIV (1881), 342–6; William Alexander Greenhill, "Medicina," in William Smith, *A Dictionary of Greek and Roman Antiquities* (London: John Murray, 1875), pp. 745–7.

experience, the art is empirical." In partial contrast Thomas Henry Huxley, renowned as "Darwin's bulldog," wrote in *"*The Connection of the Biological Sciences with Medicine" that "All true science begins with empiricism."[3] Huxley's pronouncement continues with a qualifying clause not quoted in the *OED*—"though all true science is such exactly, in so far as it strives to pass out of the empirical stage into that of the deduction of the empirical from more general truths" (343)—so he too would be no advocate of "mere" empiricism.

Serendipitists

The essence of serendipity is accidental sagacity. Horace Walpole, the eighteenth-century connoisseur and author famed for his Gothic house Strawberry Hill, his Gothic novel *The Castle of Otranto*, and his extensive correspondence, coined the word in a January 28, 1754 letter to Horace Mann. Walpole contextualizes and characterizes this word he's invented with a blend of acuteness and aristocratic nonchalance: "I once read a silly fairy tale, called *The Three Princes of Serendip*: as their highnesses traveled, they were always making discoveries, by accidents and sagacity, of things which they were not in quest of."[4] The Eastern tale to which Walpole refers concerns three princes, sons of the philosopher king Jafer of Sarendip. Highly educated by the wisest men in their father's kingdom, the princes are on their travels to gain direct experience, especially of other peoples and their customs, to complement their scholastic learning. It's important to notice that although the princes are not seeking the specific situations and details they happen upon, their travels are not purposeless. Nor are their minds unprepared. The princes' adventures on the road result in discoveries of the Sherlock Holmes sort—discoveries crucially involving, like Holmes's, the interplay of two things: accurately noticed evidence and a trained mind capable of correctly interpreting what's been observed. If the three princes were classical Greek practitioners of medicine, they'd be Methodici; for they value and profit by both direct experience and transmitted knowledge.

In a recently published, though long unfinished, monograph called *The Travels and Adventures of Serendipity: A Study in Sociological Semantics and the Sociology of Science*, Robert K. Merton and Elinor Barber patiently and elegantly follow the fortunes of the word "serendipity" from its invention to the present day, when it's widely but loosely employed. If there are many variant shades of meaning attached to "serendipity," argue Merton and Barber, the apparent ambiguities accurately represent a fundamental tension in the very idea of accidental discovery,

> ... a tension between the attribution of credit for an unexpected discovery to the discoverer on the one hand, and to auspicious external circumstances on the other. In general,

---

3   The passages quoted in the *OED* are drawn from the following sources: James Mill, *The History of British India* (London: Baldwin, Cradock, and Joy, 1817), I, 399; John Herschel, *A Preliminary Discourse on the Study of Natural Philosophy* (London: Longman and John Taylor, 1830), 71; Huxley, "The Connection of the Biological Sciences with Medicine," 343.

4   Horace Walpole to Horace Mann, 28 January 1754, in *Horace Walpole's Correspondence*, ed. W. S. Lewis (New Haven, CT: Yale University Press, 1960), 20, 407–8.

modesty demands that the writer understate the factor of "genius" or special "gift" in his own accidental discoveries, and that he stress the contribution made by external circumstances.[5]

Walpole's own mannered modesty in bringing the word "serendipity" to life has been echoed over the years by succeeding generations of observers and discoverers who display the trait (among them Austen and Darwin, both notable self-deprecators), with amateurs being likelier than professionals to downplay "sagacity" and stress "accident."

Merton himself brought the concept of the "serendipity pattern" in empirical research into the professionalized realm of the social sciences in 1946. He pointed out the scientist's unacknowledged serendipitous pattern "of observing an unanticipated, anomalous, and strategic datum which becomes the occasion for developing a new theory or for extending an existing theory" (xxi). A serendipitist in his own right, Merton realized from his trained observation of specific details that an element of creative storytelling exists in seemingly objective scientific reportage—that the rigorous logic seen as "scientific" is a fashion or convention whereby the rules of evidence prevailing at a particular time, rather than the actual sequence of events or phenomena involved in the derivation of a hypothesis, theory, or law, determine how a scientific narrative is organized.[6] The creative element involved in scientific reportage has its counterpart in scientific discovery: a distinctively groomed consciousness's imagination sparks the "eureka" moment of enlightenment.

In *Science and the Social Order*, Bernard Barber emphasizes the role of individual creative imagination in serendipitous discoveries, where one observer encounters unexpected details that have been seen but not hitherto noticed as significant by other investigators and then identifies those details as the components of a pattern. The previously overlooked particulars "are actively noticed, that is, by the scientist who has carefully studied his problem over a long time and is thereby ready, if he can create some anticipatory ideas, to take advantage of an 'unexpected' occurrence."[7] In this way accidental discovery, though it requires unexpected and anomalous data, has an element of strategy in it. As Barber sees it, successful scientists, ever alert for seemingly random details or happenings that may lead to new understandings, actively cultivate serendipity (203–5). Perhaps it goes without saying that artistic endeavor also cultivates serendipity. Characteristically striking a balance somewhere between the poles of pure fantasy and straight reportage, the imaginative sensibility accidentally or deliberately finds phenomena in life and sees, through some blend of talent, training, and luck, how these phenomena can furnish the materials, subjects, or downright details of art.

---

5   Robert K. Merton and Elinor Barber, *The Travels and Adventures of Serendipity: A Study in Sociological Semantics and the Sociology of Science* (Princeton, NJ and Oxford: Princeton University Press, 2004), p. 58. Subsequent citations of this text will be parenthetical.

6   Merton and Barber, xxii, quoting Merton's earlier book *Science, Technology, and Society in Seventeenth-Century England* (New York: Howard Fertig [1938], repr. 1970), 220.

7   Bernard Barber, *Science and the Social Order* (Glencoe, IL: Free Press, 1952), 204. Subsequent citation will refer to this edition and will be parenthetical.

Naturalist

Like "empiricist," this term's multiple and shifting meanings emerge most clearly if we pay careful attention to distinctions. Used one way, "naturalist" refers to a student of material as opposed to spiritual things, or to someone who believes that natural causes offer sufficient explanation of the world, its origins, and its development. The latter is the essence of the word as Coleridge employs it in his *Aids to Reflection*: "I am here speaking in the assumed character of a mere naturalist, to whom no light of revelation had been vouchsafed."[8] But in Coleridge's day and earlier, when in fact many British naturalists were clergymen, the word "naturalist" could also be used without the implicit opposition to "spiritual" and could simply indicate someone studying natural science—the seventeenth, eighteenth, and early nineteenth-century counterpart to what we now call a "scientist."

"Scientist" itself is a word of 1830s coinage that William Whewell introduced in his *History of the Inductive Sciences*. In this treatise, Whewell indirectly lays out some of the newly evolved distinctions between "naturalist" and "scientist." He also shows the limits on unsupplemented empiricism as a basis for substantial inductive contributions to knowledge. Induction, in Whewell's words, is "that process of collecting general truths from the examination of particular facts." Inductive science, for him, rests on a dual base: "Facts and Ideas; observations of Things without, and an inward effort of Thought; or, in other words, Sense and Reason."[9] Neither sense nor reason suffices alone. Unallied, sense offers only a practical understanding of particulars. Ungrounded, reason generates hollow if ingenious abstractions. Thus, says Whewell, "Real speculative knowledge demands the combination of the two ingredients;--right reason, and facts to reason upon. It has been well said, that true knowledge is the interpretation of nature; and therefore it requires both the interpreting mind, and nature for its subject" (6). There's a distinct Jane Austen feel to Whewell's term "right reason," which can be imagined as the strength of a well-trained sensibility reading the world as a document and naming what's to be seen in that text. Unlike Francis Bacon's insistence on fact before theory in science (a prescriptive sequence endorsed by Darwin in his *Autobiography* and elsewhere), Whewell's model doesn't specify a necessary order in which thinking and data-gathering must take place—it only insists that scientific progress must somehow involve both ideas and facts.

Ideas and facts come together thanks to what we might see as scientific serendipity. Although he does not directly invoke Horace Walpole's anecdote or use his neologism, Whewell's idea and words alike bear striking resemblance to that original account of serendipity. In *Philosophy of the Inductive Sciences* Whewell observes, "the first and great instrument by which facts ... are combined into important and permanent truths is that peculiar Sagacity which belongs to the genius of a Discoverer; and which,

---

8 Samuel Taylor Coleridge, *The Collected Works of Samuel Taylor Coleridge*, ed. John Beer, Vol. IX: *Aids to Reflection* (Princeton, NJ: Princeton University Press, 1993), 353.

9 William Whewell, *Selected Writings on the History of Science*, ed. Yehuda Elkana (Chicago, IL: University of Chicago Press, 1984), 5. Subsequent citations will refer to this edition and will be parenthetical.

while it supplies those distinct and appropriate Conceptions which lead to its success, cannot be limited by rules, or expressed in definitions" (210). Whewell, like Walpole, considers a combination of mental training and sharp observation indispensable to the discoverer's "peculiar sagacity," which maximizes the likelihood of "what are commonly spoken of as felicitous and inexplicable strokes of an inventive talent." What might look like luck to outsiders is theory and fact poised in delicate balance. Discoveries themselves "are not improperly described as happy Guesses" (211).

It hardly need be said that the discoverer's peculiar sagacity ran strong in Charles Darwin, who more clearly than any other thinker of his century (or perhaps any century) manifests what Whewell specifies as the necessary balance of right reason and facts. David Elliston Allen, whose study *The Naturalist in Britain: A Social History* shows how by Darwin's time the terms "scientist" and "naturalist" had diverged to characterize different, if complementary, approaches and preoccupations, refines on the special nature of Darwin's way of balancing reason and facts: "an essential basis of Darwin's genius was the combination in one man of two contrasting types that are normally quite separate: as well as a collector and an observer he was an experimenter and a theorist. In terms of the general run of naturalists he was thus highly uncharacteristic."[10] Although Darwin, young and old, did combine the contrasting types collector/observer and experimenter/theorist, their relative proportions changed over his lifetime. He became progressively less of the former and more of the latter. In fact, Darwin's own case could be seen as the perfect example of the old-school "naturalist" evolving into the Victorian "scientist." Allen's quoted words clearly demonstrate how the significance of the term "naturalist" had narrowed by the middle of the nineteenth century. The newly professional "scientists" distinguished between their own experimental and theoretical enterprise and the activities and orientation of the phenomenon-finding, species-describing, field-based naturalists. Darwin's ally Thomas Henry Huxley saw himself as that newly named being the scientist in a self-conscious way that shows both his difference from Darwin or Wallace and the shrinking of what "naturalist" had come to mean by mid-century: "'There is very little of the generalist in me ... I never collected anything, and species work was a burden to me; what I cared for was the architectural and engineering part of the business'" (qtd in Allen, 180). So it would seem that "naturalists" became "scientists" with the rise of the laboratory and formal experimentation. As science professionalized, the term "naturalist" came to refer more narrowly to the amateur, empirical enterprise of collecting curiosities and amassing specimens—and, concurrently, somehow to imply that people characterized by such interests did not engage in formulating concepts. The term naturalist had come to mean "mere naturalist." But Huxley's self-diagnosis also points to another and subtler difference between scientist and naturalist: the issue of being self-defined by what one loves doing. Huxley, a "scientist," preferred the large lines of theory construction; Darwin, whose passion embraced particulars, remained a "naturalist," though anything but "mere."

---

10 David Elliston Allen, *The Naturalist in Britain: A Social History* (London: Allen Lane, 1976), 176. Subsequent citations will refer to this edition and will be parenthetical.

Novelist

Deriving through French from the Latin word for "new," the term "novelist" originally foregrounded its connection with new things. "Novelist" commonly meant "innovator" in the seventeenth century, "news-monger" in the eighteenth century. At the same time, the "novelist" was a writer of "novels," a term that at first referred to "novelties" or "news and tidings," then more broadly to tales or short stories such as those of Boccaccio. Starting in the seventeenth century, says the *OED*, "novel" came to mean "a fictitious prose narrative or tale of considerable length (now usually long enough to fill one or more volumes), in which characters and actions representative of the real life of past or present times are portrayed in a plot of more or less complexity." In the seventeenth and eighteenth centuries, this term often existed in contrast to "romance," which typically referred to a shorter, less realistic prose work. In much the same way that "naturalist" is most clearly understood through distinguishing it from the related term "scientist," the novelist's goals and methods become evident in contrast with those of a related fiction-maker, the writer of romance.

In his classic study *The Rise of the Novel*, Ian Watt concurs with the common assumption of literary historians that realism is the "defining characteristic which differentiates the work of early eighteenth-century novelists from previous fiction" such as romances.[11] The exact meaning of the term "realism" has of course itself been much contested, but within the bounds of Watt's argument it refers to the general way in which the novel presents life rather than any particular content. With realism, attention shifts from types or abstractions to "concrete objects of sense-perception" (11). An observer or chronicler making this shift assumes, with Descartes and Locke, that an individual discovers truth through sense perceptions. In this way, realism is to the novelist something close to what empiricism is to the naturalist. For Watt, the novel's first duty is truth to individual experience: "since the novelist's primary task is to convey the impression of fidelity to human experience, attention to any pre-established formal conventions can only endanger his success" (13). So construed, the novelist resists models and theories, which seem to bias one's view of what is actually there rather than to aid in discovery. This rejection of abstraction and tradition in favor of experience and observation makes the novel as Jane Austen read, understood, and deployed it a narrative equivalent of empirical practice or inductive reasoning. As novelists Defoe, Richardson, Fielding, and later Austen subordinate generic conventions of plot or general human type to "the primacy of individual experience" (15) and emphasize particulars rather than universals. The novel habitually recognizes the detailed distinctiveness of characters and environments. Realistic particularity governs both characterization and the depiction of environments. Characters develop and change as they pass through time and places. Place is solid and credible, not the arbitrary backdrop of romance. Time too assumes an importance not granted it in romance; and the present state of a character or environment is the comprehensible result of past actions, events, and choices.

---

11 Ian Watt, *The Rise of the Novel: Studies in Defoe, Richardson, and Fielding* (Berkeley, CA and Los Angeles: University of California Press, 1957), 10.

In short, as Watt sees the eighteenth-century novel, it offers "a full and authentic report of human experience, and is therefore under an obligation to satisfy its reader with such details of the story as the individuality of the actors concerned, the particulars of the times and places of their actions, details which are presented through a more largely referential use of language than is common in other literary forms" (32). Such a literary task emphasizes seeing clearly, then knowing or naming rightly—a taxonomic impulse that seems to link the novelist to the naturalist.

If we conceive of novelists this way, we will understand their goal as an effort to create what Raymond Williams, writing about the nineteenth- and early-twentieth-century English novel, calls "knowable communities." Dispensing with the fantastic and improbable aspects of romance—arbitrarily chosen places that don't align with geography, history, topography, or climate as generally understood; characters whose qualities are generic or typical and whose inner lives seem inaccessible, cryptic, or nonexistent; narratives driven by plot conventions and coincidence rather than the plausible unfolding of event and consequent development of character over time—the novelist aims to show that people and their relationships can be rationally understood in communicable ways. Williams explains that this method "depends on a particular kind of social confidence and experience ... that the knowable and therefore known relationships compose and are part of a wholly known social structure, and that in and through the relationships the persons themselves can be wholly known."[12] The practical significance of Austen's "3 or 4 families in a country village" involves just this sort of belief in the knowable, a confidence that links naturalists, novelists, empiricists, and serendipitists. All assume that human societies and natural ecosystems alike work in systematic ways that we can discover and understand. We learn about such systems through close attention to their components, but then what we have learned about a system as a whole sheds light on its constituent elements. This way of knowing requires a cold, clear eye—free, insofar as such freedom is possible, from prejudices, traditions, and pre-existing theories. This eye aims to see things as they are, and right seeing leads to understood meaning.

The primacy of the eye is important here. John Locke considered thought itself a visual process; and as Ira Konisberg points out the novel as practiced by Austen and her eighteenth-century predecessors responded to this new understanding, and thereby became the dominant literary genre of the period, as it "directly confronted the problem of perception in both its narrative technique and its subject matter."[13]

---

12 Raymond Williams, *The English Novel from Dickens to Lawrence* (New York: Oxford University Press, 1970), 15. Williams writes of "knowable community" in Austen's novels in *The Country and the City* (New York: Oxford University Press, 1973), 166: "Look back, for a moment, at the knowable community of Jane Austen. It is outstandingly face-to-face; its crises, physically and spiritually, are in just these terms: a look, a gesture, a stare, a confrontation; and behind these, all the time, the novelist is watching, observing, physically recording and reflecting. That is the whole stance—the grammar of her morality. Yet while it is a community wholly known, within the essential terms of the novel, it is as an actual community very precisely selective. Neighbours in Jane Austen are not the people actually living nearby; they are the people living a little less nearby who, in social recognition, can be visited."

13 Ira Konisberg, *Narrative Technique in the English Novel: Defoe to Austen* (Hamden, CT: Archon Books, 1985), 9–10.

This is not to say that novels confine themselves to what the eye can see. Rather, thought itself is visual in novels. Reading Austen's novels, we don't merely see characters seeing the world. We also see them reacting, internally and externally. This emphasis on the visual nature of thought corresponds with the empirical or encyclopedic way of organizing and displaying knowledge in charts or tables, and with the way naturalists privilege the visual ways of categorizing phenomena, basing knowledge on criteria verifiable by the unaided or assisted eye—in the field, or through a microscope, or through a telescope.

In 1876, when he was 67 years old, Charles Darwin sketched out an autobiography, which he revised and amplified over the rest of his life. Though arguably a more artful text than it admits to being, the autobiography's stated goal is candid appraisal of the growth of a naturalist's mind, mainly for his children and grandchildren. Early in this narrative, Darwin acknowledges his inclination to share his cousin Francis Galton's belief that "education and environment produce only a small effect on the mind of any one, and that most of our qualities are innate."[14] Given this belief in nature over nurture, it is not surprising that Darwin assumed his descendants would value a record of his intellectual development. Similarly, it would make sense for him to display interest in understanding the mental powers of his own progenitors—but what's curious and intriguing is the selective nature of that interest, which focuses exclusively on his father and especially his paternal grandfather. In his Autobiography Darwin doesn't discuss the mental powers of his mother, his grandmothers, or his remarkable maternal grandfather, the ceramics king Josiah Wedgwood—and elsewhere he shows little if any concern for these potential contributors to his innate qualities. Why not? Perhaps his neglect of what the maternal side might have bequeathed to his own mental development can be explained by a blend of factors. Darwin realized that parental and grandparental characteristics recurred in subsequent generations; but, unaware of Mendel's work on genetics, he did not understand the mechanism of biological inheritance. Further, he might have been selectively and unconsciously blinkered by how his culture understood inheritance as a social and economic phenomenon. Like his fellow Victorians, Darwin was the product of a patriarchal age when the transmission of surnames, money, property, and rank characteristically followed the male line. He might unconsciously assume that the ancestors who made the chief social and economic contributions to his identity—his name, class, education, and fortune—would also be the most substantial contributors to his mental inheritance.

Whatever his reasons for the selective attention, Darwin carefully examined the mental qualities of his paternal grandfather the doctor–poet–natural-philosopher Erasmus Darwin—so famed for facile theory-spinning that Coleridge coined a term, "darwinising," to indicate bold, ambitious speculation of the sort Erasmus practiced in prose and verse alike—and his father, the highly successful Shrewsbury physician and capitalist Robert Waring Darwin. These appraisals, like the maternal-side appraisals he did not make, pose intriguing problems that call for some explanation. Charles Darwin clearly recognized that his grandfather and father possessed traits

---

14   Charles Darwin, *The Autobiography of Charles Darwin 1809–1882*, ed. Nora Barlow (New York and London: Norton, 1958), 43. Subsequent citations will refer to this text, abbreviated *A*, and will appear parenthetically.

and talents resembling some of his own—and he was well aware that his grandfather had preceded him in articulating the idea that living things evolve. But in both his autobiography and his memoir of Erasmus Darwin, Charles seems almost to go out of his way to distinguish his grandfather's and father's minds from his—and he unambiguously denies that his grandfather's evolutionary theories had any influence on his own. Of course, members of a younger generation characteristically feel a psychological need to rebel against, or at least declare independence from, their progenitors. But the case is considerably more complex than usual in the Darwin psychodrama, as we shall see.

Charles Darwin characterized his grandfather Erasmus's mind this way: "Judging from his published works, letters, and all that I have been able to gather about him, the vividness of his imagination seems to have been one of his pre-eminent characteristics. This led to his great originality of thought, his prophetic spirit both in science and in the mechanical arts, and to his overpowering tendency to theorise and generalise."[15] Charles goes on to grant that Erasmus valued experimental verification of hypotheses, possessed "uncommon powers of observation," and attended to a surprising range of subjects—but, like Coleridge, Charles sees "the incessant activity or energy of his mind" as Erasmus's dominant quality (ED 49). Charles's self-analysis recognized this mental energy as a quality he too possessed. His notebooks show that he read his grandfather's evolution-espousing *Zoonomia* as he was beginning to assemble his own thoughts on evolution. Yet he totally rejected the possibility that his ideas or chosen topics were influenced by his grandfather's. The confident vigor of this rejection seems to have risen mainly out of Charles Darwin's empirical streak.

His own mind was, like Erasmus's, capable of both observing and theorizing—but it was weighted towards valuing scrupulous observation. To Charles Darwin, patient accumulation and close examination of evidence constituted a necessary prelude to valid speculation: his wife Emma reported one of his favorite sayings as being, "'It is a fatal fault to reason whilst observing, though so necessary beforehand and so useful afterwards'" (A 159). From such a vantage point it would seem that Erasmus Darwin, Lamarck, Chambers, and most other eighteenth- and nineteenth-century evolutionists had not earned the right to theorize. Because Charles Darwin based his own theoretical contribution on laboriously accumulated observation and could bring himself publicly to avow evolution only after he had identified a mechanism by which it could plausibly proceed—natural selection, a process about which Erasmus says nothing—he felt justified in denying any influence of his grandfather's evolutionary ideas upon his own. Erasmus may have interested himself in some strikingly similar topics, but his "prophetic" speculations held no credibility with a grandson who demanded that empirical observation precede and undergird theory.[16]

---

15 Charles Darwin, *The Works of Charles Darwin*, eds Paul H. Barrett and R. B. Freeman, Vol. XXIX: *Erasmus Darwin by Ernst Krause, with a Preliminary Notice by Charles Darwin* (New York: New York University Press, 1989), 22. Subsequent citation will refer to this reprint of the 1879 John Murray edition, will be abbreviated *ED*, and will appear parenthetically.

16 Nora Barlow incisively appraises the common ground shared by Erasmus and Charles Darwin, and the grandson's reasons for not seeing the extent of their similarity, in "On Charles

Darwin asserts that his father Robert Waring Darwin, although he followed in Erasmus's footsteps and became a highly successful physician,

> ... did not inherit any aptitude for poetry or mechanics, nor did he possess, as I think, a scientific mind ... I cannot tell why my father's mind did not appear to me fitted for advancing science; for he was fond of theorizing, and was incomparably the most acute observer whom I ever knew. But his powers in this direction were exercised almost wholly in the practice of medicine, and in the observation of human character. He intuitively recognized the disposition or character, and even read the thoughts, of those with whom he came into contact with extraordinary acuteness. (ED 37)

It seems clear that even if Darwin "cannot tell" why his father failed to seem scientific to him, his next sentence implies the reason, which is the same for his disavowal of Erasmus's influence. For Charles, scientific theory could not legitimately exist without a solid foundation of facts supporting (if not proving) it. Such facts could be gathered only through a broad and deep observation of the natural world. Robert's acute observations and intuitions, centered on people he knew and especially those he treated, were too narrowly focused to be those of a scientist as understood by Charles.

The *Autobiography* takes a tack similar to the account in the memoir of Erasmus and praises Robert's talents in areas useful to scientific naturalists: "His chief mental powers were his powers of observation and his sympathy, neither of which have I ever seen exceeded or even equaled" (*A* 29). Again, however, Charles emphatically denies a "scientific" character to Robert's powerful mind: "My father's mind was not scientific, and he did not try to generalise his knowledge under general laws; yet he formed a theory for almost everything which occurred. I do not think that I gained much from him intellectually" (*A* 42). Here again, the missing element seems to have been empirical study of the natural world and systematic, responsible movement from the particular to the general. Because Robert Darwin's remarkable powers of observation were bent only on his fellow human beings, in his son's eyes he'd not paid the dues to be called "scientific."

Let us now turn to Darwin's self-scrutiny in the *Autobiography*. The retrospective Charles did not see himself as a particularly promising child, though several of the qualities evident in his boyhood—"strong and diversified tastes, much zeal for whatever interested me, and a keen pleasure in understanding any complex subject or thing" (*A* 43)—furnished rich raw materials from which a naturalist's character might be formed. His early, apparently aimless passions for field sports and beetle-collecting did not suit him for academic distinction in the classical *imitatio* that prevailed at Shrewsbury School, or for Edinburgh's medical courses centered on lectures he found tedious and dissection he found distasteful, or for Cambridge's curriculum focused on the training of future Anglican clergy. But his formal education had the advantage of putting him in touch with like-minded men whose sensibilities and accomplishments offered congenial models. Describing his Cambridge mentor John Stevens Henslow, Darwin might have been speaking of himself: "His strongest

---

Darwin and his Grandfather Dr Erasmus Darwin," Part One of the Appendix to her edition of the *Autobiography*, 149–66.

taste was to draw conclusions from long-continued minute observations" (*A* 64). Similarly, Darwin's story of a large tropical volute shell found in a gravel pit near Shrewsbury, a tale he told to the Cambridge geologist Adam Sedgwick, beautifully captures his sudden awareness of what science could do and how it worked as a mental discipline:

> Whilst examining an old gravel-pit near Shrewsbury a labourer told me that he had found in it a large worn tropical Volute shell, such as may be seen on the chimney-pieces of cottages; and as he would not sell the shell I was convinced that he had really found it in the pit. I told Sedgwick of the fact, and he at once said (no doubt truly) that it must have been thrown away by someone into the pit; but then added, if really embedded there it would be the greatest misfortune to geology, as it would overthrow all that we know about the superficial deposits of the midland counties. These gravel-beds belonged in fact to the glacial period, and in after years I found in them broken arctic shells. But I was then utterly astonished at Sedgwick not being delighted at so wonderful a fact as a tropical shell being found near the surface in the middle of England. Nothing before had ever made me thoroughly realise, though I had read various scientific books, that science consists in grouping facts so that general laws or conclusions may be drawn from them. (*A* 69–70)

Whatever his country pastimes and Cambridge associations may have contributed, Darwin believed that he owed his mind's "first real training" to the *Beagle* voyage, itself made possible through Cambridge contacts. Aboard and ashore, Darwin recollected, "I was led to attend closely to several branches of natural history, and thus my powers of observation were improved, though they were already fairly developed" (*A* 77). Throughout the five years of the voyage Darwin tirelessly collected animal and plant specimens, but he believed that his geological investigation of the places he visited was far more important because geological observation immediately called for reasoning:

> On first examining a new district nothing can appear more hopeless than the chaos of rocks; but by recording the stratification and nature of the rocks and fossils at many points, always reasoning and predicting what will be found elsewhere, light soon begins to dawn on the district, and the structure of the whole becomes more or less intelligible. (*A* 77)

Geology again offered the key when, back home in England, Darwin decided to embark on the ambitious project that was to last him a lifetime, understanding "the variation of plants and animals under domestication and in nature." Darwin resolved to follow the example of Sir Charles Lyell, whose first volume of *Principles of Geology* had shaped his *Beagle* geologizing, and determined to collect all facts bearing on the problem of variation. Darwin began his first variation notebook in July 1837: "I worked on true Baconian principles, and without any theory collected facts on a wholesale scale, more especially with respect to domesticated productions, by printed enquiries, by conversation with skilful breeders and gardeners, and by extensive reading" (*A* 119). This wholesale fact-gathering of course included first-hand observation and experimentation along with second-hand research. Its personal consequence, as understood by Darwin, seems to have been the evolution of his own mind, a strengthening of regularly exercised faculties and weakening of those neglected: "My mind seems to have become a kind of machine for grinding general laws out of large collections of facts" (*A* 139). The price Darwin believed he paid for this specialization was a loss or diminution of imaginative and aesthetic pleasures that formerly had delighted him: poetry, Shakespeare, pictures, music, scenery. "On the other hand," he confesses, "novels which are works of the imagination, though not of a very high order, have been for years a wonderful relief and pleasure to me, and I often bless all novelists" (*A* 138). It may be that Darwin's escapist way of using novels—he liked them read aloud to him, preferred happy endings, delighted in a character "whom one can thoroughly love, and if it be a pretty woman all the better" (*A* 139)—explains the endurance of this taste. But it may also be that the shared approaches and goals of naturalist and novelist allowed novels to continue appealing to Darwin after other less empirically grounded aesthetic pleasures had paled.

The *Autobiography*'s interpretation of Darwin's mental qualities is characteristically modest and self-deprecatory, though it stoutly refutes some critics' claims that "'Oh, he is a good observer, but has no power of reasoning.' I do not think that this can be true, for the *Origin of Species* is one long argument from the beginning to the end, and it has convinced not a few able men" (*A* 140).

Darwin reports that he has "become a little more skilful in guessing right explanations and in devising experimental tests; but this may probably be the result of mere practice, and of a larger store of knowledge" (*A* 136). On the other hand, verbal facility does not seem to have come with practice, though Darwin believes that his self-diagnosed deficiency in expression is offset by a consequent advantage in cognition: "I have as much difficulty as ever in expressing myself clearly and concisely; and this difficulty has caused me a very great loss of time; but it has had the compensating advantage of forcing me to think long and intently about every sentence, and thus I have been often led to see errors in reasoning and in my own observations or those of others" (*A* 136). Perhaps Darwin's self-deprecation here refers to spontaneous rather than laboriously crafted fluency. If not, the modesty is somewhat disingenuous; for the end results of Darwin's rhetorical struggles are always serviceable and sometimes brilliant. Throughout his published works, Darwin's careful qualification of claims and canny hedging of hypotheses prudently contrast with the confidence and precision of his observation and description of details. A shrewd strategist, he excels in the arrangement of particulars and generalizations—whether within paragraphs, chapters, and complete works or at the metalevel, in the sequenced pursuit and publication of his intellectual projects, one example being his decision to follow the abstract argument of *Origin of Species* (1859) with the empirically detailed monograph *On the Various Contrivances by Which British Orchids are Fertilised by Insects, and on the Good Effects of Intercrossing* (1862).[17] His habitual narrative tone of commonsensical modesty, the voice of an exhaustively

---

17 Writing to his publisher John Murray on the subject of the orchid book on September 24, 1861, Darwin observed, "I think this little volume will do good to the 'Origin,' as it will show that I have worked hard at details", *The Correspondence of Charles Darwin*, eds Frederick H. Burkhardt, Sidney Smith, Duncan M. Porter, *et al.* (Cambridge: Cambridge University Press, 1985–), IX, 29. Subsequent citations of Darwin's letters will refer to this edition, abbreviated *CCD*, and will be parenthetical.

well-informed, sagacious everyman, perfectly captures Darwin's distinctive blend of empirical caution and speculative ambition, in published and private writings alike.

As he nears the end of his *Autobiography*, Darwin lays out his ruling qualities in a tone of detachment and humility:

> On the favourable side of the balance, I think that I am superior to the common run of men in noticing things which easily escape attention, and in observing them carefully. My industry has been nearly as great as it could have been in the observation and collection of facts. What is far more important, my love of natural science has been steady and ardent ... From my early youth I have had the strongest desire to understand or explain whatever I observed,—that is, to group all facts under some general laws. These causes combined have given me the patience to reflect or ponder for any number of years over any unexplained problem. As far as I can judge, I am not apt to follow blindly the lead of other men. I have steadily endeavoured to keep my mind free, so as to give up any hypothesis, however much beloved (and I cannot resist forming one on every subject), as soon as facts are shown to be opposed to it. Indeed I have had no choice but to act in this matter, for with the exception of the Coral Reefs, I cannot remember a single first-formed hypothesis which had not after a time to be given up or greatly modified. This has naturally led me to distrust greatly deductive reasoning in the mixed sciences. On the other hand, I am not very skeptical ... (*A* 140–41)

Darwin sees himself as able to put these qualities of mind to efficient use thanks to methodical habits, the financial independence that has freed him from having to earn a living, and even his ill-health, which has insulated him from distractions even if it has also diminished his productivity (*A* 144). He concludes by attributing his success as a man of science to a complex and various array of traits:

> Of these the most important have been—the love of science—unbounded patience in long reflecting over any subject—industry in observing and collecting facts—and a fair share of invention as well as of common-sense. With such moderate abilities as I possess, it is truly surprising that thus I should have influenced to a considerable extent the beliefs of scientific men on some important points. (*A* 145)

Unlike Charles Darwin the autobiographer, Jane Austen never appraised her qualities of mind or her operating principles in a systematic or extensive way. She wrote little about the novelist's art in general or about her own particular ways of practicing it. Apart from what's demonstrated in her literary works themselves, what we can discern of her values, precepts, and strengths as a novelist comes principally from her letters; and much of the time we are obliged to operate by inference when reading them. Austen's published letters have sometimes disappointed readers who hope for something loftier, more speculative, and more "literary" rather than the prosaic, detail-dense bulletins she tends to dispatch.[18] Such readerly hopes and disappointments, though natural, are at heart unreasonable. Austen lived the sort of life she lived, and she wrote the sort of letters she and her correspondents

---

18 Jane Austen's letters, as her editor Deirdre LeFay points out, were heavily weeded and censored by her sister Cassandra, who was likelier to destroy entire letters than to excise individual portions, though to the regret of subsequent generations she did both.

(by far the most prominent among them her sister Cassandra) valued. That ought to be enough. As readers of early-nineteenth-century British correspondence, we should not be disappointed that Austen isn't as aesthetically speculative a letter-writer as John Keats or as amusingly confessional yet artful a correspondent as Lord Byron, any more than we should reproach or congratulate her for not having lived the life either Keats or Byron chose for himself.

Austen's penchant for close, clear observation—the skilled naturalist's eye trained on human society—pervades her letters. A typical passage of observation occurs in her Friday 2 September 1814 letter from London to her friend Martha Lloyd, then sojourning at Bath:

> I am amused by the present style of female dress;—the coloured petticoats with braces over the white Spencers & enormous Bonnets upon the full stretch, are quite entertaining. It seems to me a more marked *change* than one has lately seen.—Long sleeves appear universal, even as *Dress*, the Waists short, and as far as I have been able to judge, the Bosom covered.—I was at a little party last night at M[rs] Latouche's, where dress is a good deal attended to, & these are my observations from it.—Petticoats short, & generally, tho' not always, flounced.—The broad-straps belonging to the Gown or Boddice, which cross the front of the Waist, over white, have a very pretty effect I think. (*JAL* 273)

This close attention to minutiae—analogous, one might say, to Darwin's fascination with the diverse and fanciful variety in breeds of domestic pigeons[19]—indicates genuine interest. It also displays sensitivity to her audience's expectations, for one thing cherished by women living in "country villages" as did Jane Austen and Martha Lloyd was current intelligence of what fashions prevailed in sophisticated metropolitan circles. Although Austen was skilled at noticing and transmitting such trivial details, she apparently did not ascribe much value to female or male preoccupation with fashions in dress or personal accessories. Her novels contain little taxonomy of gowns or greatcoats, and when a character displays explicit interest in clothing or adornment, the trait is heavily ironized. Only the likes of dim-witted matrons like Mrs Bennet and Mrs Allen, shallow materialists like Augusta Hawkins Elton and Isabella Thorpe, simple-minded ingénues like Harriet Smith, and dunderheads like Mr Rushworth with his "pink satin cape" for *Lovers Vows* or Robert Ferrars with his obsessive concern for the design specifications of a bespoke toothpick-case display overt concern with the minutiae of fashion that constitute the substance of Austen's epistolary report; though of course any Austen heroine pronounced "elegant" must pay some attention to such matters beyond the frame of the narrative. Prosaic details in general receive this sort of double-edged treatment in Austenworld, where it seems that admirable characters have the material concerns of their lives well regulated and hence should be understood as having given a certain amount of attention to them—but where putting one's attentiveness to small details into words is nearly always presented as a laughable quality, most pronounced in the case of *Emma*'s Miss Bates, who's apparently incapable of stemming the flow of

---

[19] Darwin treats domestic pigeons in Chapters V and VI of *The Variation of Animals and Plants under Domestication*, ed. Harriet Ritvo (Baltimore, MD: Johns Hopkins University Press, 1998, repr. of the 1883 second edition), 137–235.

what Austen, in a letter advising her niece Anna Austen on novel-writing, called "too many particulars of right hand & left" (*JAL* 275). But more of this anon.

Observations on fiction—Austen's own principles and practices or those of her fellow novelists—are much less commonly encountered in her letters than are the minute particulars of real life as lived by those people among whom she passed her time. Her clearest statements on novels and their composition appear in letters to members of the younger generation of Austens who shared their Aunt Jane's penchant for fiction-writing. Letters throughout the autumn of 1814 discuss a novel being written by her niece Anna Austen, who was married in November to Ben Lefroy. Austen pays Anna's manuscript the compliment of reading it carefully and taking it seriously. She mainly offers feedback and advice centered on specific details of character, incident, motivation, and word choice. A few examples:

> We are not satisfied with M^{rs} F's settling herself as Tenant & near Neighbour to such a Man as Sir T. H. without having some other inducement to go there; she ought to have some friend living thereabouts to tempt her. (*JAL* 274–5)

> Susan ought not to be walking out so soon after Heavy rains, taking long walks in the dirt. An anxious Mother would not suffer it. (*JAL* 275)

> Newton Priors is really a Nonpareil.—Milton w^d have given his eyes to have thought of it.—Is not the Cottage taken from Tollard Royal? (*JAL* 276)

> Devereux Forester's being ruined by his Vanity is extremely good; but I wish you would not let him plunge into a 'vortex of Dissipation'. I do not object to the Thing, but I cannot bear the expression;—it is such thorough novel slang—and so old, that I dare say Adam met with it in the first novel he opened. (*JAL* 277)

Austen's overarching values—keeping faith with plausibility as empirical observation understands it, deriving details from real life, relying on fresh language rather than cant phrases—are not announced but to be inferred inductively. Her first letter, of Friday 9 to Sunday 18 September 1814 does, however, offer Anna two key principles:

> You are now collecting your People delightfully, getting them exactly into such a spot as is the delight of my life;—3 or 4 Families in a Country Village is the very thing to work on—& I hope you will write a great deal more, & make full use of them while they are so very favourably arranged. You are but *now* coming to the heart & beauty of your book; till the heroine grows up, the fun must be imperfect—... (*JAL* 275)

These remarks to Anna straightforwardly reveal Austen's own preferences—but interestingly, a close look at her words shows that one of these preferences has particularly close relevance to her current project. Throughout her novels, Austen's center-staging of unmarried but marriageable characters, with children relegated to bit parts and married adults to supporting roles, is undeniable; and all her novels follow this precept, restated later in the paragraph: "One does not care for girls till they are grown up" (*JAL* 276). Her avowed "delight" in working on the interaction of a handful of village families more accurately characterizes *Emma*, which she was writing in 1814, than any of her other works. Nonetheless, the formula loosely fits all six published novels. *Sense and Sensibility*'s Dashwood sisters are uprooted from one country neighborhood (not to say village), transplanted to another, then taken on their travels to London; so theirs is not so much a chronicle of settled village life as a discovery of new places and people. *Pride and Prejudice*'s Bennet sisters inhabit such a neighborhood, but it becomes worth writing about at the very moment when characters from the outside world arrive to shake things up and, in partial consequence, the individual Bennets gain chances to travel to other places (rural Kent, London, Derbyshire, Brighton). *Northanger Abbey*'s Catherine Morland, having just grown up, is dislodged from her village home and allowed to turn fresh eyes on the delights of Bath and the gothic charms of the novel's namesake country house. *Mansfield Park*'s Fanny Price, saved from urban squalor by being sent away from home, matures in a closed-off country-house world that for years seems to contain only two related families—the landowning Bertrams and the Norrises at the Parsonage—until death and debt bring new tenants and their relations. In *Persuasion* Anne Elliot's story, like Fanny's, involves exile—this time from, not to, a country-house neighborhood, with new experiences and perspectives contingent on Anne's re-situation at Uppercross, Lyme Regis, and Bath. Allowing for these variations on the basic theme, "3 or 4 families in a country village" is a formula that fits Austen's fiction.

In contrast to her uninflected, highly particular advice to Anna, Austen's remarks of Monday 16 to Tuesday 17 December 1816 to Anna's brother James Edward Austen, also trying his hand at novel-writing, seem arch and edgy. Austen offers her nephew an obviously facetious recommendation of plagiarism, particularly amusing in that it comes from a clergyman's daughter who never put a sermon into one of her novels and it goes to a clergyman's son: "Uncle Henry writes very superior Sermons.—You & I must try to get hold of one or two, & put them into our Novels;—it would be a fine help to a volume; & we could make our Heroine read it aloud of a Sunday Evening…" (*JAL* 323). One can't help but wonder if this whimsical suggestion doesn't contain an oblique slam at another sermon-writer, James Edward's father James, the eldest Austen son, who took over Steventon parish from his father and thus displaced his sister Jane from her settled home without intending to do so. Are James's sermons inferior to Henry's by implication? Is it a compliment for real-life sermons to be considered worth stealing by a comic-ironic novelist of Austen's sort? In any case, James Edward's own style of novel must have been quite different from his aunt's, as becomes clear when Austen recurs to the matter of prose-theft, though in a different situation. She laments over her nephew's having lost part of his manuscript:

> Bye the bye, my dear Edward, I am quite concerned for the loss your Mother mentions in her Letter; two Chapters & a half to be missing is monstrous! It is well that *I* have not been at Steventon lately, & therefore cannot be suspected of purloining them;—two strong twigs & a half towards a Nest of my own, would have been something.—I do not think however that any theft of that sort would be really very useful to me. What should I do with your strong, manly, spirited Sketches, full of Variety & Glow?—How could I possibly join them on to the little bit (two Inches wide) of Ivory on which I work with so fine a Brush, as produces little effect after much labour? (*JAL* 323)

However humorously self-deprecatory the invocation of stereotypes—dainty, feminine Jane deferring to robust, virile Edward—this passage has the potential to seem patronizing, perhaps even a bit unpleasant. Unless Edward were a pompous youth remarkably unappreciative of his aunt's published brilliance and even more infatuated than adolescent writers tend to be with his own apprentice efforts, he would very likely have squirmed at the irony. Over the years Austen's memorable metaphor "little bit (two Inches wide) of Ivory" has often been wrenched from its epistolary frame and read uninflected, as Austen's sincere self-characterization as a literary miniaturist. But the delicate balance of self-disclosure and misleading pose is what makes the passage worth considering and remembering. Austen understands full well how limited and perhaps trivial her chosen field of fiction-writing looks from certain vantage points, such as those of romancers, philosophers, moralizers, generalizers, practitioners of what Sir Walter Scott (with self-deprecation equal to Austen's) called "the big Bow-wow."[20] But from her perspective, that of the empirical novelist–naturalist, a small field's well worth intensive labor. Charles Darwin, barnacle boy and earthworm impresario, would agree with her.

The blend of irony and honesty, self-deprecation and self-confidence detectable in the letter to James Edward Austen is more continuously and unambiguously evident in Austen's correspondence with James Stanier Clarke, though the recipient himself, a man apparently tone-deaf to wryness, seems to have missed it. Clarke as self-presented in his letters to Austen seems uncannily like a comic clergyman Austen might have invented. In his role as Domestic Chaplain and Librarian to the Prince of Wales, Clarke had informed Austen that she was at liberty to dedicate any of her works to HRH the PR—and *Emma*, being the work then in progress, was duly dedicated to the Prince. Having gained his point—one a courteous subject could not decently refuse to grant the Regent—Clarke couldn't help offering Austen advice for subsequent novels in a letter of Thursday 16 November 1815. Without directly suggesting his own suitability as a protagonist, he asks Austen "to delineate in some future Work the Habits of Life and Character and enthusiasm of a Clergyman—who should pass his time between the metropolis & the Country ... —Fond of, & entirely engaged in Literature—no man's Enemy but his own. Pray dear Madam think of these things" (*JAL* 296–7).

Austen's reply of Monday 11 December 1815 should have been seen as an unanswerable demurral:

> I am quite honoured by your thinking me capable of drawing such a Clergyman as you gave the sketch of in your note of Nov: 16. But I assure you I am *not*. The comic part of the Character I might be equal to, but not the Good, the Enthusiastic, the Literary. Such a Man's Conversation must at times be on subjects of Science & Philosophy of which I

---

20 This phrase comes from a journal entry of March 14, 1826, where Scott mentions reading *Pride and Prejudice* for at least the third time: "That young lady has a talent for describing the involvements and feelings and characters of ordinary life which is to me the most wonderful I ever met with. The big Bow Wow strain I can do myself like any now going but the exquisite truth which renders ordinary common-place things and characters interesting from the truth of the description and the sentiment is denied to me", Walter Scott, *Journal of Sir Walter Scott*, ed. W. K. Anderson (Oxford: Clarendon Press, 1972), 114.

know nothing—or at least be occasionally abundant in quotations & allusions which a Woman, who like me, knows only her own Mother-tongue & has read very little in that, would be totally without the power of giving.—A Classical Education, or at any rate, a very extensive acquaintance with English Literature, Ancient & Modern, appears to me quite Indispensable for the person who w^d do any justice to your Clergyman—And I think I may boast myself to be, with all possible Vanity, the most unlearned, & uninformed Female who ever dared to be an Authoress. (*JAL* 306)

But Clarke couldn't drop the subject. He responded on Thursday [?]21 December 1815. Clarke's letter begins with some tactless bustling about *Emma*, remarkable given his previous praise of her work: "You were very good to send me Emma—which I have in no respect deserved. It is gone to the Prince Regent. I have read only a few Pages which I very much admired." Having admitted that he's not taken time for more than the merest sampling of the novel Austen has dedicated according to his suggestions and sent his way, Clarke reverts to directing Austen on what she should tackle next:

> Do let us have an English Clergyman after *your* fancy—much novelty may be introduced—shew dear Madam what good would be done if Tythes were taken away entirely, and describe him burying his own mother—as I did—because the High Priest of the Parish in which she died—did not pay her remains the respect he ought to do. I have never recovered the Shock. Carry your Clergyman to Sea as the Friend of some distinguished Naval Character about a Court ... (*JAL* 307)

So goes the formerly seagoing clerical courtier's effort to elicit Austen's interest and direct her genius. But he recognizes that besides offering himself to the provincial novelist as a potential model, he might also extend the use of his urban library:

> Pray, dear Madam, remember, that besides My Cell at Carlton House, I have another which Dr Barne procured for me at N° 37, Golden Square—where I often hide myself. There is a small Library there much at your Service—and if you can make the Cell render you any service as a sort of Half-way House when you come to Town—I shall be most happy. There is a Maid Servant of mine always there. (*JAL* 307)

The diction (especially "Cell") and the level of detail (especially the prim mention of the ever-present, potentially chaperoning "Maid Servant") are wonderfully oily enough to have come from the mouth of Mr Collins himself. But they didn't, and unfortunately Austen's reply doesn't exist.

It cannot have been too crushing, though, for a few months later Clarke wrote to offer yet another idea that flatters his own consequence while purporting to serve Austen's novel-writing interests:

> The Prince Regent has just left us for London; and having been pleased to appoint me Chaplain and Private English Secretary to the Prince of Cobourg, I remain here with His Serene Highness & a select Party until the Marriage [of Prince Leopold to Princess Charlotte]. Perhaps when you again appear in print you may chuse to dedicate your Volumes to Prince Leopold: any Historical Romance illustrative of the History of the august house of Cobourg, would just now be very interesting. (*JAL* 311)

This inspiration, as self-inflating for Clarke as it is uncongenial to Austen's talent, must have made her laugh inside; but she keeps a straight face—or at least what Clarke might take for one—in her reply:

> You are very, very kind in your hints as to the sort of Composition which might recommend me at present, & I am fully sensible that an Historical Romance, founded on the House of Saxe Cobourg might be much more to the purpose of Profit or Popularity, than such pictures of domestic Life in Country Villages as I deal in—but I could no more write a Romance than an Epic Poem.—I could not sit seriously down to write a serious Romance under any other motive than to save my Life, & if it were indispensable for me to keep it up & never relax into laughing at myself or other people, I am sure I should be hung before I had finished the first Chapter.—No—I must keep to my own style & go on in my own Way; And though I may never succeed again in that, I am convinced that I should totally fail in any other. (*JAL* 312)

Recognizing and acknowledging her strengths and limitations, Austen affirms her generic allegiance to the fictional species called novel—and her subgenre, the novel of domestic country life—as opposed to the romance. She most explicitly avows the value of the genre to which her talents are best adapted in a long digression found in Chapter V of *Northanger Abbey*, perhaps the most sustained example the novels display of Austen speaking more or less straightforwardly in her own voice.

The passage comes just after the narrator has reported that Isabella and Catherine "shut themselves up, to read novels together." It's worth quoting in full:

> Yes, novels;—for I will not adopt that ungenerous and impolitic custom so common with novel writers, of degrading by their contemptuous censure the very performances, to the number of which they are themselves adding—joining with their greatest enemies in bestowing the harshest epithets on such works, and scarcely ever permitting them to be read by their own heroine, who, if she accidentally take up a novel, is sure to turn over its insipid pages with disgust. Alas! If the heroine of one novel be not patronized by the heroine of another, from whom can she expect protection and regard? I cannot approve of it. Let us leave it to the Reviewers to abuse such effusions of fancy at their leisure, and over every new novel to talk in threadbare strains of the trash with which the press now groans. Let us not desert one another; we are an injured body. Although our productions have afforded more extensive and unaffected pleasure than those of any other literary corporation in the world, no species of composition has been so much decried. From pride, ignorance, or fashion, our foes are almost as many as our readers. And while the abilities of the nine-hundredth abridger of the History of England, or of the man who collects and publishes in a volume some dozen lines of Milton, Pope, and Prior, with a paper from the Spectator, and a chapter from Sterne, are eulogized by a thousand pens,—there seems almost a general wish of decrying the capacity and undervaluing the labour of the novelist, and of slighting the performances which have only genius, wit, and taste to recommend them. "I am no novel reader—I seldom look into novels—Do not imagine that *I* often read novels—It is really very well for a novel." Such is the common cant.—"And what are you reading, Miss ____?" "Oh! it is only a novel!" replies the young lady; while she lays down her book with affected indifference, or momentary shame.—"It is only Cecelia, or Camilla, or Belinda;" or, in short, only some work in which the greatest powers of the

mind are displayed, in which the most thorough knowledge of human nature, the happiest delineation of its varieties, the liveliest effusions of wit and humour are conveyed to the world in the best chosen language.[21]

A work demanding "the greatest powers of the mind," "most thorough knowledge of human nature," "happiest delineation of its varieties," "liveliest effusions of wit and humour," and "best chosen language" is a worthy task indeed. That Austen could see the novel this way says as much about her mind as it does about the form itself. Second- or third-rate novelists might fail in one count or in all of them—but a discipline that ideally makes use of such varied and important powers is bound to both earn the respect and showcase the talents of an empirical naturalist with a ready wit and a way with words.

Naturalists and novelists interested in "knowable communities" must frame their studies with care. Too narrow a frame and one risks observing anomaly or unconnected detail. Too large a frame and the patterns formed by particulars are lost in a vista's vast sweep. The poet–artist–engraver William Blake, a philosophical and political idealist who also, thanks to his incarnationalism, also had his feet firmly planted on the ground, voices the dream or necessity of linking great and small. Well-known lines (1–2) from "Auguries of Innocence" articulate his aspiration "To see the World in a Grain of Sand/ And Heaven in a Wild Flower/ Hold Infinity in the Palm of your hand/ And Eternity in an Hour." Blake makes this point more abstractly in *Jerusalem* (plate 91, ll. 20–21)–"… he who wishes to see a Vision; a perfect Whole,/ Must see it in its Minute Particulars"—and in "A Pretty Epigram (ll. 1–2) …"—"Nature and Art in this together Suit/ What is Most Grand is always most Minute."[22] A visionary, Blake need not offer a pedestrian means of getting from minute particulars to the perfect whole. But, as Austen and Darwin later would, one of his contemporaries, the eighteenth-century geologist James Hutton, understood how to get the scale of a study right. In *Theory of the Earth*, Hutton clearly outlines the advantages of a small-scale yet representative study as he explains why the Isle of Arran off the coast of Scotland served as an ideal case in point for his British mineral survey. Hutton began by knowing only

> that there were most eminent alpine appearances on that island, as seen from a distance; that there was granite in those mountains; and that there were, besides, in the island, coal and limestone. But these, in an island of that extent, were sufficient to make it a proper subject of natural history, and interesting as leading to the knowledge of the original constitution of our land. The island of Britain is a country too great for that purpose; that of Arran, considering its extent, is not too little.[23]

---

21 Jane Austen, *Northanger Abbey*, ed. R. W. Chapman (London and New York: Oxford University Press, 1933, repr. 1972), 37–8. This quotation comes from Chapman's third revised edition of *The Novels of Jane Austen*, as will all other quotations from her novels. Subsequent citations will use the abbreviation *NA* and will be parenthetical.

22 William Blake, *Complete Poems and Prose*, ed. David V. Erdmann (Berkeley, CA and Los Angeles: University of California Press, 1982), 490, 251, 513.

23 James Hutton, *James Hutton in the Field and the Study* (Delmar, NY: Scholars Facsimiles and Reprints, 1997), 199–200. Subsequent citations will be parenthetical.

Hutton continues that a naturalist able to recognize Arran's mineral evidence as sufficient to lead to "the knowledge of all that is necessary in the production of the land, or the surface of the earth, as a habitable world" will find the island's small size a "manifest advantage." Arran's geology can be understood empirically, but the process doesn't end there. The island's fully comprehensible yet representative nature makes it what we might think of as a geological metonym. Thus systematic principles can be inductively derived from the empirically observed data in such a way that close study of Arran can serve either of two larger purposes: theory-making or theory-testing, in Hutton's words either "forming a theory to be applied to other parts unknown" or "trying the justness of a theory formed from the various appearances collected from the different parts of the earth" (200).

Recognizing when one has found a set of minute particulars that will lead, gradually and incrementally, to the perfect, or even proximate, whole it represents in metonym requires the serendipitist's trained sagacity as well as the empiricist's clear eye. When in September 1835 the *Beagle* reached the Galápagos Islands far off the coast of Ecuador, the evidence of how geographical separation allows the individual constituents of a species to diverge over time into distinctly identifiable varieties lay right before Darwin, who had stumbled upon some perfect "knowable communities"—as did the evidence of how members of a species can vary though the generations to fill different, highly specialized niches in an ecosystem. But as Darwin explored several of the Galápagos Islands (most thoroughly the island the English called James and the Spanish Santiago, where he and a small party disembarked for a week) and collected specimens, he was not yet prepared to fathom the significance of what he saw and gathered. Unlike the fabled Princes of Serendip, he did not at the time have a mind prepared to grasp the significance of the particulars he saw.

Though called las islas Encantadas, the enchanted isles, by their Spanish colonizers, the Galápagos do not enchant the eye in a conventional way. Bare, black shores of cooled and contorted lava, dark sand beaches, intermittently productive volcanic cones, and generally sparse, scrubby vegetation give the equatorial archipelago a look of the inferno rather than of the tropical paradise the novelist Kurt Vonnegut imagines the archipelago becoming a million years hence. But the Galápagos are a naturalist's heaven, for their oddly assorted ecosystem contains a number of plant and animal species found nowhere else. As Darwin observes in his narrative of the *Beagle* voyage, published in 1839, when work had begun on classifying the specimens he had brought home in 1836, the Galápagos archipelago "seems to be a little world within itself; the greater number of its inhabitants, both vegetable and animal, being found nowhere else."[24] But Darwin recognized that these unique species were obviously related to other, familiar species; and the surprising thing was that the Galápagos plants and animals more closely resembled those of the South American mainland than those inhabiting the Cape Verde islands, a comparable equatorial island group off the west coast of Africa whose plants and animals in turn were similar to those of continental Africa.

---

24 Charles Darwin, *The Works of Charles Darwin*, eds Paul H. Barrett and R. B. Freeman, Vols II and III of *Journal of Researches* (New York: New York University Press, 1987), II, 356. Subsequent citations will be parenthetical and will use the abbreviation *JR*.

This resemblance of offshore island species to their continental neighbors rather than to the inhabitants of similar offshore islands in more distant parts of the world perplexed Darwin, who at the time of the *Beagle* voyage and for some years afterward still largely adhered to the biblical account of God creating each species distinctly. It was hard to understand why God would choose to make such dissimilar life forms to occupy habitats as similar as the Cape Verde and Galápagos islands. A more rational explanation lay in the evolutionary hypothesis that mainland species had traveled by air or water to the islands, established isolated populations that diverged from their mainland relatives, and over time become new varieties and species; but in 1839, when his *Beagle* collections had not been fully examined, the diplomatic Darwin was not willing to go too far into the realms of speculation. "We may infer," he said,

> that with the exception of a few wanderers, the organic beings found on this archipelago are peculiar to it; and yet their general form strongly partakes of an American character. ... This similarity in type, between distant islands and continents, while the species are distinct, has scarcely been sufficiently noticed. The circumstance would be explained, according to the views of some authors, by saying that the creative power had acted according to the same law over a wide area. (*JR* II, 371)

Writing solely for himself as he was cataloging ornithological specimens on the *Beagle*'s journey home, Darwin jotted down a bolder conjecture based on the island-to-island differences that he had noted in mockingbirds and on similar distinctions the Spanish Galápagos residents could discern in tortoises: "If there is the slightest foundation for these remarks, the zoology of Archipelagoes—will be well worth examining; for such facts undermine the stability of species." And in a typical rhetorical gesture, whether motivated by empirical precision or self-policing prudence, he inserted a "would" before "undermine."[25]

For many years, a vivid and enduring myth held that the Galápagos finches were the crucial species in Darwin's speculative drama, and that observing them led him to an evolutionary epiphany on the spot. Not so, as Frank Sulloway convincingly demonstrated in a series of 1982–84 articles on the Galápagos finches, the *Beagle* voyage, and Darwin's conversion from a creationist to an evolutionist who saw natural selection as the mechanism by which varieties emerged and eventually became distinct species.[26] Darwin was first drawn to gradations in Galápagos mockingbirds, while in fact the thirteen species of wonderfully varied though uniformly brown-to-black Galápagos finches initially struck him as so distinct in their forms, habitats, and diet that he failed to recognize them as related and accordingly did not see the need to carefully label his early collected specimens as to the island of origin.

---

25 Nora Barlow (ed.), "Darwin's Ornithological Notes," *Bulletin of the British Museum (Natural History). Historical Series* II (1963), 262.

26 Frank J. Sulloway, "The *Beagle* Collections of Darwin's Finches (*Geospizinae*)," *Bulletin of the British Museum of Natural History (Zoology)*, XLIII (1982), 49–94; "Darwin and His Finches: The Evolution of a Legend," *Journal of the History of Biology*, XV (1982), 1–53; "Darwin's Conversion: The *Beagle* Voyage and Its Aftermath," *Journal of the History of Biology* XV (1982), 325–96.

The members of the group we now call Darwin's finches, which descended from a common ancestral stock and gradually diverged to fill various ecological niches on the Galápagos archipelago in the absence of competition from other species, do not on the basis of mere observation seem closely related. Their beaks differ greatly in size, shape, and use. Some of the finches in fact look like finches; but others are more like warblers, wrens, or blackbirds. Their behaviors and diets vary widely. Some live on the familiar finch diet of seeds. Others feed on the flowers, nectar, seeds, and pollen of cacti. Vampire finches subsist on booby blood and eggs; tool-using finches pry grubs from decaying wood with stems or cactus spines; tick-eating finches pick their nourishment off the backs of iguanas; bark-peeling finches strip twigs and eat their tender interior parts. An apt motto for the thirteen diverse yet related Galápagos finches might invert the Latin tag the American founding fathers devised in 1776 for the thirteen separate colonies that had just united—*ex uno plura*, "from one thing, many"—but even if Darwin had indulged in classical witticisms, he couldn't have begun to envision such a genealogical possibility until after he had turned his bird specimens over to the London ornithologist John Gould for classification. Gould was excited to find so many hitherto undescribed bird specimens that were apparently unique to the Galápagos—particularly the diversely beaked brown-to-black birds that he found to be a group of finches. Aware at last of what he'd collected thanks to Gould's work of classifying, Darwin drew on the wisdom of hindsight to offer some tentative hypotheses on the finches' variation and speciation in *The Voyage of the Beagle*. But, cautious as usual, he cut off speculation before it carried him too far past what empirical evidence had shown:

> I have stated, that in the thirteen species of ground-finches, a nearly perfect gradation may be traced, from a beak extraordinarily thick, to one so fine, that it may be compared to that of a warbler. I very much suspect, that certain members of the series are confined to different islands; therefore, if the collection had been made on any *one* island, it would not have presented so perfect a gradation. It is clear, that if several islands have each their peculiar species of the same genera, when these are placed together, they will have a wide range of character. But there is not space in this work, to enter on this curious subject. (*JR* 372)

Darwin eventually came to understand that the Galápagos finches he had collected were the product of evolution through natural selection. In the twentieth and twenty-first centuries, the husband and wife research team of Peter and Rosemary Grant, Princeton-based evolutionary biologists, have annually watched the process of evolution at work in an ideally knowable community of Galápagos finches. The Grants' still-ongoing project, now regarded as a classic study of evolutionary biology and compellingly chronicled in their own scholarly publications and in Jonathan Weiner's *The Beak of the Finch: A Story of Evolution in Our Time*, has for more than thirty years involved monitoring successive generations of finches on the small island of Daphne Major.[27] Like James Hutton, the Grants understood the importance

---

27 Jonathan Weiner, *The Beak of the Finch: A Story of Evolution in Our Time* (New York: Knopf, 1994). The Grants' own accounts of their research appear in *Ecology and Evolution of Darwin's Finches* (Princeton, NJ: Princeton University Press, 1986); *Evolutionary Dynamics*

of finding a sample of the right scale for empirical observation, neither too large nor too small—and like him they chose their island well. Though centrally located in the Galápagos archipelago, Daphne Major has never been settled, or even much visited, by humans. It's a steep-cliffed stone in the sea, accessible from one sole landing spot, and only at low tide. With no beach, no harbor, no offshore anchorage possible in the deep Pacific waters, the rock called Daphne Major offers only one spot level enough for a campsite. It is springless, so drinking water and all other provisions must be hauled up a precipitous trail by the Grants and their research team. It's totally unshaded, often hot, slick with the guano of blue-footed boobies, and treacherous to circumambulate. But inhospitable though Daphne Major may be to humans, it sustains a population of finches that during the Grants' years of study has varied between a low of 300 and a high of more than a thousand.

The Grants intimately know each individual finch in this isolated finch community: they annually trap and band all but the wariest specimens, measure, weigh, and photograph the birds, and sample their blood for genetic analysis back at Princeton. Having served as the scientific census-takers for generations of finches in this environment almost impenetrably isolated from outside influences, the Grants have been able to watch Darwin's finches live out evolutionary principles that he was able only to theorize. Their observations on Daphne Major show that in the short term the branched, linear model of divergence that Darwin conceived of as resembling a tree—or, yet more aptly, coral because the living members are found at the top, above extinct predecessors that were intermediate between living types—is messy, more reticulated than branched, with the evolutionary directions varying lineages take proving to be tentative and twisty. Different lineages of the Daphne Major finches do diverge, but they also interbreed and blend. The Grants' scrupulously patient annual observation of particulars in their perfectly framed study shows that fission and fusion, competition and communion make the shaping of varieties and species subtler and less straightforward than Darwin, who had only the time of the *Beagle*'s short stay to observe and collect in the Galápagos and then was obliged to draw what conclusions he could from what data he had, could hardly have imagined.

The great gap between foresight and hindsight, the pressing but nearly impossible goal of somehow collecting all relevant details before one knows the significance of what one's gathering, and the difficulty in recognizing from a quick survey of surface features that apparently unrelated organisms are in fact closely related pose difficult enough problems for the empirical naturalist. But there's also the need to rely heavily on conjecture in deciding whether a sample, such as Hutton's Arran or the Grants' Daphne Major, is likely to be just large enough but not too large, just small enough but not too small—or in predicting how extensive the "3 or 4 families in a country village" might turn out to be. Determining whether immersion in concrete particulars will bog down or lead to general principles is likewise a matter of serendipitous guesswork. Case in point: Charles Darwin's meeting with a microscopic shell-less barnacle he whimsically called "Mr Arthrobalanus." When in January 1835 Darwin

---

of a Natural Population: The Large Cactus Finch of the Galápagos (Chicago, IL: University of Chicago Press, 1989), and many other publications.

walked along a Chilean beach where he found conch shells curiously riddled with tiny holes, he can't have suspected that his encounter with the parasitic marine animal responsible for those holes would lead to a project of epic proportions, one that would occupy nine years of his life (1846–54) and result in four hefty monographs together offering an exhaustive and definitive taxonomy of the subclass cirripedia, orders lepadidae, balanidae, and verrucidae—in other words barnacles, living and fossil, pedunculated and sessile.[28] This grand exercise in collecting, anatomizing, and classifying so filled Charles Darwin's days and dominated his domestic routine that a Darwin child was said to have asked concerning a neighbor's father, "Then where does he do his barnacles?"[29] Darwin's barnacle work was of course a consummately empirical enterprise, but it also intimately and crucially influenced his much more speculative and potentially controversial project on varieties and species—a preliminary 231-page draft of which had been finished in February 1844, set aside in a drawer with clear instructions charging his wife Emma to have the work published in the event of his death, and resurrected in September 1854, around the time the fourth and final barnacle volume was published. It's possible to view the vast yet minute barnacle project in a number of ways. As an obsession with minutiae, it undeniably distracted Darwin from his speculative work on how varieties and species arise. Yet it also enriched that greater project in a number of ways. Even the act of delay even turned out to be felicitous.

Darwin began what would come to be his nine-years' exile in the marine realm of barnacles as he was finishing the decade-long classification of his *Beagle* specimens and only one species remained to be placed, the anomalous barnacle *Arthrobalanus* collected years before on the Chilean coast. Darwin dissected the curious organism with the help of his friend J. D. Hooker, a confidant who knew the secret, tentative thoughts on natural selection recorded in Darwin's then-dormant manuscript. Hooker assisted with the laborious anatomizing by microscope and put Darwin in touch with an optician whose lens greatly improved Darwin's instrument. Darwin honed and polished his micro-anatomic techniques even as he deepened his collaborative and collegial friendship with Hooker, who had but recently returned from his own naturalist travels. Two weeks spent dissecting *Arthrobalanus* showed Darwin that "I could spend another month on it, & daily see some more beautiful structure!"[30] Understanding the particulars of these beautiful structures could come only through comparison with homologous parts in other species, so Darwin soon began borrowing

---

28 For much more on Darwin and his work with barnacles, see Rebecca Stott's learned and elegant monograph *Darwin and the Barnacle* (London: Faber and Faber, 2003).

29 Francis Darwin reports this incident in an amusing anecdote testifying to Darwin's persistence at his barnacle labors in the two-volume *More Letters of Charles Darwin* he co-edited with A. C. Seward (New York: Appleton and Co., 1903), I, 38: "This research would have fully occupied a less methodical workman, and even to those who saw him at work it seemed his whole occupation. Thus (to quote a story of Lord Avebury's) one of Mr Darwin's children is said to have asked, in regard to a neighbour, 'Then where does he do his barnacles?' as though not merely his father, but all other men, must be occupied on that group."

30 Quoted in Adrian Desmond and James Moore, *Darwin* (New York: Warner Books, 1991), p. 340.

barnacle specimens: different species and varieties at different stages of the barnacle life cycle. As was his way, an interest in one small thing widened.

In striving to understand the mysteries of *Arthrobalanus*, outrageously atypical yet undeniably a barnacle, Darwin had serendipitously begun to cultivate a fertile field of inquiry. As recently as 1830, barnacles had been classified in the wrong phylum. Barnacles had been considered members of *phylum Mollusca* rather than *Arthropoda*, until John Thompson's study of free-swimming barnacle larvae had shown that they were not mollusks but crustaceans—that though generally housed in shells and anchored throughout their adult lives to rocks, reefs, or ships, they were related to shrimp and lobsters, not mussels and limpets. In the 1830s, 40s, and 50s, when naturalists were at work examining and classifying various groups of marine creatures (Robert Grant studying sponges, Edward Forbes starfish and *medusae*, T. H. Huxley jellyfish, squid, sea squirts, and crawfish), barnacles remained comparatively neglected. Darwin felt the need to win his taxonomic spurs by coming to know everything about the entire barnacle community. Already skeptical of his grandfather Erasmus's evolutionary speculations for being too thinly supported by concrete observations, Darwin had been stung when Hooker, speaking of yet another naturalist who theorized about species, Frédéric Gérard, had dismissively stated that no one had earned the right to "examine the question of species who has not minutely described many."[31] Hooker had not meant to imply an application of these dogmatic words to Darwin's case, though in fact he did think Darwin "too prone to theoretical considerations about species"—and Darwin may have taken Hooker's criticism of Gérard personally in part because it echoed his already existing doubts of his qualification to publish on so speculative a matter and his fears that he had amassed too little specific evidence to buttress his evolutionary ideas. In any event, Darwin recognized that a thorough examination of all varieties of barnacles would gain him the empirical gravitas needed to anchor his evolutionary ideas. The deeper he went into what he meant to be the definitive taxonomic treatment of barnacles, the more problems of classification proliferated. The field expanded to include fossil barnacles as well as living varieties. But as Darwin dissected extant species and deconstructed fossils, roaming much as his grandfather Erasmus had done terrestrially and botanically in *Loves of the Plants* through a marine array of polymorphic sexuality (hermaphroditic, unisexual, bisexual, and various transitional forms, including the bizarre *Ibla* genus with relatively giant-sized females and tiny "supplemental males" that were no more than "mere bags of spermatozoa"), he found more and more evidence bolstering his notebook thoughts on evolution.

The painstaking, microscopic work of dissection and classification and the no-less-intricate task of gathering a comprehensive array of all the known living and extinct barnacles from fellow collectors at home and abroad may have consumed Darwin's energies and filled years of his life, but the apparent digression ended up putting him farther along the path towards publishing his evolutionary thoughts. During the barnacle years, Darwin had honed and polished his empirical skills in the laboratory—at a time of life when periods of bad health and the responsibilities associated with being patriarch of an ever-increasing family, landowning squire of

---

31 Quoted in ibid., p. 341.

a country neighborhood, and capitalist manager of a substantial, growing fortune combined to preclude naturalist fieldwork of the sort that had occupied him during the *Beagle* voyage. He had built a solid reputation as a systematic zoologist and thereby gained authority that, as Hooker had pointed out, would add credibility to his more speculative work. He'd recruited a worldwide team of collegial correspondents and a method for enlarging it—thereby gaining a lifelong way of reaching out from Down House to far-flung allies on whom he might rely for data, observations, insights, and support in the political and ideological debates his evolutionary ideas would spark within the rising profession of science and beyond. And, although he cannot have intended it, the nine-years' digression allowed Darwin to put away and then return to his evolving evolutionary manuscript at the right moments in his career and in the progress of scientific thought.

Remarkably for a book that might seem, at retrospective first glance, so perfectly timed—written when its author was ready to articulate its ideas and published when his audience was ready to consider them—Darwin's *Origin of Species* was both deferred and precipitated by other evolutionary texts, whose respective advents neatly bracket Darwin's barnacle years. In 1844 the reading public was buzzing, and mostly outraged, thanks to a glib, anonymous book called *Vestiges of the Natural History of Creation*—the intellectual journalist Robert Chambers's speculation-heavy, evidence-light account of how life on earth gradually evolved into ever more complex forms over long periods of time. The notoriety *Vestiges* attracted for its "heretical" and ungrounded speculations was enough to drive Darwin, who had at first feared that his ideas might be pre-empted by *Vestiges* but instead found himself warned by its hostile reception, to bury his own transformationist musings in a desk drawer—and himself in the barnacle project. Later, the 1858 receipt of Alfred Russel Wallace's manuscript sketching out a model for how species originated so closely resembling Darwin's own that, as he wrote to Lyell on June 18, "if Wallace had my M.S. sketch written out in 1842 he could not have made a better short abstract! Even his terms now stand as Heads of my Chapters" (*CCD* VII, 107). The arrival of Wallace's manuscript made Darwin put aside the "big book" on evolution he had begun to craft from his 1842 manuscript and other notes in 1856, with the barnacles behind him. Pressed by the need to get his ideas in circulation quickly, he dropped the exhaustively documented empirical study that would have taken many more years to complete and produced the stripped-down argument that, as *Origin*, would shake the world in 1859.

Like Darwin's lifelong series of projects, in one way or another all of Austen's novels concern themselves with the problem of understanding larger things through observing smaller ones and with correcting perspectives or revising hypotheses in light of carefully observed and fairly judged evidence. The three novels with abstract qualities in their titles present the epistemological issues that name them more or less straightforwardly. *Sense and Sensibility* overtly serves up a series of events demonstrating the rewards and limitations of its title's two qualities of mind as represented by two heroines, Elinor and Marianne. *Pride and Prejudice* leaves the apportionment of qualities more debatable. Is it Darcy who's proud and Elizabeth who's prejudiced? Or does each of them manifest a bit of each failing? If so, in what relative proportions? But here too the march of events, the discovery of new facts, and the fair-minded appraisal of unexpected behaviors combine to offer healthy correctives to the somewhat distorted perspectives through which two skilled and intelligent, but not perfect, observers view things. *Persuasion* also centers on right and wrong readings of evidence—and it offers its percipient protagonist Anne Elliot a longer span for mental readjustment, seeing that she and Frederick Wentworth, the romantic principals of the main story, are also those of the backstory but now eight years older and more experienced.

The two novels with place titles, *Northanger Abbey* and *Mansfield Park*, work in *bildungsroman* fashion. In these two books, we see young, mentally malleable girls transplanted, if at very different ages and stages of development, to new places. The key place in each case is the estate named in the title (though Bath serves as a way station at which Catherine Morland's initiation into adult ways of thinking begins), where the heroine learns to observe, think, and judge—partly through broadened experience and partly through the tutelage of the benevolent and perceptive older male who befriends and will eventually marry her. It's not only the principal characters who read and interpret the signs and specifics of Austenworld and are judged—by Austen, her narrator, and her readers alike—as judges of evidence. Particularly in the three novels begun after the move to Chawton, Austen depicts communities where nearly every consciousness, from the finest down to the coarsest, reveals itself dramatically through perceiving, reporting, and trying to make sense of details.

Nowhere else in Austenworld is the collection and interpretation of data as intense and widespread a preoccupation as in *Emma*, Austen's densest and most narrowly delimited novel. Many main or secondary characters manage to move beyond the direct surveillance of their fellow citizens in Highbury, "the large and populous village almost amounting to a town"[32] to which Emma's house Hartfield actually belongs in spite of its country-house features. But the comings and goings of the mobile characters and other reported or imagined happenings beyond the horizon at the Churchills' Enscombe, Mr Suckling's Maple Grove, the resorts of Weymouth and Bath, the John Knightleys' house in Brunswick Square, or the Dixons' Irish estate are also grist for the interpretative mills operated by those Highbury citizens stuck like barnacles on the spot. Among those stay-at-homes is the title character Emma Woodhouse, unique among Austen heroines in being rooted in her country neighborhood. Emma is the Austen heroine whose powers of observation and interpretation are presented and appraised in fullest detail. Yet she never spends a night away from home and only once travels more than a good country walk from her father's roof. Then she only visits nearby Box Hill, an easy day's outing from Highbury. Emma the observer—a woman whose lively mind is suited to make her a naturalist, novelist, empiricist, serendipitist, or imaginist—is confined by default to focusing, as Austen recommended in the letter to her niece Anna, on three or four families in a country village. Nonetheless, due to some of Emma's limitations, the Highbury community is less knowable than she believes.

---

32 Jane Austen, *Emma*, ed. R. W. Chapman (London and New York: Oxford University Press, 1933, repr. 1971), 7. Subsequent citations will refer to this edition, which will be abbreviated *E*, and will appear parenthetically.

If *Emma* had been written from a slightly different narrative viewpoint Highbury might, as Northanger Abbey and Mansfield Park do, suitably provide a place-name title for the novel concerning the people interacting in its milieu. Had the tale been so titled, Austen might perhaps have told her story more along the lines of George Eliot's *Middlemarch*, with many Highbury heads and hearts laid open for the author's, her narrator's, and the reader's scrutiny. Instead, Austen's title character is generally the narrative's central consciousness when the omniscient narrator is not. Despite making a few ventures into the minds of other characters, especially George Knightley, Austen's narrator habitually chooses Emma's consciousness when showing a scene from an individual's vantage point. But although we're mainly in the mind of Emma when not keeping company with the narrator, we're continuously aware that all the other inquiring minds of Highbury are busily gathering detail and evaluating evidence.

The novel's first dramatized situation involves Emma, her father, and Mr Knightley discussing details of the Weston wedding. The concluding chapter's final phrases juxtapose Mrs Elton's verdict on Emma's own wedding ("'Very little white satin, very few lace veils; a most pitiful business!—Selina would stare when she heard of it'") with the benevolent confidence of the "small band of true friends" who accurately predict "the perfect happiness of the union" (*E* 484). In between, nearly everyone's gathering data in enlightened or "mere empirical" fashion and hypothesizing solutions to the mysteries, great and small, that drive the brilliantly intricate plot. What is Harriet Smith's parentage? Why won't Jane Fairfax join the Dixons in Ireland? Who bought her the pianoforté? How did the rumor of the Coles aspiring to set up their carriage get into circulation? Is Mrs Churchill a real or an imaginary invalid? And then there are the many questions related to romantic matters. Does Mr Elton love Harriet? Is Mr Knightley attached to Emma? What is the state of Frank Churchill's feelings? From first to last, *Emma* is a tightly woven tissue of mysteries for the empirical eye to solve.

While writing the novel, Austen somewhat disingenuously referred to Emma as "a heroine no one but myself will much like."[33] A reader who dislikes Emma may well dislike the novel's narrator and Austen herself—for the three share a number of important qualities of mind and sensibility, as do those sympathetic readers who successfully negotiate the densely detailed neighborhood of the novel. Highbury, like Hutton's Arran or the Grants' Daphne Major, turns out to be perfect as an empiricist's training ground. It's a place on just the right scale for close observation that leads to something beyond mere detected fact—and thus it is also a knowable community ideal for training and exercising the mind of a novelist, naturalist, or serendipitist or, with less discipline, that of an "imaginist" like Emma. At almost the exact center of the novel lies one of the passages most crucial to the reader's understanding of Emma's mind and how it's come to be as it is. While Harriet dithers over muslins at Ford's, Emma, for once not inclined to manage her protégée's choice, instead chooses to look out of the door:

---

33 Quoted in James Austen-Leigh, *A Memoir of Jane Austen*, ed. R. W. Chapman (Oxford: Clarendon Press, 1926), p. 203.

> Much could not be hoped from the traffic of even the busiest part of Highbury;—Mr Perry walking hastily by, Mr William Cox letting himself in at the office door, Mr Cole's carriage horses returning from exercise, or a stray letter-boy on an obstinate mule, were the liveliest objects she could presume to expect; and when her eyes fell only on the butcher with his tray, a tidy old woman traveling homewards from shop with her full basket, two curs quarrelling over a dirty bone, and a string of dawdling children round the baker's little bow-window eyeing the gingerbread, she knew she had no reason to complain, and was amused enough; quite enough still to stand at the door. A mind lively and at ease, can do with seeing nothing, and can see nothing that does not answer. (*E* 233)

In another novel titled for its heroine, provincial everydayness of this sort drives another Emma, Flaubert's Madame Bovary, to ennui, extravagance, adultery, depression, and finally suicide—for Madame Bovary's a romantic fantasist. A mature naturalist, novelist, empiricist, or serendipitist would seize on such a scene of things-as-they-are, recognizing that it contains phenomena to be seen, understood, and interpreted—and Emma Woodhouse is, much of the time, capable of enjoying the observation of such prosaic phenomena. But sometimes such a mundane scene must seem confined and dull to a young woman of twenty years, described in the novel's first sentence as "handsome, clever, and rich, with a comfortable home and happy disposition," shown and said elsewhere to be the picture of health and vigor, implied to have been queen of all she surveys even before the moment she came out. As the most affluent of Austen's principal heroines and the only one living in a house that's neither entailed nor tied to a church living, Emma has no active necessity of marrying—but she likewise has no economic impediments to free and extensive traveling, to mixing and mingling in the polite society of the metropolis or the fashionable watering places. Emma's homebound by custom, kindness, and the lack of a sibling in residence. She's condemned by her charitable heart and responsible head to cosseting a valetudinarian stay-at-home father. Even poor, orphaned Jane Fairfax, destined for the governess trade, has seen more of the world than privileged Emma has. Thus it's no wonder that she can be tempted to remake her microcosm and at least some of its inhabitants into something more interesting to a young lady's scrutiny. What's wondrous is that Emma's vision is as empirically grounded and sensible as it is.

Emma's milieu as rendered by Austen's eagle-eyed narrator is a palpably material world. We don't merely know peoples' comparative standing in the social hierarchy and, in many cases, the extent of their incomes or independent fortunes.[34] More than just a socioeconomic environment, Highbury is an assemblage of minute temporal and material details. We the readers become intimately familiar with the

---

34 Though what could be a better case study for the interpreter of nuance than the impression Mr Elton's given Highbury of his fiancée Augusta Hawkins's settlement by speaking of "so many thousands as would always be called ten," and "10,000*l*. or thereabouts"? Heard by an irony-sensitive ear, these pretentiously vague phrases unintentionally convey an impression opposite to the one Elton means to transmit—and precisely because of his intentional vagueness. A clear majority of the students and other readers I've informally surveyed on the question understand Augusta Hawkins's marriage portion to be somewhat under 10,000*l*.

smallest particulars of this microcosm that confines and defines Emma—we're obliged to become fellow interpreters of the specific data she and other observers in the country neighborhood have noticed and appraised. To cite, almost randomly, a handful of specifics from the profusion: we come to know that Mr Elton's rectory is an undistinguished old edifice, too near the road but prettied up with new yellow curtains; that Emma is capable of deliberately breaking a bootlace to create a pretext for throwing Elton and Harriet together; that Emma deems Jane Fairfax and the Bates women worth a ten-minutes' social call (the precise amount of time Frank Churchill duplicitously asserts to be "all that was necessary, perhaps all that was proper" for visiting the same house) and insures that Harriet's visit to the Martin females lasts only fourteen minutes, which makes it a delicately calibrated blend of courtesy and slight; that Mrs Bates's spectacles need repair; that wax candles will be supplied in the Smallridges' schoolroom, to which Mrs Elton is hell-bent on dispatching Jane Fairfax; that Mr Perry's diplomatically agreed with his patient Mr Woodhouse about the dangers of consuming rich wedding-cake but that nonetheless his children are said to have been seen consuming hefty slices of the Westons' nuptial confection; that the December storm throwing Mr Woodhouse into consternation about being snowbound at Randalls deposits at most half an inch of snow on the road. We hear that "Hartfield pork is not like other pork," but nonetheless that Mr Woodhouse fears the unwholesomeness of roasting even the benign Hartfield product; we smile when he suggests that Emma send a loin of this exquisitely superior meat to the Bates household only to learn that she's already dispatched an entire leg; and then laugh when Miss Bates says how good it will be roasted. We learn that Harriet lightens her purse by a shilling in hopes of shaking off the menacing gypsies, and that Frank Churchill makes his first Highbury purchase, gloves, at Ford's, where he can choose between "Men's Beavers" and "York Tan." We become aware not only that Mr Knightley sends a bushel or more of apples by William Larkins to the Bates household but also that these apples come from a tree (or perhaps two) long famed for producing fruit that keeps well, that this act of generosity cleans out Mr Knightley's remaining supply and thereby displeases his housekeeper Mrs Hodges, who's indignant that he won't have another apple-tart all spring, that Miss Bates intends the apples to be baked for Jane, and that this treat will be prepared by Mrs Wallis, who bakes apples twice, not three times as Mr Woodhouse has made Miss Bates promise to have them done. All this detail and far, far more is available to the naturalist and novel-reader exploring Highbury in the company of Austen's narrator.

But despite being constructed of minute particulars, *Emma* is by no means confined to them. In fact, as suggested earlier, the attitude towards what one might call "mere empiricism" reflected in this novel—and in all Austen's others—is essentially negative. At first one might think that Austen, her narrator, or both are a bit unfair or doubleminded: willing to represent the smallest details yet equally willing to mock or implicitly condemn characters who take a demonstrable interest in concrete particulars. But in *Emma* it becomes obvious, once one considers the matter, that the superior minds of Highbury, like the inferior ones, pay attention to details. Emma's directions to servants as lady of the house (particularly when she needs to take active measures to forestall the stinting of guests that her father's valetudinarianism would inflict) and her compassionate kindness to the sick and impoverished cottagers (visited just before the encounter with Elton that makes her strategically break her bootlace) necessarily involve attention to—and articulation of—detail. Mr Knightley, a keen and active man of property who takes hands-on interest in specific agricultural matters rather than leaving them to his steward William Larkins or his tenant Robert Martin, is understood to be immersed in the details of running a country estate; but we don't hear him speak on such matters. When John Knightley is visiting from London, the brothers' shared fascination with the practical particulars of running Donwell are clearly reported, but not dramatically presented:

> The brothers talked of their own concerns and pursuits, but principally of those of the elder, whose temper was by much the most communicative, and who was always the greater talker. As a magistrate, he had generally some point of law to consult John about, or, at least, some curious anecdote to give; and as a farmer, as keeping in hand the home-farm at Donwell, he had to tell what every field was to bear next year, and to give all such local information as could not fail of being interesting to a brother whose home it had equally been the longest part of his life, and whose attachments were strong. The plan of a drain, the change of a fence, the felling of a tree, and the destination of every acre for wheat, turnips, or spring corn, was entered into with as much equality of interest by John, as his cooler manners rendered possible; and if his willing brother ever left him any thing to enquire about, his inquiries even approached a tone of eagerness. (*E* 100)

The impression implied and derived here is positive—of landed gentry actively and responsibly engaged in the daily running of an estate. George Knightley's attention to managing Donwell aligns him with Fitzwilliam Darcy, in contrast to such feckless, frivolous, absent, or detached Austen estate-owners as Willoughby, Sir Walter Elliot, Henry Crawford, and even Mr Bennet, whose reported involvement with Longbourn centers on his twin fields of indulgence, the library where he reads and the woods where he shoots. But, very significantly, Knightley's concern for his estate is reported at second hand, not singled out for word-by-word dramatization. This shrewd narratological choice is one thing that keeps him, unlike another scrupulously responsible abbey-owner, General Tilney of Northanger, who's shown discussing his estate, from seeming like a proser or a show-off. (The other markers of difference from Knightley are that Tilney's laying out of specifics centers on improvements that add to his personal comfort and prestige and that his detail-laden speech directs itself not at an informed, interested equal but at a naïve girl he aims to impress.) It's hard to imagine that a word-by-word account of the Knightley brothers' discourse on drains and gates, wheat, turnips, and corn could be anything but dullness, incongruity, or fodder for irony in a novel of the sort Austen writes: serious attention to technical minutiae would be more the province of George Eliot's realism. But even if Austen could record a conversation bogged down in agricultural specificity without mocking it, she wouldn't. One of her most consistent rhetorical strategies, in *Emma* and elsewhere, is to forge a link between reported remarks on trivial topics or material things (reports not consciously ironized by those uttering them, that is) and trivial-mindedness or materialism. Throughout Austenworld, serious-minded heroines need to make choices about dress and adornment, but they're never shown taking true interest in these petty matters—with the possible exception of Fanny Price, who worries over a chain to carry the amber cross given by her brother William, and Fanny's problem is a matter of economics, sentiment, and etiquette, not mere fashion. It's a truth that should be universally acknowledged: those directly shown speaking seriously and publicly about minute particulars in Austenworld set themselves up to be ridiculed by Austen's narrator.

This precept is never truer than at Highbury. Densely particularized though the populous village may be, those characters whose minds are confined to material phenomena and whose speech bogs down in detail are singled out for mockery, disapproval, or both—whether explicitly by Emma or implicitly by the narrator. But in nearly every case, Austen has clearly discernible subsidiary purposes for characters' long-winded, over-particularized speeches so that she never runs the risk of arraignment for charges like those Robert Southey leveled at his friend and fellow Lake District resident Wordsworth for creating the tedious sea-captain who narrates "The Thorn": "he who personates tiresome loquacity becomes tiresome himself."[35] Such personations are instructive rather than (or as well as) tedious in *Emma*. Mr Woodhouse's tiresome loquacity—manifested in rambling endorsements of gruel and prescriptions of how it should be cooked, verbosely voiced anxieties about health, safety, change, or sudden decisions, and convoluted old-school courtesies—reveals the timid, feeble, prematurely senile nature of his mind. But because readers are obliged to suffer through Mr Woodhouse's tedious prosings, they are far likelier to understand and value Emma's and Knightley's benevolent patience in bearing with him than would be the case if his fears and whims were merely reported, not set down in his own words.

Similarly, reporting Mrs Elton's relentless flow of particularity, the narrator allows her choir of vices—selfishness, insincerity, irrationality, greed, stupidity, and snobbery—to sing for themselves. There's no need for the narrator to inform the reader that this confident newcomer who vaunts her simplicity and then speaks of trimming her silver poplin dress with lace, who rhapsodizes about her passion for music and then voices the commonplace about married women giving up their instruments, who drones on about Maple Grove's substantial grounds and the Sucklings' barouche-landau, and who tries to micromanage the details of Mr Knightley's strawberry-picking party at Donwell is a hypocritical, vulgar, presumptuous bore. Seeing (and even more, hearing) Mrs Elton in full flow, the reader's disposed to like Emma more than might otherwise be the case; for Emma's worst qualities are exaggerated tenfold in Mrs Elton, and her best attributes are totally lacking. The narrator's exquisite manipulation of direct quotation and indirect report adds a further strategy for portraying Augusta Hawkins Elton in her horrid glory. Judiciously blending what we assume to be Mrs Elton's exact words with indirect discourse, the narrator at once exposes us to tiresome loquacity per se and implies that there's far more of it than we actually hear, a mass of material too voluminous and tedious to transcribe. Austen resorts to this mixed blend of quoted speech and reportage to characterize

---

35 Southey's remark, originally appearing in the *Critical Review*, XXIV, 200, is quoted in Mary Jacobus, *Tradition and Experiment in Wordsworth's Lyrical Ballads (1798)* (Oxford: Clarendon Press, 1976), 247.

Mrs Elton's first appearance: the sharply materialist appraisal of Hartfield and relentlessly forced comparison of its charms to Maple Grove's strikes the Eltonian note on first utterance, and the selective transcription implies that what the visiting bride's been saying is even worse than we can know. Later, Mrs Elton's riff on strawberries is not given totally verbatim but selectively and topically, in much the same way that Hansard published the parliamentary reports of Austen's day or that a gardeners' handbook would outline topics at the head of a chapter. This method of narration simultaneously confirms our sense of the speaker being stuck in material particulars, implies that she's worked up her horticultural expertise for the occasion, suggests that the exact words are so insincere or tiresome that we need not have them quoted in full, and accurately renders the mood swing from delight to disgust as Mrs Elton, encumbered by her "apparatus of happiness, her large bonnet and her basket," grows ever more tired (as Mr Knightley knew she would) of the rustic delights of picking strawberries:

> "The best fruit in England—every body's favourite—always wholesome.—These the finest beds and finest sorts.—Delightful to gather for one's self—the only way of really enjoying them.—Morning decidedly the best time—never tired—every sort good—hautboy infinitely superior—no comparison—the others hardly eatable—hautboys very scarce—Chili preferred—white wood finest flavour of all—price of strawberries in London—abundance about Bristol—Maple Grove—cultivation—beds when to be renewed—gardeners thinking exactly different—no general rule—gardeners never to be put out of their way—delicious fruit—only too rich to be eaten much of—inferior to cherries—currants more refreshing—only objection to gathering strawberries the stooping—glaring sun—tired to death—could bear it no longer—must go and sit in the shade." (*E* 358–9)

Through this form of free indirect discourse the narrator economically but exactly renders half an hour in Mrs Elton's company, thankfully sparing us all her exact words, which would perhaps have sprawled to something like the length of Molly Bloom's much more interesting stream-of-consciousness conclusion to *Ulysses*.

Apart from Mr Woodhouse and Mrs Elton, the other two citizens of Highbury most persistently mired in mundane particulars are Harriet Smith and Miss Bates; but empirical readers and Highburyians alike ignore the "tiresome loquacity" of these women at their peril. Both resemble Mr Woodhouse in being well-meaning but not particularly judicious or discerning. They resemble one another in being people the world can marginalize. Unlike Mr Woodhouse, whose birth, income, sex, and age entitle him to respect his mental powers could never earn, Miss Smith and Miss Bates can easily be written off. Harriet is "the natural daughter of someone," which is to say no one known to Highbury. A parlor boarder at Miss Goddard's far-from-fashionable school, she has only beauty, youth, and good nature going for her, until these qualities—and the mystery of her parentage—attract the attention of Emma, whose sponsorship gives her some reflected social cachet. Miss Bates's situation is as precarious as Harriet's or more so. Though a gentleman's daughter, she holds none of the other advantages that confer status on a woman: as the narrator waspishly pronounces, Miss Bates "enjoyed a most uncommon degree of popularity for a woman neither young, handsome, rich, nor married" (*E* 21)—the adjectival sequence echoing the initial description of Emma while denying Miss Bates the crucial attributes guaranteeing popularity to Emma, married or not. Throughout the novel, the narrator characteristically reports both Harriet's and Miss Bates's exact words, however banal; for one reason these characters exist in the novel is to sound naively shallow in one case, tediously long-winded in the other. It's all too easy for a reader to do as the citizens of Highbury (especially Emma) might and write off Harriet's observations or tune out Miss Bates's many-more-than-three-things-very-dull-indeed.

But failing to pay attention to what Harriet and Miss Bates have to say is a mistake on at least two grounds. Condescending to the one and ignoring the other, a negligent reader commits the very sins she or he may, in superior fashion, be charging to Emma.[36] The second drawback of marginalizing the words of these unmarried women is more substantial. Harriet Smith and Miss Bates will never win prizes for their cerebral skills, but they're much better observers than they get credit for being. Miss Bates's remarks may never transcend daily particulars, and Harriet's conclusion-drawing may be naïve at best; but both women are surprisingly fair-minded and clear-sighted observers of things as they are. A reader who ignores what they see and say—especially details buried in Miss Bates's effusions—misses clues necessary to solving the many mysteries that preoccupy their country neighborhood.

The narrator presents Miss Bates in full-flow stream-of-consciousness several times in the course of *Emma*. The style and structure of these palpably material, unfailingly appreciative, absurdly specific performances emerges clearly in miniature mimicry as Emma, debating with Mrs Weston about whether or not Mr Knightley might aim at marrying Jane Fairfax, imagines the chatterbox aunt as a sort of effusively grateful ghost disturbing Donwell's peace:

> How would he bear to have Miss Bates belonging to him?—To have her haunting the Abbey, and thanking him all day long for his great kindness in marrying Jane? "So very kind and obliging! –But he always had been such a very kind neighbour!" And then fly off, through half a sentence, to her mother's old petticoat. "Not that it was such a very old petticoat either—for still it would last a great while—and, indeed, she must thankfully say that their petticoats were all very strong." (*E* 225)

Miss Bates's first actual, rather than imagined, effusion comes in the first chapter of Volume II, when Emma cannily calls under the assumption that the Bates ladies won't recently have heard from Jane Fairfax, learns to her chagrin that Jane has in fact just written, is obliged to hear the whole substance of the letter along with digressions on Jane's penmanship, her economy of paper, and other matters, and only just escapes before the letter already characterized in fullest detail can be read aloud to her. Miss Bates next holds forth in Chapter IX of Volume II. This gush of words is set off by Emma's preliminary "I hope Mrs Bates and Miss Fairfax are—,"

---

36 Confessional moment: it was not until my third or fourth time through the novel that I, having on earlier readings impatiently skipped bits of Miss Bates's seemingly interminable monologues and given no credit to Harriet's statements, found that I'd fallen into a cleverly set narratological trap. If my readerly manners and morals were no better than Emma's interpersonal ones, how could I presume to judge her?

a commonplace inquiry curtailed by Miss Bates's almost four-page medley on Jane's health, Mrs Bates's spectacles and Frank Churchill's repair of them, the complete history of their latest batch of baked apples, and the dark, narrow twistiness of their staircase, up which she conducts Emma and Harriet (*E* 236–9). The virtually uninterrupted monologue terminates only because Miss Bates and her guests enter the sitting-room occupied by Jane, Frank, and old Mrs Bates. Still later in the second chapter of the third volume, on her arrival at the Westons' ball, Miss Bates launches into yet another epic of mundane detail, some of the topics being the rain, her thick-soled shoes, the festive look of the Crown's ballroom, Jane's health and looks, greetings to the various guests, and renewed compliments on the hospitality, with the conclusion "Everything so good!" (*E* 322–3). Miss Bates's monologue is almost directly followed by an equally detailed if briefer discourse from Mrs Elton that, though comparably tedious, highlights the key difference in the two bores, the one warmly outgoing, the other coldly self-involved. A few days later on Box Hill, Miss Bates, with amiable self-mockery, is about to venture the "three things very dull indeed" option Frank Churchill has proposed for Emma's amusement along with its alternatives, "one thing very clever, be it prose or verse, original or repeated—or two things moderately clever"—but Emma cuts her off with "Ah! Ma'am, but there may be a difficulty. Pardon me—but you will be limited as to number—only three at once" (*E* 370). After Emma's callous snub at Box Hill, Miss Bates's volubility is curbed, but only temporarily. When Emma pays her penitential visit the next day, all it takes is a friendly inquiry after Miss Fairfax to precipitate a long, detailed account of Jane's having accepted a governess position in the neighborhood of Maple Grove, at the Smallridges' (*E* 379–83).

If Miss Bates is hard to bear, it's because she talks too much. Harriet Smith's discourse is discredited for a different reason: she often seems indecisive, ignorant, or both. There are several reasons why we should be careful of feeling too certain about Harriet's innate limitations, though. First, Harriet is young. At seventeen, she's a contemporary of *Northanger Abbey*'s heroine Catherine Morland, whose at-home education seems not much better than Harriet's at Miss Goddard's school—and Catherine strikes most readers as youthfully naïve, not stupid. Harriet seems as dim or wrongheaded as she does because we see her chiefly in conversation with Emma, whose stronger, more sophisticated mind makes Harriet's look even weaker and simpler than it is and whose guidance (as opposed to Henry Tilney's mentorship of Catherine) misleads Harriet as much as, or more than, it improves her. Harriet Smith can be easily written off as an airhead; but a close look at her principal speeches shows that in fact she's a good, close observer of detail—and not just physical detail either, but emotions as well. She may be no judge of a letter, but she can accurately understand the language of faces, voices, and bodies. In an early utterance, Harriet shows herself sharp-eyed and retentive of details pertaining to the Abbey-Mill Farm where she stayed the previous September, right down to the upper-maid who has been there twenty-five years and the "eight cows, two of them Alderneys, and one a little Welch cow, a very pretty little Welch cow indeed" (*E* 27). She recalls that Robert Martin has "been bid more for his wool than any body in the country" and remembers what books he's read and not read (*E* 28–9). She may not be able to gauge the quality of his written proposal with Emma's acuteness ("it is but a short letter too," *E* 54) or to puzzle out the meaning of Elton's obsequious charade on "courtship" ("Can it be Neptune? ... Or a trident? or a mermaid? or a shark?," *E* 72–3). But the indirect discourse relayed through Emma's reacting mind conveys Harriet's impressions of her 14-minute reunion with the Martins in a way that shows her capable of clear, accurate perceptions when things and feelings are straightforward:

> They had received her doubtingly, if not coolly; and nothing beyond the merest commonplace had been talked almost all the time—till just at last, when Mrs Martin's saying, all of a sudden, that she thought Miss Smith was grown, had brought on a more interesting subject, and a warmer manner. In that very room she had been measured last September, with her two friends. There were the pencilled marks and memorandums on the wainscot by the window. *He* had done it. They all seemed to remember the day, the hour, the party, the occasion—to feel the same consciousness, the same regrets—to be ready to return to the same good understanding; and they were just growing again like themselves, (Harriet, as Emma must suspect, as ready as the best of them to be cordial and happy,) when the carriage re-appeared, and all was over. (*E* 186–7)

Silly and sentimental enough to cherish a leftover bit of court-plaster and a leadless pencil nub as relics of Elton, Harriet (badly underestimated by Emma) is emotionally perceptive enough to feel more gratitude for Mr Knightley's rescuing her from partnerlessness at the ball than for Frank Churchill's driving away the gypsies, and wise enough to understand which man is worthier of her respect, admiration, and love. That Harriet remains as off-the-mark as she does for most of the novel is due more to Emma's active misleading than to her mind's innate errancy. Left to her own devices—or advised by an Emma who gave full credit to the excellence she couldn't help discerning in Robert Martin's letter of proposal and whose comparative social placement of both Martin and Harriet derived from empirical observation rather than romantic imagination—Harriet Smith would have changed her surname to Martin shortly after Miss Taylor became Mrs Weston rather than weeks before Emma married Mr Knightley. And how different the story would have been.

Emma's move away from cherishing imaginism to preferring empirically based reasoning, and her eventual decision to get on with her own life rather than attempt to manipulate others as proxies for living herself, are rendered as parts of a delicately detailed and far from straightforward evolutionary process. Emma's mind and spirit seem mature and confident when we first encounter her—and she's perfectly capable of keen observation and clear appraisal of what she sees. The problem is that Emma, like most people, has blind spots—but she doesn't know it, a particularly dangerous situation for someone who prides herself on her powers of perception. Emma's bored and lonely without exactly recognizing that she is. Because she doesn't face or understand her own feelings, she can't take full account of how they might mislead her. The story has only just started when the first conversation between Emma and Knightley reveals Emma's rational strengths and limitations. As they discuss the recent Weston marriage, she claims, "I made the match, you know, four years ago" (*E* 10–11). Knightley disagrees and asserts that her idea of "making the match ... means only your planning it, your saying to yourself one idle day 'I think it would be a very good thing for Miss Taylor if Mr Weston were to marry her'" (*E* 12–13). As Knightley sees it, Emma's merely made "a lucky guess." But it seems to Emma, something of a serendipitist, that "a lucky guess is never merely luck. There is always some talent in it" and, further, that there is something between the polarities of "the do-nothing" and the "do-all" in managing relationships from the outside: "If I had not promoted Mr Weston's visits here, and given many little encouragements, and smoothed many little matters, it might not have come to any thing after all" (*E* 13). Knightley again differs, believing that rational adults are best left to handle their own concerns and that Emma's interference is likelier to have hindered than promoted the eventual outcome.

This first encounter between the bright but overconfident heroine and her commonsensical, equally confident lifelong mentor sets the pattern for subsequent disagreements between Emma and Knightley. They quarrel over Harriet Smith's refusal of Robert Martin's proposal and Emma's role in thwarting a match that in Knightley's view would have offered much more benefit to Harriet than to Martin. They disagree on whether Elton needs someone to find a wife for him and whether Frank Churchill is truly confined to Enscombe at the whims of Mrs Churchill. They are at odds about whether there might be a secret understanding between Frank and Jane Fairfax and about what degree of friendship and attention Emma should properly show Jane, whose accomplishments highlight the limited nature of Emma's own and whose reserve exasperates her. But in day in, day out matters of practical conduct, Emma and Knightley are often shown to be in complete agreement. They are alike in their concern and respect for old Mr Woodhouse and his shaky equanimity. A few words between them can smoothly settle the matter of departing from Randalls in a snowstorm, for their basic values are as similar as their shared taste for spruce-beer. The consistent pattern: Emma, like Knightley, is fundamentally observant, humane, and rational; but where and when her powers of imagination get involved, she doesn't see things as they are. Emma likes to play idle games, whereas Knightley is businesslike. She casts people in roles to act out dramas she stages in her mind's theater—and would like to produce on the boards of real life. Thus for Emma, Harriet *must* be of gentle birth. The Churchills *must* be to blame for Frank's failure to pay a prompt wedding visit to Highbury. Jane *must* have a secret love— and this undisclosed amoroso *must* be the plain, married Mr Dixon rather than the handsome, eligible Frank Churchill, who *must* instead vainly love Emma. In Emma, we're shown how the imaginist's peremptory needs can intermittently blind the sharp empirical eye of observation. But Emma's powers of observing and reasoning aren't always impaired; and her mind's much more interesting (to the reader, the narrator, Austen herself, and probably Knightley) because it's such a blend of strength, talent, benevolence, arrogance, and self-delusion.

Emma's preference for being an artist who creates rather than an empiricist who observes emerges full-blown in Chapter VI of Volume I, where we see her in various roles: as a metaphorical choreographer or dramatist aiming to manipulate people's motions and emotions alike, as an actual artist sketching Harriet, and as an actress-director playing the sketcher's role in her staging of a tableau vivant that centers on Harriet's beauty and encourages Elton to admire it, this second act preceded by one in which she stimulates Harriet's appreciation of Elton's charms and eligibility. The chapter begins with a report of Emma's smugness at managing that first objective, which she believes to be the start of a promising attachment: "Emma could not feel a doubt of having given Harriet's fancy a proper direction and raised the gratitude of her young vanity to a very good purpose, for she found her decidedly more sensible than before of Mr Elton's being a remarkably handsome man" (*E* 42). Despite Emma's complacency, this sentence raises a number of red flags. Emma works on Harriet's fancy—a mental trait even less grounded than imagination is—and cultivates her vanity rather than fostering some virtue. We also notice early evidence of a volatile phenomenon Emma will try to exploit in crafting her portrait of Harriet, that handsomeness or beauty aren't stable, objectively discerned properties but shifting impressions that can be enhanced or diminished through artful strokes, whether words or a pencil are being wielded.

Elton is of Emma's mind in noticing and professing to value the artistic improvement of people, though Emma misreads his perception as proof of a growing attachment to Harriet rather than as a fawning compliment to herself. The language of art, literal and figurative, pervades their calculated conversation: "'You have given Miss Smith all that she required,'" says Elton. "'Harriet only wanted drawing out,'" replies Emma, her words figuratively foreshadowing what Knightley will later in the chapter diagnose as the literal fault of her sketch of Harriet. "'Skillful has been the hand,'" pronounces Elton, with "a sort of sighing animation, which had a vast deal of the lover" (*E* 42–3). The analytical scrutiny of Elton's mode of delivery and cool awareness of its affective excess seems to be Emma's, for the narrator is in her consciousness at the time. But, as so often proves true in the novel, Emma observes the phenomenon accurately but is mistaken about its cause: Elton means to praise her, not Harriet.

Without even starting a new paragraph, the story jumps forward a few days to the dramatized incident of Harriet's sitting for her portrait. Emma deviously sets up the scene by asking Harriet if her likeness has ever been taken, then, when Harriet's out of the room, leading on Elton with a casual confession of her own penchant for sketching. "Let me entreat you," he cries out, following his entreaty with effusive praise of Emma's landscapes and flower and figure-pieces displayed at Hartfield and Randalls. She rightly gauges the undiscerning nature of his compliment—"Yes, good man!—thought Emma—but what has all that got to do with taking likenesses? You know nothing of drawing. Don't pretend to be in raptures about mine. Keep your raptures for Harriet's face" (*E* 43)—but makes a show of yielding to the encouragement she's actually invoked, then, with Elton's support, easily prevails on Harriet to pose.

Next follows a perusal of Emma's portfolio containing her various attempts at portraiture—many beginnings in diverse genres and media. The narrator gives us access not just to the portfolio but to Emma's thoughts about it and about her artistic accomplishments in general, thoughts that blend basic good taste and disillusioned self-knowledge with vanity in the sphere of public opinion:

> She played and sang;—and drew in almost every style; but steadiness had always been wanting; and in nothing had she approached the degree of excellence which she would have been glad to command, and ought not to have failed of. She was not much deceived as to her own skill either as an artist or a musician, but she was not unwilling to have others deceived, or sorry to know her reputation for accomplishment often higher than it deserved. (*E* 44)

This meta-appraisal of Emma's powers of self-assessment aims not to educate the heroine, now in full thrall to her delusions of grandeur, but to train the reader in the empirical skills necessary to see things as they are in the mannered microcosm of Highbury. The following lines, characterizing Harriet's and Elton's undiscriminating responses to Emma's oeuvre and implicitly juxtaposing their ignorance with the narrator's educated eye and critical brain, remarkably condense a great deal of keen observation into a few well-chosen words, at once epigrammatic and axiomatic:

> There was merit in every drawing—in the least finished, perhaps the most; her style was spirited; but had there been much less, or had there been ten times more, the delight and admiration of her two companions would have been the same. They were both in extasies. A likeness pleases every body; and Miss Woodhouse's performances must be capital. (*E* 44–5)

There's much to consider here. What kind of artistry shows itself to best effect in the subgenre of *nonfinito*? Probably raw talent without much discipline or technical skill. What sort of people could be equally pleased by styles with Emma's degree of spirit or "much less" or "ten times more"? Unreasoning observers, as the word "extasies" suggests. Is the observation of a likeness universally pleasing? Perhaps that's a truth worth granting in one sense of the word "likeness" but not the other: the human mind does seem to delight in detecting resemblances, but pleasure in viewing a portrait depends on a number of circumstances. In any case, "Miss Woodhouse's performances must be capital" is a claim whose inevitability is clear only to uncritical beings like Harriet and Elton, one thinking Emma flawless out of simple gratitude (or, more intricately, the beneficiary's pragmatic inclination to idealize the benefactor), the other meaning for Emma to believe he thinks her flawless to further his own purposes of ingratiation.

Emma's portfolio of likenesses is limited to faces and figures from the Hartfield family circle. As docent to her collection of portraits, Emma displays candor and good taste in pointing out the strengths of each attempt at portraiture and explaining the psychological contexts of each exercise. What she judges to be her best work, a picture that's very like its subject, only too handsome and flattering, is a full-length miniature of John Knightley, nearly finished but "put away in a pet" when Isabella offered "cold approbation": "'Yes, it was a little like—but to be sure it did not do him justice'" (*E* 45–6). Not deceived about her level of expertise but wanting her skills recognized for at least as good as they are by others, Emma couldn't bear to think of this sketch "apologized over as an unfavourable likeness, to every morning visitor in Brunswick-square" (*E* 46)—and so, paradoxically, her best effort was the one that made her put away her paper, pencils, paints, and brushes in a huff. If a likeness pleases everyone, an expressed sense of a portrait's unlikeness can displease the artist and the viewer in equal measures but different modes.

The critical detachment necessary to judge art as art is evident only in the artist herself as Harriet sits, Emma sketches, and Elton gazes with fatuous admiration that allows him to "discern a likeness almost before it was possible. She could not respect his eye, but his love and his complaisance were unexceptionable" (*E* 47). Again, the narrative emphasizes both Emma's ability to see things as they are and her inclination to connect those effects she's discerned with causes she's imagined. When a more numerous party assembles to see the picture the next day, each viewer responds in a way that illuminates his or her habitual way of interpreting. The dramatized scene offers an empirical reader clear evidence of how people think, feel, speak, and judge at Highbury—particularly how they think about, feel for, speak of, and judge Emma.

> Every body who saw it was pleased, but Mr Elton was in continual raptures, and defended it through every criticism.
> "Miss Woodhouse has given her friend the only beauty she wanted,"—observed Mrs Weston to him—not in the least suspecting that she was addressing a lover.—"The expression of the eye is most correct, but Miss Smith has not those eye-brows and eye-lashes. It is the fault of her face that she has them not."
> "Do you think so?" replied he. "I cannot agree with you. It appears to me a most perfect resemblance in every feature. I never saw such a likeness in my life. We must allow for the effect of shade, you know."
> "You have made her too tall, Emma," said Mr Knightley.
> Emma knew that she had, but would not own it, and Mr Elton warmly added,
> "Oh, no! certainly not too tall; not in the least too tall. Consider, she is sitting down—which naturally presents a different—which in short gives exactly the idea—and the proportions must be preserved, you know. Proportions, fore-shortening.—Oh, no! it gives one exactly the idea of such a height as Miss Smith's. Exactly so indeed!"
> "It is very pretty," said Mr Woodhouse. "So prettily done! Just as your drawings always are, my dear. I do not know any body who draws so well as you do. The only thing I do not thoroughly like is, that she seems to be sitting out of doors, with only a little shawl over her shoulders—and it makes one think she must catch cold."
> "But, my dear papa, it is supposed to be summer; a warm day in summer. Look at the tree."
> "But it is never safe to sit out of doors, my dear."
> "You, sir, may say any thing," cried Mr Elton; "but I must confess that I regard it as a most happy thought, the placing of Miss Smith out of doors; and the tree is touched with such inimitable spirit! Any other situation would have been much less in character. The naiveté of Miss Smith's manners—and altogether—Oh, it is most admirable! I cannot keep my eyes from it. I never saw such a likeness.' (*E* 47–8)

In this series of responses to the likeness, we detect Mrs Weston's discerning eye and kind heart in her willingness to exaggerate Emma's skill and, having noted Emma's enhancement of Harriet's beauty, to see it in the most benevolent possible light. Mr Knightley's economically penetrating way of getting to the heart of things is equally evident in his blunt "You have made her too tall, Emma"—as are Emma's characteristic recognition that he's right and concomitant unwillingness to admit it. Mr Woodhouse's response voices his dithering, detail-obsessed valetudinarianism and his childlike inability to distinguish between life and art. Elton's obsequious, pretentious, half-educated personal style is perfectly captured in his jumbled jargon and fragmentary (probably because his ideas are logically uncompletable) grammatical constructions. In a community so carefully delineated, there is ample evidence allowing empirical readers to know local facts and understand larger truths of human nature, so long as we look, attend, think, hypothesize, doubt, and revise—

a process Emma fails to follow once the portrait's done and Elton, who volunteers to take it to London for framing, accepts his charge with a "tender sigh" and a canting phrase, "What a precious deposit!"

> "This man is almost too gallant to be in love," thought Emma. "I should say so, but that I suppose there may be a hundred different ways of being in love. He is an excellent young man, and will suit Harriet exactly … but he does sigh and languish, and study for compliments rather more than I could endure as a principal." (*E* 49)

The portrait-sketching episode, like the earlier incident of Emma reading and judging Robert Martin's epistolary offer of marriage, presents one of many potential forks in the narrative's path. As was true in the earlier scene, what a different turn the story would here have taken if Emma had thought critically about the specific details she'd noticed so accurately and not been blinded by premature commitment to an ill-formulated hypothesis. Austen, however, has determined that the empirical education of Emma Woodhouse is to proceed much more gradually: no epiphanies until Volume III, when she learns in rapid succession that she's badly erred in her behavior to Miss Bates, missed the clues that point towards an engagement between Frank Churchill and Jane Fairfax, failed to understand that the object of Harriet's confided romantic attachment has been Mr Knightley rather than Frank Churchill, and most crucially been ignorant of her own heart. Austen resorts to one of her rare instances of pulling out the suspense-building stops (such as rhetorical questions, figurative language, and syntactic structures that reserve the point for the end of a phrase, sentence, or paragraph) for the scene of Emma's moment of self-knowledge, which comes hard on the heels of Harriet's avowal that she cares for Knightley and that he, perhaps, may return her affection:

> Emma's eyes were instantly withdrawn; and she sat silently meditating, in a fixed attitude, for a few minutes. A few minutes were sufficient for making her acquainted with her own heart. A mind like her's, once opening to suspicion, made rapid progress. She touched— she admitted—she acknowledged the whole truth. Why was it so much worse that Harriet should be in love with Mr Knightley, than with Frank Churchill? Why was the evil so dreadfully increased by Harriet's having some hope of a return? It darted through her, with the speed of an arrow, that Mr Knightley must marry no one but herself! (*E* 407–8)

Self-knowledge and an appreciation for unbiased empiricism as opposed to wishful imaginism comes late in the novel for Emma Woodhouse; but even if she fails to learn the epistemological lesson of Volume I's portrait-drawing scene and many others like it, a reader can. That early chapter's sharp focus on individual behavior and communal interaction epitomizes how subsequent events will proceed in Emma's Highbury circle, how they'll be rendered by the narrator, and how the agents and observers alike will evaluate them. If attentive, trained readers draw the conclusions Emma willfully fails to draw throughout Austen's densely detailed presentation of a few families in an evolving country neighborhood, they can savor ironies that everywhere elude the intellectually over-confident protagonist. And if they fail to read evidence correctly until well into the novel, fresh pleasures and perceptions will await them when they examine the evidence afresh on re-reading.

In various ways, the relations of small to large and the sense of how these matters of scale build communities knowable to empiricists and serendipitists, naturalists and novelists, have been central themes in my assessment of Darwin's and Austen's minds, characters, and writings. That a certain sort of novelist's eye can see the world in a grain of sand is proved when Austen shows how Emma's "Ah! ma'am ... only three at once" can shake the foundations of communal civility as the temporarily uprooted representatives of three or four families sit like leisurely, more decorously clad Olympian gods on Box Hill with Dorking, Mickleham, and other villages in Surrey's "garden of England" spread below them. A similar kind of naturalist's eye is at work in Darwin's serendipitous encounter with *Arthrobalanus*, as what for most beachcombers would be the idle act of picking up a shell led to Herculean labors of collection, examination, interpretation, and classification, the taxonomic odyssey that grounded and fortified Darwin for his world-changing argument in *Origin of Species*. Austen's voice began this essay, so let Darwin's conclude it, with words describing his life's great project to his cousin, friend, and fellow naturalist William Darwin Fox. Resembling Austen in his sense and sensibility alike, Darwin here envisions the potential link between trivial phenomena and vast consequences—as with a mixture of humility and ambition he dedicates himself to following serendipity and the empirical eye where they will take him:

> I forget whether I ever told you what the objects of my present work is,—it is to view all facts that I can master (eheu, eheu, how ignorant I find I am) in Nat. History, (as on geograph. distribution, palaeontology, classification Hybridism, domestic animals & plants &c &c &c) to see how far they favour or are opposed to the notion that wild species are mutable or immutable: I mean with my uttermost power to give all arguments & facts on both sides. I have a *number* of people helping me in every way, & giving me most valuable assistance; but I often doubt whether the subject will not quite overpower me.[37]

---

37 CD to W. D. Fox, Feb. 21, 1855, *CCD* V, 294.

Chapter 2

"An Entangled Bank," or Sibling Development in a Family Ecosystem

> It is interesting to contemplate an entangled bank, clothed with many plants of many kinds, with birds singing on the bushes, with various insects flitting about, and with worms crawling through the damp earth, and to reflect that these elaborately constructed forms, so different from one another, and dependent on one another in so complex a manner, have all been produced by laws acting around us.[1]

Thus Darwin begins the famous concluding paragraph of *Origin of Species*, with its memorable image of an exquisitely complex little world where the "war of nature" is played out. This war involves a struggle for existence within species and among species vying for food and shelter, and for the chance to reproduce. What Darwin metaphorically calls "natural selection" determines the war's winners and losers, with the results being divergence of character and extinction of less-improved forms. From a Darwinian perspective, the human nuclear family can be seen as a variation on the theme of "entangled bank," a place where individuals cooperate and compete for necessities in limited supply, nurture, reject, challenge and change one another, flourish or fade according to their success in finding a niche to occupy in the family ecosystem.

This second of four essays considers the parallels between Darwin's ideas on adaptive variation (how species diverge to fill unoccupied niches in a particular environment) and the ways siblings, especially sisters, develop in relation to one another and to their parents in Austen's novels. Science historian Frank Sulloway's Darwinian theory of sibling differentiation will serve as a template for the assessment of personality development in sibling groups from all six Austen novels—and, incidentally, in the Austen and Darwin families. As younger children in large families, Jane Austen and Charles Darwin grew up markedly different from their siblings (especially from Cassandra and Erasmus, the immediately older, sole same-sex siblings in the Austen and Darwin families) and from their parents. To a considerable extent, it seems that Austen and Darwin developed along the lines set forth by Sulloway's Darwinian model of sibling personality formation; and the

---

[1] Charles Darwin, *On the Origin of Species: A Facsimile of the First Edition of 1859, with an Introduction by Ernst Mayr* (Cambridge, MA: Harvard University Press, 1964), 489. As will be the case elsewhere unless otherwise noted, this quotation from *Origin* comes from the first edition (London: John Murray, 1859). Throughout the book's six editions, Darwin continually bolstered, qualified, and reconsidered his "one long argument," a theory expressed in its freshest and most straightforward form in the first edition.

theory accounts convincingly for the diverging personalities of siblings in Austen's fiction. The Dashwood, Ferrars, Steele, Darcy, Bingley, Lucas, Bertram, Price, Crawford, Woodhouse, Knightley, Thorpe, Morland, Tilney, Musgrove, and Elliot sibling groups will all come under consideration; but the most detailed appraisal will center on the Bennets of *Pride and Prejudice*, five all-but-unprovided-for sisters of marriageable age all competing for suitors at the same time.

A distinguished contribution to the emerging field of evolutionary psychology, Frank J. Sulloway's *Born to Rebel: Birth Order, Family Dynamics, and Creative Lives* uses Darwinian theory to help answer a pair of puzzling questions. What accounts for the revolutionary genius that allows a Darwin, a Newton, or a Copernicus to radically alter our understanding of the world? And why, in a period of contested radical shift, are some people open to a new worldview while others adhere to the old dogma? Although Sulloway recognizes that in lifelong learners like humans "individual behavior needs to be explained as the product of complex interactions between proximate and ultimate causes," he sees the family as the site where personality traits develop.[2] His interactionist perspective acknowledges a wide range of variables as potential shapers of individual consciousness and behavior. Gender, social class, and hereditary traits all contribute. But, argues Sulloway, the Darwinian struggle for existence plays a major role: "Western history can be seen as an often nasty contest over the right to reproduce. More often than we realize these battles have been fought *within the family*" (67). Furthermore, Sulloway claims, these family battles are not the intergenerational rivalry posited by psychoanalysts: an Oedipal son fighting his father or a daughter seeking to displace her mother in her father's affections. Instead of competing with their parents, siblings vie with one another for the parental attention and favor that will help them to survive, thrive, and eventually reproduce.

The family, then, can be seen as a Darwinian "entangled bank" where resources are limited, competition and cooperation are different ways of gaining those resources, and a range of ecological niches are available for habitation. Recent personality studies have shown that siblings raised in the same family nearly always differ as much from one another as unrelated individuals do.[3] These sibling differences, says Sulloway, are the result of Darwin's "principle of divergence" (83–4). Brothers' and sisters' personalities and behaviors diverge according to the same evolutionary principle that accounts for how the Galápagos finches have fanned out to occupy

---

2   Frank J. Sulloway, *Born to Rebel: Birth Order, Family Dynamics, and Creative Lives* (New York: Pantheon, 1996), 63. Subsequent citations will be parenthetical.

3   Personality studies of this sort include Judy Dunn and Robert Plomin, *Separate Lives: Why Siblings Are So Different* (New York: Basic Books, 1990); John C. Loehlin, *Genes and Environment in Personality Development* (Newbury Park, CA: Sage Publications, 1992); Robert Plomin *et al.*, "Parent-Offspring and Sibling Adoption Analyses of Parental Ratings of Temperament in Infancy and Childhood," *Journal of Personality* LIX (1991), 705–32; Robert Plomin and Denise Daniels, "Why Are Children in the Same Family So Different from One Another?", *Behavioral and Brain Sciences* X (1987), 1–60; Sandra Scarr and Susan Grajek, "Similarities and Differences among Siblings," in *Sibling Relationships: Their Nature and Nurture Across the Lifespan*, eds Michael E. Lamb and Brian Sutton-Smith (Hillsdale, NJ: Lawrence Erlbaum, 1982), 357–81.

a range of niches: ground finches and tree finches, seed-eaters, cactus-eaters, leaf-eaters, insect-eaters. As in the natural world, divergence within the human family minimizes competition for resources, whether those resources be a finch's food and habitat or a child's parental affection and support.

In the Western families examined in Sulloway's study centering on how the personalities of scientific and intellectual revolutionaries have developed, many interacting factors shape a child's emergent behaviors. Temperament, class, parental conflict, parental loss, and gender are all important—particularly the last. But birth order is second only to gender—and of particular interest to Sulloway. A family is different for each sibling because the vantage point afforded by each position in birth order is unique. If the primary benefit of diversifying from one's siblings is the likelihood of increasing parental investment (98), the task of finding a distinctive niche will be different for each sibling according to the niches occupied by each of the others.

Sulloway asserts that "the first rule of the sibling road is to be different from one's brothers and sisters, especially if one happens to be a laterborn" (118). In a normal, functional family, the most obvious ecological niche available to a child is that of parental emulator. This role will generally be appropriated by the firstborn. Later siblings must seek different, unoccupied niches if they are to enhance their chances for parental attention. Thus siblings differ systematically in identifying with one parent or the other, with "split parental identifications" especially pronounced for the first sibling pair. Other disparities are generally the most pronounced in the first pair, with the second pair (the second and third child) being the next most disparate (96). Pairs of brothers or sisters find it more necessary to diversify from one another than a brother–sister pair would. Birth interval plays a part too. Children with a three- to five-year gap in their ages tend to be the most competitive. When the sibling gap is smaller, family circumstances are likelier to be similar for both members of the pair; when the gap is greater, the older child is likely to be beyond needing the same sort of parental attention the younger child requires. In each of these scenarios, there is less need for sibling competition than in families with the moderate three to five year gaps between siblings (136).

Sulloway argues that the way siblings distinguish themselves from one another enacts disruptive selection, the Darwinian principle that favors, and thereby preserves, individual differences. The typical pattern involves firstborns, the likeliest parental emulators, becoming authorities or authoritarians, leaders of their siblings and supporters of the established family order. Laterborns, filling other niches out of necessity, are typically more flexible, more open to new things and experiences, more rebellious against the domestic status quo. Just as siblings settle into different niches within the family ecosystem, they also diverge in terms of social attitudes. They acquire and cultivate differing habits of mind that in adult life will be important in such matters as selecting a mate, choosing an occupation, favoring a political candidate, and supporting or opposing a revolutionary movement. Sulloway's research into the individual personalities of scientists and other creative thinkers shows that firstborns are much likelier than laterborns to endorse conservative ideas and to oppose revolutionary ones, such as Copernicus's argument for a heliocentric solar system or Darwin's theory of evolution. The reverse is true of laterborns, who are made more likely by birth order to challenge authority themselves and to embrace causes or movements that do so.

Sulloway's idea of the family as Darwinian microenvironment where children diverge into different niches to maximize their chances of thriving seems to account plausibly for personal behaviors in a remarkable number of circumstances, even when a particular case might at first seem to contradict the pattern. For instance, the astronomer Galileo was a firstborn. Thus according to Sulloway's general principles of birth order he'd seem unlikely to be a thinker so fiercely opposed to authority that he'd defy the Papal Inquisition and be convicted of heresy. But Stillman Drake's account of Galileo's family shows that his father Vincenzo, who revolutionized musical theory by demonstrating that harmonic intervals violate Pythagorean principles, trained his son in music—and by example served as his son's precursor in basing iconoclastic mathematical claims about physics on experimental verification. For the younger Galileo, then, shattering established paradigms was a way of identifying with, rather than rebelling against, his father. It was, in a way, the family business.[4]

In like manner, Jane Austen's and Charles Darwin's respective places in their families can be seen as contributing to the distinctive qualities of mind that made for their accomplishments. Sulloway observes that Darwin's laterborn, second-son status helps to explain the personality that resulted in his revolutionary genius and methodological style alike: "Throughout his illustrious career, Darwin's most abiding scientific hallmark was his penchant for elevating the inferior and the insignificant into the superior and the significant ... He valued questions over answers, curiosity over conviction, and perseverance over prerogative" (359). These observations taken into the literary sphere could account for laterborn, second-daughter Austen's characteristic approach to constructing fiction—and, some of the time at least, for the characteristic outcome of her novels, where the typical ending involves raising a woman whose social position is comparatively inferior and insignificant, though her personal qualities make her superior and significant, through the defining act of marriage.

Jane Austen, as mentioned earlier, was the second daughter and penultimate child in a family of eight siblings. James (1765–1819), who became a clergyman, succeeded his father at Steventon. George (1766–1827), deaf and mentally handicapped, lived away from home but in the neighborhood. Edward (1768–1852) was adopted by rich relations, the Knights, whose surname he took and whose estates Godmersham in Kent and Chawton in Hampshire he inherited. Henry (1771–1850) led a dashing, unsettled youth—a brilliant Oxford student, militia officer, second husband to the Austens' French-Revolution-widowed cousin Eliza Comtesse de Feuillide, banker, Receiver-General of Oxfordshire—but subsided in middle age to a country clergyman. Francis (1774–1865) trained at the Royal Naval Academy and eventually rose to be Admiral of the Red Fleet, thus the world's most powerful naval officer in his day. He was knighted and made GCB. (Knight Grand Cross of the Bath). Charles (1779–1852) followed his brother into the navy and also succeeded, if

---

4   Stillman Drake, *Galileo Studies* (Ann Arbor, MI: University of Michigan Press, 1970), 43–62.

a bit less dramatically. He became a rear admiral, a CB (Companion of the Bath), and Commander-in-Chief of the East India Station. Cassandra (1773–1845), two-and-a-half years older than Jane, was her lifelong companion. In her twenties, Cassandra was engaged to Thomas Craven Fowle, a clergyman who died abroad in the service. Cassandra never married and lived with a gradually diminishing household that first lost her father, then Jane, and finally her mother, until she was left alone at Chawton Cottage. Cassandra, named after her mother, was reputed to be intelligent, undemonstrative, moody, with regular habits, conventional opinions, and a reserved exterior. She was Jane's closest confidante and the recipient of most of her letters, some of which she censored or destroyed on Jane's death.

The patterns of adaptive divergence Sulloway lays out seem to hold true for the Austen siblings. All the sons followed career paths conventional for their class and time, but the eldest obviously took the most conservative role by going directly into the church and even succeeding to his father's principal living. The next two brothers were eventually removed from fraternal competition—George by his handicapped exile from the household, Edward by rich relations taking him up according to the Frank Churchill model, though his personality, adoptive name, and South-of-England estates make him seem more like George Knightley. Henry, six years junior to James, followed a path that sometimes replicated his brother's and sometimes radically diverged but eventually brought him to a similar ending-point. Both James and Henry attended their father's Oxford college, St John's, on scholarship as Founder's Kin. James, scholarly and contemplative, gained a college fellowship, then took orders and was granted the parishes of Overton and Deane. He succeeded to Steventon on his father's retirement in 1805. Brilliant Henry—Jane's favorite brother, whereas the good-natured, generous, practical Edward was Cassandra's—was said to be handsomest of the handsome brothers. For all his talent, he did not win a college fellowship; and his laterborn early life was far more adventurous and uneven than James's smooth, straight path. The militia—two broken engagements—marriage to the heiress-cousin-wife with whom he was nearly apprehended when they traveled to France during the 1802 Peace of Amiens in hopes of recovering her guillotined first husband's property—a bank that prospered, then failed. Henry, with a character that must have been altogether more rackety than those of his older brothers James and Edward, finally settled down as a 45-year-old to the family business of preaching sermons. The fifth and sixth sons, laterborns open to new possibilities, thought alike in choosing the navy, though their temperaments apparently were quite different in predictably adaptive ways. The elder of the pair, Francis—"neat, practical, and intrepid" from childhood—grew into a man who was considered a pious, stern, and just leader. Charles seems to have been warmer, livelier, and more demonstrative as a child. As a man he became an officer "regarded by his men with unbounded affection."[5]

Although the Austen brothers were educated at home along with their father's boarding pupils until it was time for them to go away to Oxford or the Royal Naval Academy, Mrs Austen was apparently too busy with other domestic duties to instruct

---

5   John Halperin, *The Life of Jane Austen* (Baltimore, MD: Johns Hopkins University Press, 1984), 24. Subsequent citations will be parenthetical.

her daughters, who were first sent, when Jane was seven in 1783, to Mrs Cawley's school in Oxford, then to the more prestigious and salubrious Abbey School of Mrs Latournelle in Reading. The sisters were brought home in 1787, Cassandra now old enough to assist her mother in the large household's labors. But the end of formal schooling offered Jane what would be her "real education" (Halperin, 26), better than anything available at either of the female academies she'd attended. She read in her father's well-stocked library—perhaps under his direction or one of her older brothers'. Her informal curriculum included large doses of Shakespeare, Milton, Pope, Thomson, Gray, Hume, Sheridan, Blair, Gilpin, Johnson, Cowper, Crabbe, Goldsmith, and eighteenth-century novelists.[6] She also acquired ornamental female accomplishments and practical womanly skills: French, Italian, pianoforte, drawing, sewing, embroidery. And she began an apprenticeship in writing. Her brothers James and Henry had both contributed to *The Loiterer*, an Oxford publication with essays that, among other things, criticized the emotional excesses of sentimental fiction. With an irony just as detached as her brothers' and far more ferocious than that pervading her adult works, the adolescent Jane followed their lead, albeit in a different vein, and amused herself and her family by mocking the excesses of sensibility and other conventions of literature and etiquette alike in such miniature burlesques as "Love and Freindship" and "The Beautifull Cassandra."

It would be a mistake to assume that in Austen's case or most others art simply reflects life. Nonetheless, the gallery of bad or indifferent mothers in her novels seems to rise out of a distance between Jane and her mother Cassandra Leigh Austen—a woman who may, like a better-born and better-bred Mrs Price, have been too busy running a large household full of sons to have had much time for her second daughter—who may, like Mrs Bennet, have preferred her helpful and more conventional first daughter to her witty second—and who may, like Mr Woodhouse, have demanded endless patience for her lifelong hypochondria that increased with the years. Cool or sharp-edged remarks about Mrs Austen appear throughout Jane's letters, and her extensive correspondence contains not one letter addressed to her mother. The omission silently speaks volumes about the relationship, whether Jane never wrote them or Mrs Austen, anomalous among her correspondents, did not save them or Cassandra, the self-appointed guardian of Jane's reputation, felt obliged to destroy them.

Like her creation Elizabeth Bennet, Austen loved her father, probably endured her mother, and found in her older sister a complementary spirit and lifelong companion of the sort that Jane Bingley would have been to Elizabeth had Darcy and Bingley (or acceptable substitutes) never arrived at Longbourn asking for their hands. Cassandra's niche as assistant to the mother whose name she bore —and perhaps, in her relations with Jane, surrogate for that mother—may have pushed Jane to identify

---

6   For a thoroughly contextualized account of the Enlightenment qualities of Jane Austen's fiction, see Peter Knox-Shaw, *Jane Austen and the Enlightenment* (Cambridge: Cambridge University Press, 2004). Other important treatments of this theme are found in Mary Waldron, *Jane Austen and the Fiction of Her Time* (Cambridge: Cambridge University Press, 1999) and Claudia L. Johnson, *Jane Austen: Women, Politics, and the Novel* (Chicago, IL: University of Chicago Press, 1988).

more with her father and consequently may have freed her to develop the rich inner life that bore fruit in her novels. But despite or because of their differences, the more traditional Cassandra and the more intellectually adventurous Jane shared their deepest thoughts and their living spaces throughout life, until Jane died in Cassandra's arms in rented rooms in Winchester. On the surface, they could be seen as a pair of reserved spinsters in a country neighborhood—women wiser and quieter than Miss Bates but comparably situated, with a respectable clerical background but limited, declining means. At heart they were as different as a cactus-eating finch and a seed-eater.

The Darwin family and Charles's place among his siblings offer comparably intriguing illustrations of Sulloway's principles of personality development at work. Like Jane Austen, Charles Darwin was the next to the last child in a large group and had a single older sibling of his own sex. Six children were born to Dr Robert Darwin and Susanna Wedgwood, the wife chosen for him by his father, the brilliant and multi-talented Dr Erasmus Darwin: Marianne (1798–1858), Caroline (1800–1888), Susan (1803–66), Erasmus Alvey (1804–81), Charles Robert (1809–82), and Emily Catherine (1810–66). Conformity and rebellion, as evidenced by career or marital choices, are hard to unbraid among the Darwins, an inbred group whose members, even when rebelling, proved true to type. Robert Darwin, the youngest of three sons born to Erasmus Darwin (himself a younger son) by his first wife Mary Howard, followed his father's career path, if with less *éclat*, and became a highly successful medical practitioner. He also became a rich, shrewd man of property. His wife Susanna was the daughter of first cousins Sarah Wedgwood and Josiah Wedgwood, the founder of the famous pottery manufactory and friend of Erasmus Darwin in the liberal intellectual group called the Lunar Society. Susanna's marriage portion of 25,000 pounds combined with Robert's considerable earnings to give their family, ensconced in a house called the Mount on the outskirts of Shrewsbury, a lifestyle surpassing that of the Austens and more comparable to that of Jane Austen's prosperous, genteel characters—whose near-contemporaries the Robert Darwins would have been, were the boundary between life and art a permeable membrane.

Much ink has been spilled concerning the nature of Charles Darwin's relations with his father. Some historians, particularly Freudians, have seen Robert as a domineering autocrat who failed to detect his son's genius and tried to force him along uncongenial paths, first making him study medicine at Edinburgh, then obliging him to prepare for a church career at Cambridge.[7] Some of the cited evidence for

---

7   For instance, Dr Robert Waring Darwin is both verbally and visually figured as an overbearing patriarch in Jonathan Miller and Borin Van Loon's lively and lucid intellectual comic book *Darwin for Beginners* (New York: Pantheon, 1982). Here, the plus-sized doctor's well-known silhouette portrait recurrently serves to suggest the heavy, repressive father overshadowing the son. The black silhouette of Robert Darwin tortures his son on the rack while saying, "Look, son, since your medical career is a dead loss, I'm sure you'll agree that it's best for you to go to Cambridge and study holy orders" (57). The paternal shadow is felled by a knockout punch from Uncle Josiah Wedgwood (whose face is wittily superimposed on the body of Michelangelo's David) after having been "enraged" by Henslow's invitation for Darwin to take the naturalist's post on the *Beagle* (63) and later, along with a vast image of the benucha or "great black bug of the pampas," looms over a cowering Charles Darwin

Dr Darwin's repressive power comes from the childhood impressions of Charles's wife and first cousin Emma Wedgwood (herself the youngest of seven children, three brothers and four sisters), who grew up 20 miles off at Maer Hall in a freer and livelier household. Robert Darwin certainly had a large, imposing presence, a highly sensitive and possibly irritable temperament, and a sense of authority, consequence, and gravitas that, though as natural for a real man of his time and station as for a fictive Sir Thomas Bertram or Fitzwilliam Darcy, offends the more egalitarian eye looking back over almost two centuries. But as a young man Robert Darwin himself had suffered from a high-powered father's blend of domineering expectations and personal neglect, undesired interference and unwillingness to give needed help. Janet Browne observes that in compensation "he vowed never to treat his own children in similar fashion."[8]

Although Robert Darwin wanted both Erasmus and Charles to follow him into medical practice and accordingly sent them to Edinburgh, seat of Britain's finest medical faculty, he eventually freed both sons to follow their own inclinations rather than his own—and he generously supported them in their choices. For instance, though initially disinclined to allow Charles to embark on the *Beagle* voyage that turned out be the making of his scientific career, Robert was flexible enough to say that he'd yield if one rational advocate (whom Charles easily found in his uncle Josiah Wedgwood) argued in favor of the adventure. Won over by Wedgwood, Robert Darwin ungrudgingly paid Charles's considerable expenses during the five-year voyage. In turn, Charles's accounts of and behavior towards his father consistently and convincingly bespoke a lifelong, sincere, and uncomplicated affection, not the contorted filial emotions that would be aroused by an overbearing, disapproving patriarchal bully.

It may be that, like Jane Austen, Charles Darwin suffered more from lack of involved maternal love than from a deficiency of paternal approval. Susanna Wedgwood, like many others in her family, was a confirmed invalid—and at a time when even healthy rich women might not have much more to do with child-rearing than does the sofa-loving Lady Bertram of *Mansfield Park*. Susanna died when

---

(88–9). This last image figures in a section that lays out possible reasons for Darwin's lifelong ill-health and, after citing Chagas disease caused by a benucha bite as one possibility, states "The alternate explanation is that Darwin was crippled by the burden of an overbearing father." Also see John Chancellor, *Charles Darwin* (London: Weidenfeld & Nicolson, 1913), a study characterizing Robert Darwin as a "dominating and unlovable" (144) and "crassly unimaginative" father who "never attempted to understand his son's gifts" (53). For a more recent and specifically Freudian reading, see Julian Huxley and H. B. D. Kettlewell, *Charles Darwin and His World* (New York: Viking, 1965). Huxley and Kettlewell describe Robert Darwin as an "autocratic" father whom his son "subconsciously resented" (66) and suggest that Charles's eventual invalidism proceeded from a youthful "guilt-complex toward his father" (12). Yet another Freudian take on the relationship between Charles Darwin and his father appears in Phyllis Greenacre, *The Quest for the Father: A Study of the Darwin–Butler Controversy, As a Contribution to the Understanding of the Creative Individual* (New York: International Universities, 1963), 54–6, 88–92.

8   Janet Browne, *Charles Darwin: Voyaging* (Princeton, NJ: Princeton University Press, 1995), I, 43. Subsequent citations will be parenthetical and will use the abbreviation *CDV*.

Charles was eight years old, yet he claimed that "I can remember hardly anything about her except her death-bed, her black velvet gown, and her curiously constructed work-table" (*CDV* 19). Robert Darwin's powerful but reticent grief might have contributed to this strange gap in Charles's recollections—as might his elder sisters' "never being able to speak about her or mention her name."[9] And Susanna's invalid state meant relative isolation long before the absolute separation of death. The consequence of Susanna's death, for Charles Darwin and his significantly older sisters, was a proxy matriarchy, with three young women running the household and supervising the two siblings young enough to be at home. Until she married Henry Parker in 1824, Marianne ran the household. Caroline, who later married the Josiah Wedgwood of her generation and who most resembled her mother in character and looks (*CDV* 21), became a loving if didactic mother substitute in a sweeter vein than her junior Susan, Charles's sharp, humorous so-called "Granny." All three sisters, and later the youngest Catherine, inherited their mother's piety, which they tried to nurture in "dearest Charley" (or "Bobby"). At the Mount, the sisters pursued a high-minded, busy life of housekeeping, leisure activities appropriate for their class, and good works suitable to their family's liberal leanings. With their father's active support they maintained a local infant school based on progressive educational principles. They supported abolition and other causes dear to the Wedgwood–Darwin heart. And, when their brother Charles was far from female control on distant seas, they sent letters from Shropshire reminding him of the country parsonage that they meant to be his eventual cozy lot in life.

Benignly ruled by the eldest three sisters, Charles developed in relationship mainly to his adjacent siblings Erasmus and Catherine. He and Catherine were children together in a bereaved household, playmates until she became old enough to make common cause with her sisters and enlarge the chorus of female fussing over Charles. Charles's reminiscences speak of how much quicker his little sister was than he and how much more extensive her memories of Susanna were. Erasmus, five years older, was far enough ahead in school that Charles was always following in his sedate wake. As sole brother Erasmus was at once the sibling from whom, of all others, it was necessary for Charles to distinguish himself and the one who could be, as Cassandra Austen was for Jane, his family confidant. Erasmus, young and old alike, did not live the typical conforming, achieving life of an eldest son. Perhaps because he was preceded by three strong sisters, perhaps because his laterborn father was a strongly dominant presence, perhaps because he had prospects of financial security without landed responsibility, perhaps because of hereditary and environmental tendencies towards invalidism, Erasmus in his maturity was not a rebel so much as a quiet idler—unless we think of cultivated indolence as a somewhat contrarian posture in the nineteenth-century England's upwardly mobile professional classes.

---

9   Janet Browne observes that Darwin's remarkably few memories of his mother, her death, and its aftermath must have been suppressed, this bereavement being "the first compelling occasion in a life spent struggling with the desire to push all unpleasant things to one side." But Browne goes on to warn that it would be a mistake to "project modern ideas about parent–child relations onto this particular family or to suggest that Darwin failed properly to grieve" (*CDV* 20).

He and Charles, who both bore the burden of Darwin family history in their first and second names alike, shared many scientific interests, the first being their youthful infatuation with chemistry. They attended the same schools and universities: Shrewsbury, Edinburgh, and Christ's College Cambridge, though Erasmus received his Cambridge degree before going to Edinburgh, whereas Charles joined his brother at Edinburgh for a few terms before shifting to Cambridge. Unlike Charles, Erasmus did actually qualify as a doctor, though he never practiced medicine.

In adulthood, the brothers' choices and lives were notably different yet complementary. Erasmus, who inherited the largest share of his father's substantial estate, savored the domestic tranquility and social stimulation of a bachelor bon vivant in London. His relationships with women were intense friendships (some with married women, such as Jane Carlyle and his cousin Hensleigh Wedgwood's wife Fanny) without the potential for becoming more demanding attachments. If the good-natured, witty, lazy Eras lived the life of a well-off metropolitan do-nothing, Charles, in sharp contrast, chose rural seclusion, uxorious attachment to one worthy woman—his cousin Emma Wedgwood, who bore him ten children—and a dogged work ethic that resulted in extraordinary productivity in spite of invalidism even more pronounced than Erasmus's. Janet Browne attributes Darwin's industriousness to being a younger brother desperately trying to catch up with a naturally talented older brother (*CDV* 11)—a trait that may also explain why, as their sister Caroline observed, Charles failed to perceive the extent of his father's respect for him: "I wish some years ago, I had known that Charles thought my Father did not understand or know what ability & power of mind he had—really he was so proud as well as fond of him that I often felt afraid that Erasmus might feel mortified & feel undervalued" (qtd in *CDV* 18). But Erasmus's sweet nature prevented either his noticing any disproportion in paternal pride or his minding even if he did notice—and the two brothers were exceptionally close, necessary to one another in the way of Jane and Cassandra Austen. Emma Darwin was an extraordinarily compatible wife and a well-educated partner for Charles, but even so there were limits to what they could share. Conventionally feminine and conventionally pious, Emma had no particular interest in or knowledge of Charles's scientific pursuits, and his ever-growing religious doubts actively disturbed her. Erasmus, a like-minded but differently oriented brother who need not be battled as a rival, was the family member with whom Darwin could speak openly about things that could or should not be shared with Emma.

Post-mortem character analysis of the sort appearing above entails guesswork. Even interpreting a living person's character inevitably involves extrapolation. However scrupulous and thorough the evolutionary psycho-biographer may be, he or she can never know all there is to know about an individual's personal circumstances. With real people what's discernible is something akin to the proverbial iceberg tip, much remaining undetected and undetectable. In contrast, literary characters have no secrets from readers. What's to be known about them is available to us; what's unknown is strictly speaking nonexistent, outside the frame of the fiction; and our inferences, if responsible, must take these limitations into consideration. For example, a reader interested in arguing whether or not Sir Thomas Bertram of *Mansfield Park* has slaves working on his Caribbean estate can deploy learned socio-cultural contextualizing, psychological subtlety, and close attention to details of the novel to argue for or against Sir Thomas's status as slaveholder, colonial landowner without slaves, or (less likely) outright abolitionist.[10] Nonetheless, the inferences drawn cannot be proved

---

10 The classic extrapolative statement that Sir Thomas's Antiguan plantation depends on slave labor comes in Edward W. Said, *Culture and Imperialism* (New York: Alfred A. Knopf, 1993): "Sir Thomas's property in the Caribbean would have had to be a sugar plantation maintained by slave labor" (89). Following Said's lead, various critics have written about the relation between slavery and Austen's novel as if Sir Thomas's slave-owning status is a proven fact or a foregone conclusion. See Clara Tuite, "Domestic Retrenchment and Imperial Expansion: The Property Plots of Mansfield Park," in *The Postcolonial Jane Austen*, eds You-me Park and Rajeswari Sunder Rajan (New York: Routledge, 2000), 93–115; Carl Plasa, *Textual Politics from Slavery to Postcolonialism: Race and Identification* (New York: St. Martin's Press, 2000), 32–59; Brian Southam's particularly convincing "The Silence of the Bertrams: Slavery and the Chronology of Mansfield Park," *TLS* (17 February 1995), 13–14; Maaja A. Stewart, *Domestic Realities and Imperial Fictions: Jane Austen's Novels in Eighteenth-Century Contexts* (Athens, GA: University of Georgia Press, 1993), 105–36; and Moira Ferguson, "Mansfield Park: Slavery, Colonialism, and Gender," *Oxford Literary Review*, 13 (1991), 118–39. For a thoughtful reply to these and other recent postcolonial renderings of Austen's novel, see John Wiltshire, "Decolonising Mansfield Park," *Essays in Criticism* LIII.4 (October 2003), 303–22.

Although sugar cane was the dominant cash crop of colonial Antigua in Austen's time and actual sugar plantations then generally exploited slave labor, Sir Thomas's landholdings are fictive. Thus in the absence of detail from the novel itself, we can't do more than imagine how extensive Sir Thomas's property might have been, what it would have produced, or how it might have been run. Extrapolating from historical, political, geographical, and economic matters outside the novel, an approach made possible by the way Austen grounds her fiction in empirical observation, leads to the conclusion that Sir Thomas would most likely have slaves on his Antiguan property. But reasoning from personal interactions and traits of character within the novel itself rather than from historical contextualizing might suggest that, if anything, Austen meant Sir Thomas to be a friend to abolition rather than a slave-owner. On his return from Antigua Fanny takes the initiative of engaging him in conversation on the slave trade. Having admitted to Edmund that "'I love to hear my uncle talk of the West Indies'" (*MP* 197), Fanny finds herself pressed by her cousin to speak more in the presence of Sir Thomas, who is favorably disposed towards her. The discussion continues,

"But I do talk to him more than I used. I am sure I do. Did not you hear me ask him about the slave trade last night?"

"I did—and was in hopes the question would be followed up by others. It would have pleased your uncle to be inquired of farther."

"And I longed to do it—but there was such a dead silence! And while my cousins were sitting without speaking a word, or seeming at all interested in the subject, I did not like— I thought it would appear as if I wanted to set myself off at their expense, by shewing a curiosity and pleasure in his information which he must wish his own daughters to feel." (198)

High-minded, oppressed Fanny Price seems a most unlikely friend of slave-owning. As timid as she is principled, Fanny seems just as unlikely to take the bold step of confronting a slave-owner on a subject that, in a time when the growing abolitionist movement had accomplished some of its goals and was moving towards others, would put him on the defensive. It also seems psychologically implausible that Sir Thomas, as Austen draws him, would have taken pleasure in discussing the details of his plantation if he owned slaves or that Fanny, as depicted,

or disproved. The novel simply doesn't say, either directly or indirectly, whether or not Sir Thomas owned slaves. But if drawing conclusions about the personalities of literary characters is an inevitably limited enterprise, within those limitations a careful reader can be confident of finding everything available for interpretation. Turning to the sibling groups that appear in Austen's novels, we can draw conclusions that take complete account of what needs noticing, whereas we would have to be satisfied with approximation if studying real family groups. Sulloway's Darwinian model of siblings diversifying in somewhat predictable ways to occupy different niches within the family ecosystem accounts with striking success for the brothers and sisters Austen portrays. Perhaps this evidence supports the validity of Sulloway's theory; perhaps it affirms Austen's skill as an observer of personality.

When the thought-experiment I'm presently engaged upon plays by any rules apart from those of common sense and clarity, it follows conventions and strictures drawn from literary criticism rather than those of social science. Despite this disciplinary allegiance, it will be efficient to preface the upcoming discussion of siblings in Austenworld by a pair of tables which, if they do nothing else, will eliminate the need of supplying the title of a novel each time a particular family or character is mentioned. The first table, organized according to novel, lists the sibling groups that will be discussed and where possible supplies ages, birth dates, or other information that can help to establish birth order and sibling gaps. The second table is a taxonomy that organizes the six novels' sibling groups according to their various configurations. In this second table, I follow Sulloway's claim that only-child status is, if only *in potentia*, a sibling position.

The mere act of organizing Austen's characters in this fashion foregrounds some problems with theorizing about siblings and personalities—especially in fiction, where what we have to go on is what details are in the text. In some cases, what constitutes the entangled bank called a family is entangled indeed. For instance, do John Dashwood and his three half-sisters Elinor, Marianne, and Margaret belong to two families or one? With different mothers and a probable age gap of at least ten years between John and Elinor, they did not compete for parental attention. Yet they share a father and, through him, the connection to Norland, the estate where the sisters have grown up and to which their half-brother will eventually succeed. One might ask a similar question about Henry and Mary Crawford and their older half-sister Mrs Grant. Then too, several Austen characters have birth orders that can only be inferred, because there aren't details confirming the inference. For example, Fanny Dashwood, authoritarian, already married, and the mother of a four-year-old, seems to be the firstborn Ferrars sibling; but it's never directly stated that she's older

---

would have been tactless enough to raise and enjoy the topic under such circumstances. Thus if a reader confining interpretation to specifics within the novel itself infers anything about the details of Sir Thomas's Antiguan plantation, it's likely to be that Sir Thomas is an exception to the slave-owning majority. Of course, it is possible that everyone else in the room during Fanny's interchange with her uncle is aware of the Antigua plantation's slave economy, thinks it a dirty secret, and maintains "dead silence" for that reason. But for that scenario to be true, Fanny would have to be woefully uninformed about the state of the Bertrams' affairs—and it would still be necessary to account for Sir Thomas's pleasure at her expression of interest in a topic on which the rest of the family is silent.

Table 2.1 Sibling Groups in Jane Austen's Six Novels

Novel	Sibling Groups
Sense and Sensibility	**Brandon**: unnamed older brother (dead), Col. Brandon, unnamed sister in Avignon. **Dashwood**: John, older half-brother to Elinor (19), Marianne (16–17), Margaret (13). **Ferrars**: Edward (23–24); Robert (younger); Fanny, Mrs Dashwood (presumably older). **Jennings**: Mary, Lady Middleton (26–27); Charlotte, Mrs Palmer (younger). **Middleton**: John (about 6), William, Annamaria (3), unnamed youngest. **Steele**: Anne (nearly 30), Lucy (22 or 23).
Pride and Prejudice	**Bennet**: Jane (22), Elizabeth (20), Mary, Catherine, Lydia (15–16). **Bingley**: Charles (22), Louisa, Mrs Hurst; Caroline. **Darcy**: Fitzwilliam (28), Georgiana (16). **Fitzwilliam**: earl with undisclosed title and Christian name, Lady Anne Darcy, Lady Catherine de Bourgh. **Gardiner**: Edward, Mrs Bennet, Mrs Phillips. **Gardiner, Mr and Mrs Edward**: two unnamed girls (8 and 6), two younger boys. **Lucas**: Charlotte, Mrs Collins (27); Maria, younger girls and boys.
Mansfield Park	**Bertram**: Tom (25), Edmund (24), Maria (21), Julia (20). **Crawford**: Mrs Grant (older half-sister), Henry, Mary. **Price**: William (19), Fanny (18), John, Richard, Susan (14), Mary (dead), Sam (11), Tom (9), Charles (8), Betsey (5). **Ward**: Mrs Norris (eldest); Maria, Lady Bertram; Frances, Mrs Price (youngest).
Emma	**Hawkins**: Selina, Mrs Suckling (elder); Augusta, Mrs Elton. **Knightley**: George (37–38), John (younger). **Knightley, John and Isabella**: Henry (eldest), John, Bella, George, Emma. **Martin**: Robert, Elizabeth, another sister. **Woodhouse**: Isabella, Mrs John Knightley (elder); Emma (20).
Northanger Abbey	**Morland**: James (at Oxford), Richard, George, Catherine (17), Sarah (16), Harriet, four others, ranging down to "a boy and girl of six and four years old." **Thorpe**: Isabella (21), John (at Oxford), Edward, Anne, Maria. **Tilney**: Frederick (eldest), Henry (24–25), Eleanor (youngest).
Persuasion	**Elliot**: Elizabeth (29), Anne (27), Mary, Mrs Charles Musgrove (23). **Harville**: Captain, Fanny. **Hayter**: Charles (eldest), others. **Musgrove**: Charles, Richard (died), Henrietta (20), Louisa (19), enough others to comprise "a numerous family." **Musgrove, Charles and Mary**: Charles, Walter. **Wentworth**: Sophia, Mrs Croft, Edward, Frederick.

Table 2.2   A Taxonomy of Austenworld Sibling Configurations

Sibling Configuration	Novel; Names
Sisters	*Sense and Sensibility*: Dashwood (grown half-brother), Jennings, Steele. *Pride and Prejudice*: Bennet. *Mansfield Park*: Ward. *Emma*: Woodhouse, Hawkins. *Persuasion*: Elliot.
Sisters and brothers	*Pride and Prejudice*: Lucas. *Mansfield Park*: Bertram, Price. *Emma*: John Knightleys. *Northanger Abbey*: Morland, Thorpe.
Sister with brothers	*Sense and Sensibility*: Ferrars. *Northanger Abbey*: Tilney. *Persuasion*: Wentworth.
Brother with sisters	*Pride and Prejudice*: Gardiner, Bingley, the anonymous earl, living or dead, whose sisters are the late Lady Anne Darcy and Lady Catherine De Bourgh. *Emma*: Martin. *Persuasion*: Musgrove.
Brother–sister pair	*Pride and Prejudice*: Darcy. *Mansfield Park*: Crawford (older half-sister), Harville (no other siblings as far as we know).
Brothers	*Emma*: Knightley.
Younger brothers*	*Sense and Sensibility*: Brandon. *Pride and Prejudice*: Fitzwilliam.
Older brother†	*Emma*: Weston. *Persuasion*: Hayter.
Implied younger bro.	*Mansfield Park*: Yates.
Only children‡	*Sense and Sensibility*: Willoughby, Grey. *Pride and Prejudice*: Collins, Wickham, De Bourgh. *Mansfield Park*: Rushworth. *Emma*: Fairfax, Smith, Churchill. *Persuasion*: Walter Elliot, Miss Carteret.

* Those whose elder brothers and any other siblings aren't direct actors in the story.
† Those whose younger brothers or younger siblings aren't in the story.
‡ Insofar as one can tell.

than 23- or 24-year-old Edward. The Hon. Mr Yates in *Mansfield Park* may, in light of his honorific, be a baron's firstborn or laterborn son or an earl's laterborn son; but whatever the rank of his father, it seems highly likely that he's a younger son. Were Yates a peer's heir, he would from his first appearance at Mansfield Park have seemed a highly eligible catch to the Bertrams, a family worldly-minded enough to accept the untitled Rushworth, whose estate and fortune counterbalance his folly, as a son-in-law. And we simply can't tell about the Bingley sisters. The married Louisa Hurst and the desperately Darcy-stalking Caroline seem older than 22-year-old Charles, who has the laid-back personality of a younger sibling. Nonetheless, the siblings' birth order remains conjectural.

One remarkable feature of nearly all sibling groups in Austen's novels: although infant and childhood mortality were relatively high during the late eighteenth and early nineteenth centuries, they seem to have almost no effect on the sibling groups Austen surveys. Perhaps she felt no need to imagine juvenile characters who would have nothing to do with her stories, or perhaps the high survival rate reflects the extraordinary health of her own sibling group.

Sulloway's investigation studies children without siblings in light of their conservatism, flexibility, and openness to experience, and concludes that in such matters they fall between firstborns and laterborns. Given that his subject is how the personalities of creative revolutionaries are formed, Sulloway does not consider the qualities most commonly attributed to only children by popular wisdom: selfishness and social awkwardness. Austen's attitudes on only children seem to follow the popular perception that being an only child is an obstacle to character development, for except in *Emma* only children in Austen's novels are always negative characters to a greater or lesser extent. A majority of the marital prospects it would be a mistake for a worthy person actually to wed—whether because of their stupidity, ill nature, bad health, unscrupulousness, immorality, or selfishness—are apparent only children: Willoughby, Miss Grey, the Rev. Mr Collins, Wickham, Miss De Bourgh, Rushworth, Mr Elliot, Miss Dalrymple. It is almost possible to add another only child, Frank Churchill, to this list. To be sure he, like only children Willoughby, Wickham, and Walter Elliot plus the pattern-breaking older brother Henry Crawford, is a variation on the theme of the manipulative seducer who plays with women's minds and hearts. But the uprooted and adopted Frank Churchill's mixed character, a seeming blend of his Weston heredity and his Churchill environment, is redeemable—and it will be redeemed because he has both the good judgment to engage himself to another, better only child, the orphaned Jane Fairfax, and the good fortune to keep her. It's worth speculating on whether Frank and Jane's shared status as orphaned or semi-orphaned, adopted or quasi-adopted, uprooted only children is as important as their respective charms in drawing the two temperamental opposites together. In any case, their singleton status, like that of the "natural daughter of somebody" (*E* 22) Harriet Smith, points to a practical literary reason that can explain why Austen made them, and perhaps the other only children in her other novels, singletons. Austen created Frank Churchill, Jane Fairfax, and Harriet Smith, to differing degrees all outsiders to the long-established Hartfield–Donwell coterie at the heart of this most densely particularized of her books, to fill particular functions relative to the novel's title character and her little world. All three must be given relatively complex, believable personalities; but supplying them with sibling relationships that, in their turn, would require some degree of appraisal would blur the focus of a fictional experiment elegantly centered, for all its exquisite, realistic, and seemingly random but actually significant detail, on one chief thing, the evolving character of Emma Woodhouse.

Sibling relationships and the attendant differences in character and behavior are often important components of Austen's plots, but not always. Children too young to go out into society typically exist as human accessories or props rather than receiving attention in their own right. Austen doesn't individuate or appraise the Gardiner children in *Pride and Prejudice*, the John Knightley brood in *Emma* (children shown in their fullest detail on drawing-paper, as Emma has sketched them for her portfolio), or the younger Morlands in *Northanger Abbey*. Similarly, the unspecified younger children in the Lucas family don't count as individual characters, although one spirited boy is allowed to proclaim that if as rich as Mr Darcy, "'I should not care how proud I was. I would keep a pack of foxhounds and drink a bottle of wine every day'" (*PP* 20). Had Austen set herself up to write Darwinian *bildungsromans* rather than novels of manners, this selective inattention to preadolescents would be a shame, for all these children are in the phase when family interactions are most strongly forming their personalities.

If the relationships of brothers and sisters still in the nursery or the schoolroom are seldom important to Austen's purposes, the sibling relationships of mature characters are sometimes irrelevant or outside the narrative frame. What matters in some such cases are the psychological or social consequences of simply having grown up with brothers, sisters, or both. It's subtly useful to know that Mr Elton has sisters, mainly because that knowledge carries with it the implication that he doesn't have a brother (therefore neither direct competition nor early experience at interacting with males of his generation) and the possibility that he's accustomed to being dominated by females, as he will be on marrying "the charming Augusta Hawkins." The fact that Fanny, the dead fiancée of Captain Benwick, is Captain Harville's sister serves principally to explain the unusually close bond between Benwick and the Harvilles. Mr Weston's brothers (probably younger because they went directly into trade, whereas he did so only after marriage to Miss Churchill of Enscombe proved too expensive for a young lieutenant's private means) are mere background figures Austen never brings to Highbury. Colonel Brandon's ailing sister in Avignon and deplorable, defunct older brother are not significant in and of themselves but exist to fulfill peripheral plot functions, the former as an alternative to the young Miss Williams as potential focus for Brandon's sudden concern on receipt of a mysterious letter, the latter as the reason Brandon's family did not allow his heiress cousin Eliza to follow her heart and give him rather than the elder son and heir her hand and her fortune. Selina Hawkins Suckling, whose marital situation at Maple Grove provides the chief grist for her sister Augusta's conversational mill, never comes to Highbury with her husband in their storied barouche-landau; but being equipped with a married older sister gives Mrs Elton an idée fixe to run into the ground—and adds a further reason for us to see her as an obnoxious analogue to Emma.

In family groups where some or all of the siblings are selectively left unindividuated, whether because they're too young or too marginal, even the unindividuated fill plot functions. The Gardiner children are a multipurpose collective accessory. Among other things, their existence explains why Mr Gardiner's fortune can't go towards propping up his inadequately provided-for Bennet nieces and allows Jane Bennet's maternal potential to shine forth. Similarly employed if more prominently displayed, John Knightley's five children, granted names but not their own personalities, evoke significant behaviors in others. The young Knightleys exist as testimony to their parents' ardent domesticity, and as an important subject on which their maternal aunt and paternal uncle (whose respective interactions with the children show what a loving parent each would be) can always agree, whatever their opinions on other matters. They are also eyewitnesses that even vigorous Mr Knightley can pine with lovesickness ("'I believe I did not play with the children quite so much as usual. I remember one evening the poor boys saying, 'Uncle seems always tired now'"—*E* 465).

Large Austen families can contain a few children crucial to the novel of manners, with others left obscure. It would be difficult to imagine anything but a full-blown family saga that could offer an equal display of the Morlands as ten instances of adaptive variation at work. In *Northanger Abbey* Catherine, the fourth sibling and first daughter, is the novel's protagonist; and James, the firstborn, is by dint of family position quarry for the fortune-hunting Isabella Thorpe. Sarah, the second daughter and younger sibling next to Catherine, has a bit part as confidante. Catherine's relationships with Sarah, and yet more importantly with James—whose pronouncements Catherine first unquestioningly accepts as authority, then doubts as she develops her own powers of judgment—shed light on the emerging individuality of a young woman gaining confidence and insight, both through experience and as a loving sister. (In this sisterly affection Catherine resembles Eleanor Tilney and differs from Isabella Thorpe, who both are, like Catherine, oldest or only sisters in families containing brothers either older or nearly the same age.) Because the novel's focus is on Catherine's character maturing in the wider world rather than being formed in the family environment, the other seven siblings, some named and some not, can remain in the shadows. Likewise *Pride and Prejudice* pays a great deal of attention to Charlotte Lucas, the spinster firstborn in a large though uncounted sibling group, and some comparative attention to the second sister Maria, who takes after her father in displaying a simple-minded credulity that stands in contrast to Charlotte's sharpness and that of Elizabeth Bennet, Charlotte's friend and Maria's fellow houseguest at the newlywed Collinses'. It is important that there be other, younger Lucases. Their very existence reinforces "sensible, intelligent" Charlotte's firstborn duties as surrogate parent—particularly because she's the daughter of a fatuous knighted provincial who talks only of St James' and "a very good kind of woman, not too clever to be a valuable neighbor to Mrs Bennet" (*PP* 18). Being first in a sibling parade intensifies the innate pragmatism that makes Charlotte, unlike laterborn Elizabeth, settle for financial and social security and marry a lout she can't love or esteem.[11] Charlotte's younger siblings are given a chance to applaud her anti-romantic prudence in saying "yes" to Collins, a choice that stands to benefit

---

11 Cf. Sulloway, 151: "Large sibships reinforce the firstborn's duties as a surrogate parent. Parenting responsibilities increase the likelihood that eldest sisters will become mother-identified, and hence conforming to parental authority."

them. "The younger girls formed hopes of *coming out* a year or two sooner than they might otherwise have done; and the boys were relieved from their apprehension of Charlotte's dying an old maid" (*PP* 122). This being done, the younger Lucases vanish from the scene, having fulfilled their limited purpose in a narrative chiefly engrossed by the particularized sibling relations in another family with the need to marry off daughters, the Bennets.

What of the siblings Austen is interested in distinguishing from one another? Surveying the firstborns and laterborns that populate the pages of her six novels reveals something far richer and messier than two opposing camps of conservative, authoritarian, rigid firstborns and rebellious, iconoclastic, flexible laterborns. Austen's empirical eye noticed many of the variables that present-day psychology sees interacting to shape human personality. Such influences as wealth or its absence, social position, conflict with or loss of a parent, family size, presence of additional relatives, gender, and gender of other siblings all add nuances to individual matters of sibling difference in Austen's novels. Difficulty with parents is an especially prominent complicating factor in Austenworld, where readers must look hard to find an intact married couple made up of two reasonably responsible, effective, loving—and living—parents. There are only two such couples, the Morlands and the Musgroves. Neither pair is idealized, but each offers an example of something surprisingly rare in Austen's novels: a secure, stable, loving, two-parent home. Interestingly, both the Morlands and the Musgroves are, as family groups, subjected to a fairly heavy dose of narratorial satire. It seems that Austen is determined to be unsentimental about large, intact, generally happy families—almost certainly because of their size, which she recognized as a heavy burden on the woman who, however wealthy and well provided with domestic help, unavoidably bore the costs and faced the risks of labor and delivery. In the Morland and Musgrove domestic ecosystems the individual personalities and relationships take a shape that's more difficult to appraise than is usual in Austenworld. Not totally commendable but certainly not deplorable, the younger generations of Morlands and Musgroves behave in a way that's believably normal.

The healthy normality of the entire Morland ménage comes in for mockery in the opening lines of *Northanger Abbey*. The ostensible target of Austen's irony is the improbability of family circumstances and personal character in Gothic fiction. According to Gothic standards the unglamorous, prosaic Morlands are anomalous. But the further irony is that surveying Austen's six novels shows the Morland family to be as uncharacteristic in her fiction as it would be in Ann Radcliffe's:

> No one who had ever seen Catherine Morland in her infancy, would have supposed her born to be an heroine. Her situation in life, the character of her father and mother, her own person and disposition, were all equally against her. Her father was a clergyman, without being neglected, or poor, and a very respectable man, though his name was Richard—and he had never been handsome. He had a considerable independence, besides two good livings—and he was not in the least addicted to locking up his daughters. Her mother was a woman of useful plain sense, with a good temper, and, what is more remarkable, with a good constitution. She had three sons before Catherine was born; and instead of dying in bringing the latter into the world, as any body might expect, she still lived on—lived to have six children more—to see them growing up around her, and to enjoy excellent

health herself. A family of ten children will be always called a fine family when there are arms and legs enough for the number; but the Morlands had little other right to the word, for they were in general very plain, and Catherine, for many years of her life, as plain as any. (*NA* 13)

Taught by her parents (writing and accounts from her father, French from her mother), not gifted or trained in the female spheres of drawing or music ("the day which dismissed the music-master was one of the happiest of Catherine's life"—*NA* 14), preferring "cricket, base ball, riding on horseback, and running about the country at the age of fourteen, to books—or at least books of information" (*NA* 15), Catherine, an eldest daughter with older brothers and six younger siblings, is largely left to shift for herself as womanhood dawns. But the solid foundation offered by ordinary loving parents serves her better than accomplishments, knowledge, sophistication, or elegance serve other Austen heroines with more ornamental, less stable, less loving families.

We see rather little of Catherine's interaction with eight of her nine siblings—unsurprising, given that she's away at Bath or Northanger Abbey for the bulk of the novel. But when James, the first child and eldest brother, turns up at Bath in company with his aggressively stupid Oxford friend John Thorpe, we are treated to brother–sister interactions much more real, if less concertedly charming, than Henry Tilney's with his younger sister Elinor. Though infatuated with Isabella Thorpe, James, a brother of amiable disposition who's sincerely attached to Catherine, greets her with as much pleasure as he can feel when Isabella's at hand—and he's honest but tactful enough to answer his sister's "'how good it is of you to come so far on purpose to see *me*'" by replying "with perfect sincerity, 'Indeed, Catherine, I love you dearly'" (*NA* 51). As elder brother, James is used to dominating and Catherine to submitting; so it's a major advance in her maturation when Catherine recognizes that the two of them have different opinions about John Thorpe and suspects that hers is the correct one:

> Little as Catherine was in the habit of judging for herself, and unfixed as were her general notions of what men ought to be, she could not entirely repress a doubt, while she bore with the effusions of his endless conceit, of his being altogether completely agreeable. It was a bold surmise, for he was Isabella's brother; and she had been assured by James, that his manners would recommend him to all her sex; but in spite of this, the extreme weariness of his company ... induced her, in some small degree, to resist such high authority, and to distrust his powers of giving universal pleasure. (*NA* 66–7)

Here we have a laterborn female author sympathetically if ironically portraying a sister's tentative declaration of independence from her firstborn brother. Catherine's assurance grows in a later encounter when the Thorpes and James, a trio needing Catherine's presence to make their intended excursion more decorous, urge her against keeping an earlier engagement with the Tilneys. James unfairly reproaches Catherine with "'you were not used to be so hard to persuade; you once were the kindest, best-tempered of my sisters.'" Catherine's stoutly sensible reply is "'I hope I am not less so now, but indeed I cannot go. If I am wrong, I am doing what I believe to be right'" (*NA* 99–100). This totally ordinary struggle of wills with her older brother helps prepare Catherine to move towards thinking for herself later on—even at an abbey, even when her male authority is Henry Tilney. As the story proceeds further, we see both James and Catherine make mistakes in judgment, his biggest being engagement to the fortune-huntress Isabella, hers being the inference that General Tilney had done away with his wife. These two Morland siblings are no prodigies, but their good-hearted mutual attachment is never in doubt.

Like the Morlands, the Musgroves of *Persuasion* are announced with the tonal equivalent of a wryly raised eyebrow: "The Musgroves, like their houses, were in a state of alteration, perhaps of improvement. The father and mother were in the old English style, and the young people in the new. Mr and Mrs Musgrove were a very good sort of people; friendly and hospitable, not much educated, and not at all elegant. Their children had more modern minds and manners" (*P* 40). As elsewhere in Austen, the word "improvement" here carries something of a negative connotation; but the narrator also seems cooler about "old English style" than does her previous counterpart in *Emma*, where the adjective "English" (meaning "admirable") is explicitly associated with the significantly named Knightleys of the just-as-significantly-named "old style" abbey of Donwell. Uppercross, the manor inhabited by the stylistically evolving Musgrove family, has an "old-fashioned square parlour, with a small carpet and shining floor, to which the present daughters of the house were gradually giving the proper air of confusion by a grand piano forte and a harp, flower-stands and little tables placed in every direction" (*P* 40). The interior décor's tension between "old English style" and "improvement" is equally evident in the exteriors of the two Musgrove houses, "the mansion of the 'squire, with its high walls, great gates, and old trees, substantial and unmodernized," and the heir's "farm-house elevated into a cottage ... with its viranda, French windows, and other prettinesses" (*P* 36).

In Austen as in Darwin, change is change but not necessarily "improvement." The Musgroves, old style and new style alike, are as mixed as their milieu. Charles Musgrove, the young 'squire, is discerning enough to have wanted to marry Anne, undiscriminating enough to have settled for Mary, human enough (and, unlike Anne, unrepressed enough) to get annoyed with the annoying Mary, sometimes to voice his annoyance, and often to take refuge from an ill-run household in field sports. His sisters Henrietta and Louisa, similarly mixed and real in their natures, can regret that Anne's not their sister-in-law without disliking Mary. Unlike the Bertram sisters, they can both fall for and briefly spar over an attractive newcomer without losing sisterly regard—and without being so inflexibly devoted to Captain Wentworth that Henrietta's longstanding attachment to her cousin Charles Hayter and Louisa's newfound affinity for Captain Benwick can't satisfy them. The unfashionable, not remarkably intelligent senior Musgroves display, like the Morlands or the even more mockable Mrs Jenkins of *Sense and Sensibility*, warm parental hearts and nurturing ways that count for more than education or elegance. They appreciate Anne's superiority and notice Mary's defects without pining for the might-have-been daughter-in-law or being cold to the daughter-in-law they have. Mrs Musgrove, whose "large fat sighings" over her dead sailor-son are subject to what is probably the most unfairly satiric comment in the whole Austen canon, is able, along with her whole family, to retrospectively sentimentalize "poor Richard," the troublesome lad sent to sea and lost there, even if

> The real circumstances of this pathetic piece of family history were, that the Musgroves had had the ill fortune of a very troublesome, hopeless son; and the good fortune to lose him before he reached his twentieth year; that he had been sent to sea, because he was stupid and unmanageable on shore; that he had been very little cared for at any time by his family, though quite as much as he deserved; seldom heard of, and scarcely at all regretted, when the intelligence of his death abroad had worked its way to Uppercross, two years before. (*P* 50–51)

This passage exposes the imperfections of its narrator as much as those of her subjects of scrutiny. Richard, when we come right down to it, is a fictive contrivance concocted merely to have been the recipient of some Wentworthian kindness and to have died at sea. But if we play along with literature's make-believe and grant him and his fellow Musgroves imaginative status as real people, we must recognize that the family members improving Richard in retrospect and mourning the idea more than the actual son and brother are being no more selective than is the reifying narrator, who diminishes both an adolescent formerly obnoxious but now dead and those survivors who grieve for him to easy targets for witty cynicism.

Long story short: the Musgroves, as individuals and as a family unit, display resilience, inconsistency, mixed tempers, and cohesion over time. Though supporting characters they are, as parents and siblings, as real as family ecosystems get in Austenworld. Uppercross, crammed for the holidays with the Musgroves' own children and grandchildren plus the little Harvilles, is the site of Austen's only delineated scene of normal multi-generational family interaction: some bossing, more fun, much noise. It is a "fine family piece" in fact, despite the overstimulating effect it might have on a fastidious introvert.

> Immediately surrounding Mrs Musgrove were the little Harvilles, whom she was sedulously guarding from the tyranny of the two children from the Cottage, expressly arrived to amuse them. On one side was a table, occupied by some chattering girls, cutting up silk and gold paper; and on the other were tressels and trays, bending under the weight of brawn and cold pies, where riotous boys were holding high revel; the whole completed by a roaring Christmas fire, which seemed determined to be heard, in spite of all the noise of the others. (*P* 134)

This homely vignette, more characteristic of Dickens than Austen, is saved from sentimentality by being filtered through the melancholy, peace-loving sensibility of Anne Elliot—and, beyond her, through the intermittently discernible viewpoint of the narrator, more satiric and less tolerant of absurdity than Anne is. But even if domestic cordiality in this register is not Anne's preference, she recognizes its sustaining power for other kinds of people, especially the children who grow up taking its security for granted.

Such security is rare in the family circles central to Austen's novels, where bad parenting is rampant and competent mothering, in particular, something close to a death warrant for a woman. The three mothers who apparently were highly respected for their good hearts and heads—Mrs Tilney, Mrs Woodhouse, and Lady

Elliot—all have died long before we enter into the lives of their surviving families. Mr Dashwood, about whom there's nothing to deplore apart from his misfortune in expiring so soon after he succeeds to Norland estate, dies as his daughters' story starts. The ruling-class parents who survive to shape and launch children in Austen are a mixed bag, some benevolent but flawed, some downright culpable, few if any as admirable as readers extrapolating beyond the limits of the novels might imagine and hope those parents' rightly matched offspring will be when they in turn become parents. The dysfunctional gallery includes fecklessly optimistic Mrs Dashwood, noisy Sir John and cold, empty Lady Middleton, cynically detached Mr Bennet, obstreperously vulgar Mrs Bennet, the lightweight Lucases, domineering Lady Catherine De Bourgh, stern and worldly if principled Sir Thomas Bertram and his unbelievably passive Lady (their parental partnership made worse by aunt Norris's officious blend of malevolence and flattery), the over-fertile, under-funded, far-from-shipshape Prices, dim and timid Mr Woodhouse, calculating, tyrannical General Tilney, and vain, stupid Sir Walter Elliot.

The prevalence of bad parenting in Austen's novels means that, according to Sulloway's Darwinian theory, normal patterns of sibling divergence will be altered in various ways. Some of the potential differences are obvious to the eye of common sense: children being less likely to adopt their parents' values, firstborns being more likely to invest emotionally in their younger siblings at the expense of their parents (Sulloway, 125), daughters being more rebellious especially if the difficult parent is the mother (166). According to Sulloway, "substantial conflict with parents raises radicalism, especially in firstborns" (121). Perhaps because the ruling-class manners of the day entailed formal respect for parents (however bad), there's little outright intergenerational conflict in Austen's families—and thus little discernible radicalism among ill-parented firstborns. Those firstborns who "rebel" characteristically do so by developing strengths that compensate for parental deficiencies (Elinor Dashwood, Jane Bennet, Charlotte Lucas) rather than failing to follow parental principles (Tom Bertram). Many other firstborns seem to perpetuate their parents' virtues, vices, charms, or foibles: Fitzwilliam Darcy, George Knightley, Charles Musgrove, Fanny Ferrars Dashwood, Frederick Tilney, Elizabeth Elliot, Isabella Woodhouse Knightley.

At one time or another, Austen's novels show us both good and bad consequences of most phenomena or practices: of primogeniture and of less orthodox ways of bequeathing property, of respecting social precedence and of ignoring it, of allowing young women the freedom to be "out" and of sheltering them. Austen's empirical eye discerned that real life offered evidence on both sides, and her novels reflect chromatically shaded complexities rather than black-and-white polarities. Given her penchant for subtle variations on a theme and her sharp-eyed respect for truth to life in all its shadings, it's not possible to generalize whether being a firstborn is good or bad for the development of personal character in Austen's novels. A fair number of firstborns display mainly the negative effects of their birth order: self-indulgent Tom Bertram and Captain Tilney, overconfident Mrs Norris, Elizabeth Elliot, and Fanny Ferrars Dashwood if indeed she's older than Edward. Other firstborns are close to being paragons (at least as Austen's narrators apparently mean us to see them): Elinor Dashwood, Jane Bennet, George Knightley, Fitzwilliam Darcy after he's been chastened by Elizabeth's rejection, though in fact the 12 years between him and Georgiana make him in effect an only child. But apart from Mr Knightley, significantly farther into adulthood than the others (he's reached Colonel Brandon's advanced stage of life, in fact), each of these admirable firstborns pays a clearly discernible psychological price that is the shadow side of the privileged position, as do the more modestly admirable firstborns Charlotte Lucas and Charles Musgrove.

Edward Ferrars provides an interesting off-the-chart example here, an apt illustration of family niches trumping cultural stereotypes. Despite being the firstborn brother in a landed family, Edward does not display the confident, assertive, conservative nature characteristic of that role. He lacks the virtues and flaws generally associated with the eldest male for various special reasons: the estate isn't entailed on him, he has a (probably) older sister who has obviously identified with her strong-willed mother, he has formed a clandestine engagement his domineering mother and sister would not approve, his father seems to have been dead for a long time (at least long enough that he's never mentioned in the novel), and as an adolescent he had been isolated from his peers by a private education, unlike his younger brother who was socialized partly for good and mostly for ill at Westminster public school. Unable and unwilling to confront the duties and assert the rights of the first son and heir—in his case, these would include pursuing a worldly calling the women in his family would respect and courting the heiress Miss Morton—Edward instead chooses the psychological challenges of another family niche. In his quiet, depressive way, he seems born to rebel in a family of mean-minded fools.

Despite such exceptions as the Ferrars and De Bourgh families afford, the ordinary way of passing down landed estates in Austen's novels is primogeniture, the socioeconomic arrangement favored for keeping a landowning family's wealth and power concentrated and the family name consequential over generations by transmitting an estate intact to the oldest son (or, in the absence of a son, to the closest male relation) rather than dividing it into parcels shared out among all sons or all siblings. The subject of primogeniture will surface again in the chapter centered on marriage. Here, the main point to keep in mind is that a personal consequence of this system of handing down estates is the enhancement of typical firstborn traits and of masculinity in firstborn males. In Austen's novels, think of George Knightley and Fitzwilliam Darcy, twin towers of both conventional manliness and actual masculine virtue, but also of Captain Tilney, Henry Crawford, and Tom Bertram, whose dissipations are the stereotypical transgressions of beneficiaries of primogeniture behaving badly. Then notice the dilution or modification of conventional masculinity in younger sons portrayed by Austen, brothers who grow up inferior to the firstborn heir, prove likelier to question the rural status quo because they have less stake in it, and need to be flexible enough to make a living, to pursue life as something other than a landed country gentleman. Examples here might be Henry Tilney and Edmund Bertram, who have distinguished themselves from badboy big brothers by being responsible—but responsible in a gentler, more sensitive vein than the firstborns Darcy and Knightley. It's felicitous that the younger Tilney and Bertram are destined, thanks to family influence, for church livings, because their less emphatically masculine laterborn temperaments suit them for a pastoral vocation. It's equally interesting and similarly fortunate (if anything can be said to depend on fortune in the well-made microcosm of an Austen novel) that John Knightley's not been given a church living in Donwell parish, Highbury, or elsewhere. His character is distinct from his older brother's, just as Henry Tilney's and Edmund Bertram's are—but he's not any less masculine than George. Because the elder Knightley's character is commendable rather than lamentable—and partly because the Knightley brothers have a good decade's maturity on the Tilneys and the Bertrams—John Knightley is drawn, not like Henry Tilney and Edmund Bertram as a desirable contrast to his older brother, but rather as what Fritz Oehlschlaeger terms a "more intense and more narrowly focused" version of the Knightley virtues,[12] a laterborn variation on the theme. Both brothers are decisive, country-loving, clear-headed, and good-hearted. The differences: John, whom interestingly enough we never see on his own turf, either his self-made home in Brunswick Square or his ancestral home Donwell, is less patient and more irritable than is George in the status of guest at Hartfield and Randalls—and he has a clearer view of the potential consequences of Emma's playing at Cupid.

John Knightley's disposition may be moodier than his brother's for the purely practical reason that Austen doesn't want to put two suns in her novel's sky. Or she may have meant to depict in John and Isabella, both as individuals and as a married couple, a degree of excellence that comparative assessment shows his older brother and her younger sister, alone and as a team, will eventually be able to surpass. But Darwinian divergence is also at work. It may be that John Knightley's less-perfect disposition is partly a consequence of mild but deep-seated insecurity that rises out of not growing up as the heir to Donwell but as the laterborn brother who one day will need to make his way in the wider world. He has done so with notable success. Indeed, by establishing himself in London at the bar, marrying a good woman (if not his mental equal), fathering a family, and devoting himself to that family's nurture, he is ahead of his elder brother in fulfilling the basic goals of existence in a Darwinian ecosystem. Just as George Knightley's firstborn bachelor existence at Donwell has its downside, John's laterborn lot as urban paterfamilias carries certain costs. Because the brothers are alike in their values though dissimilar in temperament, love of their ancestral land is a pronounced attribute of both, as is evident on their reunion at Hartfield. In an already quoted passage, the narrator relates that George Knightley, "as a farmer, as keeping in hand the home-farm at Donwell ... had to tell what every field was to bear next year, and to give all such local information as could not fail of being interesting to a brother whose home it had equally been the longest part of his life, and whose attachments were strong" (*E* 100). Given his "strong attachments," growing up under the shadow of banishment from the estate on which he was reared could very likely have darkened John Knightley's disposition a bit; and the ways London life and legal practice would grate on a sensibility better suited to rural retirement could aggravate the problem.

Differences in domestic circumstances contribute to the brothers' temperamental divergence. George, a childless bachelor and country squire, faces the potential risks of lonely melancholy—his effective remedies being regular calls at Hartfield and

---

[12] Fritz Oehlschlaeger, *Love and Good Reasons* (Durham, NC: Duke University Press, 2003), 96.

active involvement in the Highbury community. John, an urban professional, married, blessed and encumbered with five children, and housed in an urban residence far less spacious than Donwell, is bound to face more daily annoyances. Life with Isabella, a woman as mildly irritating as she is fondly indulgent to his irritability, and with small children, who cannot all have filled the family niche of paragon, is bound to offer John Knightley some challenges his brother has yet to experience—though to be sure uprooting from Donwell and moving to Hartfield, with increased exposure to Mr Woodhouse, an older, self-centered, even more valetudinarian male version of his elder daughter, will test George Knightley's temper even as it demonstrates his fervent desire to marry Emma.

The English landed gentry's practices of primogeniture and entailment, then, play significant roles in determining the differences in brothers' developing characters and behaviors in Austen's novels. When these inheritance conventions are in play, there's an unambiguously predestined niche for the eldest son to occupy in the family ecosystem—and younger brothers diverge accordingly. The custom of leaving an intact estate in one male heir's hands has consequences to daughters' personalities as well. A private fortune, like beauty, charm, accomplishments, and social position, helped a young woman compete in the Darwinian struggle for an eligible mate—but it also made life without a man easier. Emma's problem is self-justifying overstatement, not error, when she pronounces to Harriet Smith, "It is poverty only which makes celibacy contemptible to a generous public!" (*E* 85). The presence, absence, and size of a private fortune might, in some cases, also influence personality development. Lack of money no doubt enhances Lucy Steele's calculating shrewdness, but also intensifies Elinor Dashwood's prudence, a more praiseworthy quality. Possession of money makes many Austen women, among them Lady Catherine De Bourgh, Mrs Ferrars, Fanny Dashwood, Augusta Elton, Emma Woodhouse, and Sophia Grey, confident, overbearing, or peremptory. Even a woman whose character has apparently developed without regard to her financial status might be forced to recognize that money could crucially shape her future. Mr Collins, dim and dense though he generally may be, argues rationally when he doubts the sincerity of Elizabeth's rejection of his proposal on the grounds that "'in spite of your manifold attractions, it is by no means certain that another offer of marriage may ever be made you. Your portion is unhappily so small that it will in all likelihood undo the effects of your loveliness and amiable qualifications'" (*PP* 108). But the influence of money—or any other individual factor—on character, marriage, or destiny is far from straightforwardly predictable.

Austen's clearest example of the unpredictable nature of the circumstances that interact to shape sibling character is the three Ward sisters, whose equal starting-points but widely divergent paths are delineated in the first paragraph of *Mansfield Park*:

> About thirty years ago, Miss Maria Ward of Huntingdon, with only seven thousand pounds, had the good luck to captivate Sir Thomas Bertram, of Mansfield Park, in the county of Northampton, and to be thereby raised to the rank of a baronet's lady, with all the comforts and consequences of an handsome house and large income. All Huntingdon exclaimed on the greatness of the match, and her uncle, the lawyer, himself, allowed her to be at least three thousand pounds short of any equitable claim to it. She had two sisters to be benefited by her elevation; and such of their acquaintance as thought Miss Ward and Miss Frances quite as handsome as Miss Maria, did not scruple to predict their marrying with almost equal advantage. But there certainly are not so many men of large fortune in the world, as there are pretty women to deserve them. Miss Ward, at the end of half a dozen years, found herself obliged to be attached to the Rev. Mr Norris, a friend of her brother-in-law, with scarcely any private fortune, and Miss Frances fared yet worse. Miss Ward's match, indeed, when it came to the point, was not contemptible, Sir Thomas being happily able to give his friend an income in the living of Mansfield, and Mr and Mrs Norris began their career of conjugal felicity with very little less than a thousand a year. But Miss Frances married, in the common phrase, to disoblige her family, and by fixing on a Lieutenant of Marines, without education, fortune, or connections, did it very thoroughly. She could hardly have made a more untoward choice. Sir Thomas Bertram had interest, which, from principle as well as from pride, from a general wish of doing right, and a desire of seeing all that were connected with him in situations of respectability, he would have been glad to exert for the advantage of Lady Bertram's sister; but her husband's profession was such as no interest could reach; and before he had time to devise any other method of assisting them, an absolute breach between the sisters had taken place. It was the natural result of the conduct of each party, and such as a very imprudent marriage almost always produces. (*MP* 3–4)

Although they began life with the same social position, the same private fortune, and, if Huntingdon's taste is to be relied on, the same degree of beauty, the Ward sisters cannot have begun with distinct personalities. The widely different circumstances of their adult lives don't suffice to explain their extreme differences in temperament, character, and behavior. A close look at how the sisters have turned out shows the multifaceted nature of psychological development in action. Innate characteristics, birth order, socioeconomic contingencies, and interaction with one another and with other people have worked together in the process of adaptive variation that makes these sisters the individuals they are.

Mrs Norris displays classic firstborn traits of a strong will and an inclination to manage things. She has an apparently innate or very early acquired "spirit of activity" (*MP* 4), in notable contrast to her younger sisters. Her tireless energy and dominant nature are used mostly for bad purposes in *Mansfield Park*—perhaps partly because of her marital circumstances, which situate her and her husband in a role of dependence on her brother-in-law's patronage and just below the bottom limit of genteel income as calculated by F. M. L. Thompson, 1000 pounds a year.[13] "Nobody knew better how to dictate liberality to others: but her love of money was equal to her love of directing..." (*MP* 8). "Having married on a narrower income than she had been used to look forward to" (*MP* 8), thanks to expectations raised

---

13 F. M. L Thompson, *English Landed Society in the Nineteenth Century* (London, Routledge & Kegan Paul, 1963), 112.

by her younger sister's grand marriage, Mrs Norris began practicing frugality out of principle but now does so from choice or ingrained habit. She hoards at home, "spunges" handouts from the housekeeper at Sotherton, and even steals the green baize not needed for stage furnishings when Sir Thomas's return ends the amateur theatricals. She makes herself indispensable at Mansfield Park in order to live at the Bertrams' expense rather than her own. When it's suggested that Fanny could console Mrs Norris's widowhood by living at the White House, to which she moves when the Grants succeed her and the late Mr Norris at Mansfield parsonage, she recoils in horror. Without any children of her own to raise, she spoils the Bertram girls, especially Maria, like herself a handsome elder sister—and she's so rigidly set in her opinions and feelings that Maria's adulterous elopement means only that aunt Norris's "attachment seemed to augment with the demerits of her niece" (*MP* 464).

The niche, temperament, and behavior of Maria, Lady Bertram, are polar opposites to her firstborn sister Norris's. Lady Bertram, initially described as "a woman of very tranquil feelings, and a temper remarkably easy and indolent," (*MP* 4) is a memorable example of how disposition, birth order, marital choice, and family dynamics can converge to exaggerate a character's innate tendency. Naturally lazy, she's made more so by being able to rely on an active, authoritarian husband and a bustling older sister. "Guided in everything important by Sir Thomas, and in smaller concerns by her sister," (*MP* 20) she spends most of the novel lolling on her sofa engaged in needlework "of little use and no beauty, thinking more of her pug [the canine equivalent of her needlework] than her children" (*MP* 19). It's easy to feel contempt for Lady Bertram; but in fact Austen points out that she, a flexible laterborn, has better values than does her stronger-minded but (self-)misguided older sister the clergyman's widow. Lady Bertram may be shallow and self-centered, but her essentially correct thoughts and feelings can't be moved. Grown accustomed to loving and needing her niece Fanny, she'll accede to Sir Thomas's persuasion that Fanny needs to go to Portsmouth but can't be convinced, however vigorously Mrs Norris tries, that she won't miss her (*MP* 371). Fanny's return to a Mansfield Park in crisis over Tom's illness and Maria and Julia's respective elopements involves a small and touching moment of Lady Bertram behaving out of usual character in testimony to overwhelming feelings, a convincingly real blend of sincere, grateful love and self-interest: "Lady Bertram came from the drawing room to meet her; came with no indolent step; and, falling on her neck, said, "'Dear Fanny! now I shall be comfortable'" (*MP* 447). She can be more so because, unlike her older sister, she's fortunate enough to have both a laterborn's tractable nature and an essentially right-minded guide: "Lady Bertram did not think deeply, but, guided by Sir Thomas, she thought justly on all important points" (*MP* 449).

Miss Frances Ward, the youngest sister, offers abundant evidence in favor of Sulloway's observation that laterborn siblings are likeliest to rebel. With one sister who's made a brilliant marriage and another who's married prudently, to a man whose professional interests can be effectively promoted by her brother-in-law, she weds "to disoblige her family"—then spawns a brood her husband, an ungentlemanly Marine lieutenant retired on shore pay, can't support in comfort. Not, at least, with her as wife. For if Mrs Price plays favorites like Mrs Norris—"Her daughters never had been much to her. She was fond of her sons, especially of William, but Betsey was the first of her girls whom she had ever much regarded" (*MP* 389)—she has the natural laziness of Lady Bertram without the means to indulge it.

> Of her two sisters, Mrs Price very much more resembled Lady Bertram than Mrs Norris. She was a manager by necessity, without any of Mrs Norris's inclination for it, or any of her activity. Her disposition was naturally easy and indolent, like Lady Bertram's; and a situation of similar affluence and do-nothing-ness would have been much more suited to her capacity, than the exertions and self-denials of the one, which her imprudent marriage had placed her in. She might have made just as good a woman of consequence as Lady Bertram, but Mrs Norris would have been a more respectable mother of nine children, on a small income. (*MP* 390)

The hypothetical role reversal concisely sketched in the last sentence displays the brilliance of Austen's empirical speculation. The imagined reversal of the sisters' fortunes amuses readers with a glimpse of what is not—but it also obliquely reminds us of some easy-to-overlook features of what is. Notice the different force of the subjunctive verbs: Mrs Price "might" have equaled Lady Bertram as a baronet's wife—no particular compliment there. But Mrs Norris "would" have done a better job of raising a large family on a tight budget. In a narrative where the details and tone often seem calculated to demonize Mrs Norris, this speculation acknowledges that, placed in other circumstances, the hardheaded firstborn with too much energy could have harnessed her powers to better effect. An imagined alternate station for Lady Bertram is amusing by its absence. The narrator's silence on that score loudly proclaims that Lady Bertram, by virtue of everything heredity and environment have given her, is fit for nothing but a life of sofas and pugs, with a deferential niece within earshot of her languid drawl.

Given her fiction's focus on female protagonists growing through widened experience of people and places and defining themselves through marriage, it's unsurprising that Austen is more interested in the comparative development of sisters' characters than in brothers'. The Wards, though Austen's sole group portrait of married sisters whose circumstances have diverged and whose life experiences have completely solidified their personalities, are only one of several groups of differentiated sisters in Austen's novels. In at least two families comprised of multiple male and female children (and presumably three, because Colonel Fitzwilliam's existence as an earl's younger son and as cousin to Darcy and Miss De Bourgh presupposes Lady Anne and Lady Catherine having a brother, whether he's still alive or not), Austen shows more interest in describing and differentiating daughters than sons. Prudent, analytical Charlotte Lucas is distinguished from her credulous younger sister Maria, with the younger children left a pack of sons and daughters; Fanny and Susan Price display different temperaments but comparable good instincts against a backdrop of stair-step siblings, a progression in which the eldest son William's drawn in detail, the remaining sisters are minimally sketched (Mary as the dead bequeather of a silver knife to Susan, Betsey as the spoiled baby), but the younger brothers still at home are just five noisy young fellows who most likely will go to sea. Two pairs of sisters are hard to fit into a pattern. The fashionable, hypocritical Bingley women, less important to the Bennet-centered plot than their brother is, seem to differ mainly in that Louisa is married and that Caroline very much wants to be—and thus, with a husband still to be bagged, has a much more active part to play in the romance-centered plot. The Bertram sisters, like their brothers, emerge as individuals, with the pattern established by Tom and Edmund holding true, if a bit less dramatically, with Maria and Julia. Being firstborn daughter and Mrs Norris's spoiled favorite makes Maria develop into a more actively deplorable character than Julia—a contrast demonstrated subtly throughout but never more vividly than on the excursion to Sotherton and later stated clearly, if baldly, in the final chapter's "Let other pens dwell on guilt and misery" summation:

> That Julia escaped better than Maria was owing, in some measure, to a favourable difference of disposition and circumstance, but in a greater to her having been less the darling of that very aunt, less flattered, and less spoilt. Her beauty and acquirements had held but a second place. She had been always used to think herself a little inferior to Maria. Her temper was naturally the easiest of the two, her feelings, though quick, were more controulable; and education had not given her so very hurtful a degree of self-consequence. (*MP* 466)

But over all Austen proves much less interested in how the Bertram sisters differ from one another than in how they both differ—in temper, education, self-consequence—from their exemplary cousin Fanny.

The site for most clearly seeing how birth order affects the choice of family niche should be same-sex siblings groups, because that's where the need to differentiate to achieve adaptive advantage would be greatest. Austen's novels offer a good number of characters reared from childhood in all-female sibling groups. Along with the three Ward sisters whose diverging marriage choices furnish the preamble to *Mansfield Park*, there are the three Dashwoods (all born after their half-brother John would be old enough to be away at school), two Steeles, and two Middletons of *Sense and Sensibility*, the Woodhouse and Hawkins pairs in *Emma*, the three Elliots of *Persuasion*, and, furnishing the most striking example of Darwinian divergence, the five Bennets of *Pride and Prejudice*, all within about six years of one another and all, imprudently, "out." Austen does not use any two of these sisterhoods in exactly the same way, but what crucially interests her is how sisters who have radiated out into different family niches will further define themselves through the ordering dance of marriage—for the characters and social and economic positions of the men they wed will significantly shape them, in much the same way that marrying Sir Thomas Bertram rather than Lieutenant Price has been indispensable in Lady Bertram's becoming what she is when we encounter her.

Some sister pairs or groups fill mainly subsidiary functions. The Jenkins and Steele sisters' respective sibling relations serve mainly to contrast with the Dashwoods' loving involvement with one another. Nancy and Lucy Steele, the elder silly, shallow, and desperate for beaux, the younger shrewd, vulgar, and predatory, are merely differentiated without their differences being accounted for. They are a Wollstonecraftian nightmare: uncongenial, uneducated, unmarried, mature sisters kept together by nothing but the necessity of pooling their limited resources. Mrs Jenkins' well-married daughters are, like the Steeles, grown opposites who demonstrate no feeling for one another. They don't exchange a word or glance that's reported in the novel; and Lady Middleton's obsession with motherhood apparently doesn't extend to paying a call when her younger sister delivers a son and heir. The contrast between these sisters is so absolute as to seem contrived. Lady Middleton: "her face was handsome, her figure tall and striking, and her address graceful. Her manners had all the elegance which her husband's wanted. But they would have been improved by some share of his frankness and warmth ... Though perfectly well-bred, she was reserved, cold, and had nothing to say for herself beyond the most common-place inquiry or remark" (*SS* 31). Charlotte Palmer: "several years younger than Lady Middleton, and totally unlike her in every respect," "short and plump, had a very pretty face, and the finest expression of good humor in it that could possibly be. Her manners were by no means so elegant as her sister's, but they were much more prepossessing. She came in with a smile, smiled all the time of her visit, except when she laughed, and smiled when she went away" (*SS* 106). Like her older sister in one thing at least, Charlotte has a husband so different from her as to seem unsuitable, "a grave looking young man ... with an air of more fashion and sense ... but of less willingness to please or be pleased" (*SS* 106). In the Jenkins sisters, Austen illustrates several points she makes elsewhere: that noisy, undiscriminating warmhearted natures may not be totally admirable but are to be preferred to more polished manners united to colder hearts, that men attracted to the youth-and-beauty brigade can go badly wrong and marry women whose minds and dispositions don't match their own, that like the marriage bond a blood relation does not necessarily imply a meaningful personal relationship.

In contrast to the Steele and Jenkins sisters, the Dashwoods love, like, respect, and interact with one another, even at the times when their behaviors seem least compatible and their thoughts and feelings least shared. And they resemble one another in marrying men they can love, like, and respect, men who can love, like, and respect them. When I say the Dashwoods, I mean the older two. Delineating the Dashwood sisters, Austen's eye seems to glaze over at a point when attentive observation would be at odds with the generic needs of romance fiction and the specifically dualistic demands of a novel titled *Sense and Sensibility*. Three sisters within six years of one another, observed in real life, would develop and interact in complex ways—differentiating themselves, according to Sulloway's Darwinian view, as two pairs. For Austen's fictional purposes only Elinor and Marianne are relevant, partly because marriageable status is generally what constitutes importance in Austenworld and partly because spinning out the contrast between a "sense" sister and a "sensibility" sister involves one dyad, not a pair of them or a triad. Whatever the reason, 13-year-old Margaret is cursorily dismissed in the last paragraph of the expository first chapter as "a good-humoured well-disposed girl; but as she had already imbibed a good deal of Marianne's romance, without having much of her sense, she did not, at thirteen, bid fair to equal her sisters at a more advanced period of life" (*SS* 5). In other Austen novels, young women no more promising than Margaret metamorphose from larvae to butterflies in the crucial years that will come next—as witness Catherine Morland and Fanny Price when they turn 17 and 18 respectively. Given a few years and her own story, Margaret Dashwood might be a heroine in her own right, but she's not needed as one in this story—though the narrator changes her tune in the penultimate paragraph of the novel's summing-up: "fortunately for Sir John and Mrs Jennings, when Marianne was taken from them,

Margaret had reached an age highly suitable for dancing, and not very ineligible for being supposed to have a lover" (*SS* 380).

By contrast, Austen attends more carefully to the third member of a six-year-spanning trio of sisters in *Persuasion*, where her chief interest centers on the middle sister and both the eldest and the youngest exist mainly for comparative purposes. Although it's far more obvious from dismissive scenes played out at Kellynch and Bath alike that Elizabeth Elliot's shallow, stupid, but supremely confident vanity has driven Anne, also a beauty before her first bloom faded with romantic disappointment, to stake out a drastically different niche herself, the equally differentiated relation between Anne and Mary, four years her junior, is also treated, principally during Anne's sojourn at Uppercross. Mary, growing up junior to a responsibility-shouldering, self-effacing paragon, has thereby been enabled to cultivate self-centered discontent and valetudinarianism. Joined with her own share of Sir Walter's and Elizabeth's snobbish fixation on the grandeur of the Elliot name, these features make Mary's demanding, aggrieved personality a dreary backdrop against which Anne's selfless, benevolent, capable nature shines—as is recognized by Mary's husband Charles, her in-laws the Musgroves, and Captain Wentworth. But perhaps because as far as one can tell she's never been a beauty (and now is "coarse") and she's had the good fortune to marry into a warm, generally functional family and to have children (however inadequately she mothers them), Mary is humanized in a way denied to the icy Elizabeth.

If all the Elliot virtues and talents belong to one daughter, the middle one, the carefully observed joint heroines Elinor and Marianne Dashwood both possess virtues and talents alike—both have the capacity for "sense and sensibility." They have, however, diverged in the Darwinian way that might be predicted likeliest in a family less than perfectly functional but far better adjusted than the Elliots are. The Dashwoods' father, with only a life-interest in Norland but a "cheerful and sanguine" temperament, (*SS* 4) and his equally sanguine wife, with "a sense of honour so keen, a generosity so romantic" that any offense against delicacy "was to her a source of immoveable disgust" (*SS* 6) might, unlike Sir Walter, be good parents under auspicious conditions. But in an uncertain or adverse world, neither could inspire the confidence that would make an eldest child emulate him or her. Instead, Elinor takes it upon herself to provide the substitute for, rather than the junior embodiment of, parental seriousness:

> Elinor, this eldest daughter whose advice was so effectual, possessed a strength of understanding, and coolness of judgment, which qualified her, though only nineteen, to be the counsellor of her mother, and enabled her frequently to counteract, to the advantage of them all, that eagerness of mind in Mrs Dashwood which must generally have led to imprudence. She had an excellent heart;—her disposition was affectionate, and her feelings were strong; but she knew how to govern them: it was a knowledge which her mother had yet to learn, and which one of her sisters had resolved never to be taught. (*SS* 6)

That sister, Marianne, bears a name that through its association with the French Revolution implies the unrestrained fervor the conservative landed classes of England generally associated with that movement. If Elinor has specialized in the sense their mother lacks, Marianne distinguishes herself from her older sister by emphasizing the good and bad features of the maternal model: "Marianne's abilities were, in many respects, quite equal to Elinor's. She was sensible and clever; but eager in every thing; her sorrows, her joys, could have no moderation. She was generous, amiable, interesting: she was everything but prudent. The resemblance between her and her mother was strikingly great" (*SS* 6).

Knowing that "what Marianne and her mother conjectured one moment, they believed the next—that with them, to wish was to hope, and to hope was to expect" (*SS* 21), the fatherless Elinor finds herself the still-teenaged head of her all-female family—if by that term we mean her nuclear family, not the dynasty indicated by the novel's opening sentence: "The family of Dashwood had been long settled in Sussex" (*SS* 3). One of the novel's most productive Darwinian ironies stems from the different ways this opening statement is and is not true. Norland Park, childhood home of the Dashwood sisters, becomes their father's property only when his old uncle dies—and only for a year, when he too dies and the estate passes by decree of his uncle's will to John Dashwood, the girls' half-brother, in trust for his four-year-old son Henry. Bequeathing Norland in the traditionally patriarchal way may be good for the long-term continuance of the ancestral name (or the Dashwood "species" as a whole) in Sussex. But it's bad for the women whose family home the country house has been, the individual members, if you will, of the "Dashwood" species population. Adding to the Dashwood women's misfortunes are their selfish half-brother and even more selfish sister-in-law. The latter ascribes to a nuclear rather than extended view of "family," and takes a ruthless attitude towards her husband's half-siblings that, did she but know it, comes right out of post-Darwinian psychology as well as out of Wollstonecraft's contemporary observations.[14] Fanny Dashwood believes that

---

14   When I say "post-Darwinian psychology," I am thinking especially of the "selfish gene" theory, implicit in Darwin's theory of kin selection and later adumbrated by William D. Hamilton in the 1960s. The best-known statements on the topic appear in Edward O. Wilson's *Sociobiology: The New Synthesis* (Cambridge, MA and London: Belknap Press of Harvard University Press, 1975) and Richard Dawkins's *The Selfish Gene* (New York: Oxford University Press, 1989). The selfish gene, according to Dawkins, "is not just one single physical bit of DNA but all replicas of a particular bit of DNA, distributed throughout the world" (88). Dawkins theorizes that organisms are simply "survival machines" by which means selfish genes become more frequent in the gene pool. Self-serving behavior in organisms would thus serve to ensure the survival of genes.

If viewed from this vantage point, even acts of apparent altruism are essentially selfish—selfish for the gene, not for the individual. While parents may act altruistically towards offspring, such behaviors remain self-serving insofar as the ultimate goal is the perpetuation of genes common to both parent and child. The financial ill-treatment of Elinor, Marianne, and Margaret by John and Fanny Dashwood offers an example of behavior consistent with "selfish gene" theory: Fanny's selfish quest to disinherit John's half-sisters stems from a biological desire to maximize resources for her young son Harry, who will carry her genes into the next generation. Mary Wollstonecraft, arguing empirically, makes a similar observation concerning the fate of an unmarried sister living in her brother's household in *A Vindication of the Rights of Men with A Vindication of the Rights of Woman and Hints*, Cambridge Texts in the History of Political Thought, ed. Sylvana Tomaselli (Cambridge: Cambridge University Press, 1995). Such women live "with a tolerable degree of comfort" so long as the brother does not marry. But "when the brother marries," the unmarried sister is viewed by the wife "as an intruder, an unnecessary

her son's interests and those of John's half-sisters are opposed. She is directly said to be a "caricature" of her husband's narrow-mindedness and selfishness, but the ungenerous case she makes would, stripped of its superlatives and absolutes, make perfect sense in terms of genetic heredity:

> And what possible claim could the Miss Dashwoods, who were related to him only by half blood, which she considered as no relationship at all, have on his generosity to so large an amount. It was very well known that no affection was ever supposed to exist between the children of any man by different marriages; and why was he to ruin himself, and their poor little Harry, by giving away all his money to his half sisters? (*SS* 8)

Facing selfishness from the wider family, Elinor must cope with improvident folly within her nuclear family. Mrs Dashwood believes she can save enough surplus from 500 pounds' annual income to make improvements to Barton Cottage; Marianne claims to disdain wealth and to ask only a competence but then reveals that to her "competence" means 2000 pounds a year, twice the sum that signifies "wealth" to Elinor, whom Marianne sees as calculating. Elinor endures heavy and often undeserved criticism from her mother, sister, and many readers for the self-repressed, tactful, expedient sense that she's obliged to cultivate, seeing that no one else in her family will—and for not displaying the sensibility that, in a family of self-dramatizers, she's better off concealing. But the harsh circumstances of life and Elinor's interactions with parent and siblings inevitably intensify the responsible quasi-maternal behaviors and values associated with her firstborn role. Only late in the novel, when crises have been managed, can she indulge the luxury of her own sensibility—a moment that fills Marianne with typically dramatic self-reproach. But, again typically, the object of Elinor's sensibility is an unprepossessing young man who needs nothing so much as maternal nurturing.

An interesting problem with *Sense and Sensibility* is that though Elinor, the "sense" sister, has a character that seems to rise from heredity and family environment working inevitably and perhaps irresistibly together, Marianne's "sensibility" character, formed in a similar way, is meant to be understood as something she can and should put behind her. Chastened by disappointment in Willoughby and serious illness, sobered by awareness of her sister's admirable conduct, finally granting more importance to Colonel Brandon's loving benevolence than to his age and flannel waistcoats, Marianne rises from what seems a prolepsis of the Victorian novel's Significant Sickbed and experiences a change of heart that bears fruit in what might seem to be radically altered conduct and character.

Perhaps this malleability is what can be expected from a heroine who's only 17 (the lower of heroine status threshold in Austenworld)—a simple act of growing up.

---

burden on the benevolence of the master of the house, and his new partner" (141). Wollstonecraft goes on to describe a ruthless jealousy on the part of the wife that post-Darwinian readers might attribute to gene selfishness: "The wife, a cold-hearted, narrow-minded woman ... is jealous of the little kindnesses which her husband shews to his relations ... is displeased at seeing the property of her children lavished on a helpless sister" (142). But these examples don't mean that Wollstonecraft, Austen, or indeed Darwin (who saw adaptive advantages in altruistic behavior practiced by communal animals) would endorse or excuse selfishness.

In some ways, however, Marianne's transformation is the problematic consequence of practical demands imposed by Austen's genre conflicting with what realistic observations of character would tell her. From its very title onward, *Sense and Sensibility* promises to have a prescribed and tidy outcome. In contrast, evolution in family ecosystems is a matter that in real life would offer far less closure and clarity at the end of a young woman's eighteenth year. Unlike Marianne's predictable and arguably semi-convincing changes of heart and behavior, the dramatic changes that take place in Emma Woodhouse and Anne Elliot, younger sisters like Marianne, seem realistic—whether because these changes themselves derive from carefully chronicled incremental challenges to their established habits of mind and behavior, or because the two heroines are 20 and 27 rather than 17, or because *Emma* and *Persuasion*, as novels of Austen's thirties rather than her early twenties, embody a psychological realism subtler than the satirical formal contrasts of *Sense and Sensibility*.

Apart from being laterborn protagonists of their respective novels, Emma and Anne seem at first to share few traits of character and behavior. The former is "handsome, clever, and rich," overflowing with health, energy, and imagination, and apparently trapped at home in Highbury with her father. The latter when first encountered is "haggard," delicate, wistfully regretful about having been prudent to a fault, shackled to a dysfunctional landed family on the way down, and about to be uprooted from Kellynch. Besides their domestic stagnation, Emma and Anne are alike in having older sisters who identified with fathers whose qualities they inherit and behaviors they enact, fictional firstborn embodiments of Sulloway's claim that in personality development "family niches often override biology, just as they transcend cultural stereotypes" (149). Isabella Woodhouse Knightley mirrors her father in lacking "strong understanding or any quickness," in displaying delicate health, valetudinarianism, hypersolicitude for her children, "many fears and many nerves," and, more positively, in "a general benevolence of temper, and a strong habit of regard for every old acquaintance" (*E* 92). Appraising Mr Woodhouse, Fritz Oehlschlaeger ascribes these shared qualities, which seem more culturally appropriate to a woman than to a ruling-class estate-owning male, to anxiety that rises out of having failed to confront and grieve for Mrs Woodhouse's death (95). Not accepting death and change takes a different form when played out in Emma's stronger character—a character whose raw materials most likely came from the mother she can recall only indistinctly but whom Mr Knightley characterizes as "the only person able to cope with her. She inherits her mother's talents and must have been under subjection to her" (*E* 37). In like manner, Elizabeth Elliot takes after her father in all ways: "Vanity was the beginning and the end of Sir Walter Elliot's character; vanity of person and situation" (*P* 4)—a pronouncement that could be made with equal truth of the firstborn daughter, "very handsome, and very like himself" (*P* 5). Anne, "with an elegance of mind and sweetness of character, which must have placed her high with any people of real understanding," (*P* 5) is patterned on her dead mother, who had been "an excellent woman, sensible and amiable" who "had humoured, or softened, or concealed his [Sir Walter's] failings, and promoted his real respectability for seventeen years; and though not the very happiest being in the world herself, had found enough in her duties, her friends, and her children, to attach her to life" (*P* 4). Take away the children and the seventeen years, and the description of Lady Elliot's lot, as well as her stoical response to it, would be equally applicable to her daughter Anne, who also has inherited as confidante and advisor Lady Russell, the woman who was Lady Elliot's intimate friend.

In Marianne Dashwood, Emma Woodhouse, and Anne Elliot we see laterborn sisters who identified with mothers where their firstborn sisters either identified with fathers or, in Elinor's case, compensated for an absence of adult leadership in the family. The psychic task given each young woman is self-improvement, but the task is different for each. Marianne, with a negative maternal example and a positive role model in her sister Elinor, must curb her excesses and cultivate what's commendable in her sister's restraint. Emma and Anne, with admirable dead mothers and firstborn sisters they couldn't and shouldn't emulate, must learn to make the best of their innate laterborn excellences. Emma must moderate her "imaginism," stop playing at life through proxies, face the real world of change, death, and love that she inhabits, and discover her own true feelings. Anne, having yielded to Lady Russell's prudent persuasion when she was Emma's age and "learned romance as she grew older" (P 30) must, when given a second chance at happiness after more than seven years in the emotional wilderness, trust her heart and head. Both heart and head counsel Anne, rebellious in a genteel but typically laterborn way, to turn her back on her landed origins and commit herself to the rising meritocracy, attractively embodied in the person of her once-rejected suitor Captain Wentworth.

Sisters in a family ecosystem are bound to compete unless felicitous circumstances intervene—but adaptive radiation diminishes the competition. It's convenient for their mutual regard that Elinor and Marianne, thanks to their divergent tastes and temperaments, would be unlikely to fall in love with the same man. At least Marianne could never fancy such unpromising romantic material as Edward Ferrars, and once the maternal Elinor's given her heart to him she's not about to develop a rival crush on the more glamorous Willoughby. But, as Mrs Jenkins is blunt enough to point out, eligible men are a limited commodity in the Dashwood sphere; and if one sister gains Colonel Brandon and Delaford, the other won't. Similarly, Mr Elliot can't court both Anne and Elizabeth. A sister who has made a good match can help her unmarried siblings, though—and similarly though unfairly, one woman's folly can taint all the unmarried females of her household. Concern for his daughter Julia (and his nieces Fanny and Susan) means that Sir Thomas must harden his heart and bar his door to adulterous Maria.

Nowhere in Austen do we see so brilliantly intricate a depiction of siblings diverging, competing, cooperating, and damaging one another than in *Pride and Prejudice*. For all the bright, light, witty tone, the substance of this novel is family Darwinism at its potential darkest. In several ways, the Bennet women are situated more precariously than any other Austen heroines, Fanny Price included. Consider: they live on an entailed estate worth 2000 pounds a year. They have no brother to inherit it. Their mother's fortune is only 4000 pounds. Due to Mr Bennet's detachment and Mrs Bennet's extravagance, little has been put away out of Longbourn's annual income; and the five Bennet daughters will have a total of only 5000 pounds from their father to be settled upon them when their parents die. The sisters, neither sent off to school nor provided with a governess, have received a minimalist laissez-faire education: as Elizabeth puts it, "we were always encouraged to read, and had all the masters that were necessary. Those who chose to be idle, certainly might" (*PP* 165). With so little formal instruction and almost no accomplishments—among the sisters, only Elizabeth and Mary even play and sing, and not well enough to teach—they are not equipped to earn livings in the governess-trade. Nor are they are trained to manage a modest household, to be the sort of women who could exist, if need be, with few or no servants. Mrs Bennet, having dismissively accounted for Charlotte Lucas's absence as probably being needed at home to help with mince pies, proudly tells Bingley, "For my part, Mr Bingley, *I* always keep servants that can do their own work; *my* daughters are brought up differently" (*PP* 44). There are no rich relations to help support the Bennet sisters after their father's demise: Mrs Bennet's foolish sister Phillips is married to a mere Meryton lawyer; her capable, gentlemanly brother Gardiner, in trade in London, is responsible for a young family of his own. Mr Bennet's sole surviving relation seems to be his heir Mr Collins, with whose father he had quarreled—and Elizabeth rejects the marriage offer Collins has charitably if pompously made, an offer that is, in spite of his personal buffoonery, a potential life-preserver for all the Bennet women. Unlike the Lucas sisters, who will progressively enter the social scene at strategic intervals, all five unmarried Bennet sisters, from 22-year-old Jane down to 15-year-old Lydia, are "out" from the start of the story. A believer in chumming rather than skillful angling, Mrs Bennet has saturated the social stream with marriageable daughters. And, as far as one can tell from the excitement induced by the arrival of the Bingley party at Netherfield and of fresh militia officers at the Meryton garrison, their neighborhood suffers a pronounced scarcity of those single men whose fortunes are large enough to mean that they "must be in want of a wife" (*PP* 3) because, as maternal logic runs, so many women are in want of a husband.

There's a direct connection between all five Bennets being "out" and Austen being seriously concerned with the whole interacting sisterhood, though it is hard to say which is the cause and which the effect. As in *Sense and Sensibility*, Austen is most interested in the characters and romantic fortunes of the elder two sisters. But here as nowhere else she pays close attention to how all the sisters in the group have differentiated and how they can help or harm one another's prospects. Sulloway's Darwinian rules of personality development are strikingly accurate in accounting for the variation among these daughters of ill-matched, culpably incompetent or negligent parents. As Sulloway would predict for children of dysfunctional parents, the Bennet sisters tend to invest emotionally in one another rather than in their parents—and, again predictably, the eldest two in particular vary systematically as to their parental affiliation. Jane substitutes for her ineffectual mother; Elizabeth reflects certain attributes of her father. All five sisters, in their distinctive ways, have found adaptive compensations for inhabiting a family ecosystem so unstable and unsatisfying. In terms of natural gifts, however, the eldest two sisters have far more than an equal share of the family's total portion of beauty, brains, and good temperament.

Jane, the firstborn and the acclaimed beauty of the group, "united with great strength of feeling, a composure of temper and a uniform cheerfulness of manner" (*PP* 21). Although just as capable as Elizabeth is of reason—together the two have often attempted to explain to their obtuse mother the nature of an entail (*PP* 62) or to correct the behavior of their younger siblings—she is reluctant to draw conclusions that reflect badly on other people. When Elizabeth reports what Darcy has disclosed to her about why he didn't grant Wickham the parish living intended for him, Jane would like "to clear one, without involving the other" (*PP* 225). Although Elizabeth doesn't disclose half of Wickham's villainy, Jane "would willingly have gone through the world without believing that so much wickedness existed in the whole race of mankind, as was here collected in one individual" (*PP* 224–5). She is almost as reluctant to think ill of womankind. It takes overwhelming evidence to make Jane see Caroline Bingley's hollow professions of friendship for the hypocrisies they are. Jane's problem in recognizing human wickedness when confronted by it is emotional rather than rational. A conservative firstborn, she's conditioned herself to resist following negative perceptions to the logical conclusions they would imply in her domestic environment, where doing so would confront her with facts too painful to face about her father, mother, and sisters. Darcy's epistolary appraisal of the Bennet family failings, so deeply mortifying to Elizabeth, would have been far more wounding to Jane. Elizabeth, in an uncharacteristic gesture of reserve, "dared not relate the other half of Mr Darcy's letter, nor explain to her sister how sincerely she had been valued by his friend" (*PP* 227). For all Jane's excellences—and these include a judgment that's sometimes fairer than Elizabeth's, for instance in their respective first impressions of Mr Darcy—she must be shielded from knowing how her parents' and sisters' follies have foiled her hopes of Bingley. Elizabeth recognizes that Jane occupies a niche that won't allow for detached scrutiny of her family. The nonjudgmental sweetness Elizabeth cherishes in her combines with Jane's remarkable beauty to make her the second favorite child of her mother; her good heart and sound sense to make her second favorite of her father. She is thus the Bennet daughter most popular overall with her parents, a position particularly to be cherished by a firstborn. But the seriousness with which she takes her firstborn duties probably means that, had Jane not met Bingley and thus had an unattached heart (one that, the narrator says, had never been touched before) when Collins came calling and first settled on her, she probably would have responded to his proposal in the practical style of Charlotte rather than in Elizabeth's bravely romantic way. For responsible Jane, sacrificing herself to an ass would probably matter less than keeping Longbourn available as a home for her mother and sisters.

Too much detachment from her family rather than too little is the peril facing Elizabeth, her father's favorite and her mother's least favored daughter. Indeed, after Darcy's epistolary apologia convinces her that "Till this moment, I never knew myself" (*PP* 208), Elizabeth, without acknowledging or indeed at first recognizing it, shifts to sharing Darcy's viewpoint even before realizing that his perspective has in turn been radically modified by her cogent rebuke of him. But long before Elizabeth adopts a Pemberley perspective on Longbourn she has already distanced herself from her mother and younger sisters and has distinguished herself from Jane, the commendable substitute mother, by identifying with the father whose cynical temperament she partly shares. Where Jane dutifully stays within traditional female roles, Elizabeth ignores strictures that are mere genteel custom—and is the more attractive a woman for it. Her fine eyes sparkle with free thought; the sun tans her skin; and if independent cross-country walking dirties her petticoats, the Bingley sisters may disapprove but Darcy certainly doesn't. In blazing a path that diverges from her older sister's, Elizabeth effectively reduces the competition between them: like Elinor and Marianne Dashwood, the two eldest Bennets are unlikely to attract or be attracted by the same men. In a super-civilized arena, they have settled matters as have the Catskill wolves Darwin describes naturally diverging to hunt different prey: "one with a light, greyhound-like form, which pursues deer, and the other more bulky, with shorter legs, which more frequently attacks the shepherd's flocks."[15] Like the wolves, each sister must do what she can to thrive; but complementing, rather than competing, is the better arrangement for adjacent siblings who love, rely on, and invest in one another more than in any other family member.

Poor Mary. The best-looking two Bennet sisters, closely bonded as a complementary pair, precede her; the just-as-tightly-connected Kitty and Lydia follow her—and besides being the unpartnered leftover she's also the least lovely of the lot. Loneliness among her sisters and lack of beauty drive Mary to choose a studious niche in the family ecosystem; but though she labors over books and music, she derives little apparent benefit from her studies. Mary is a sort of female counterpart to her ponderous cousin Collins, a weak performer who humiliates Elizabeth, at least, by her attention-seeking but ridiculous public displays. When the rest of her family is devastated by Lydia's elopement, Mary's hours of reading have given her nothing but pompous, unfelt commonplaces to utter—"'This is a most unfortunate affair; and will probably be much talked of. But we must stem the tide of malice, and pour into the wounded bosoms of each other, the balm of sisterly consolation'" (*PP* 289). And,

> "Unhappy as the event must be for Lydia, we may draw from it this useful lesson; that loss of virtue in a female is irretrievable—that one false step involves her in endless ruin—that her reputation is no less brittle than it is beautiful,—and that she cannot be too much guarded in her behaviour towards the undeserving of the other sex.'" (*PP* 289)

When the sisterly migration north that concludes *Pride and Prejudice* leaves Mary the only daughter at home, she is "necessarily drawn from the pursuit of accomplishments by Mrs Bennet's being quite unable to sit alone" and obliged to mix more with the world; "and as she was no longer mortified by comparisons between her sisters' beauty and her own, it was suspected by her father that she submitted to the change without much reluctance" (*PP* 343). This alteration shows how changes in the family environment can, as in the natural world, bring about modification of longstanding patterns of behavior.

Kitty and Lydia form a dyad as strong as that of Jane and Elizabeth—the difference being that the elder pair displays mutual attachment, complementary strength, and equality whereas the younger pair consists of leader and follower, one willful egoist and one weak imitator. With three older sisters and an overbearing younger one, Kitty might seem a sibling without a niche of her own—except that her special role is to have a weak character and constitution alike. Kitty's distinctive feature seems to be her coughs, concerning which Mr Bennet facetiously observes that she "lacks discretion ... she times them ill." Apart from coughing, Kitty follows Lydia's

---

15 Darwin, *On the Origin of Species*, 91.

lead in everything, particularly in chasing militia officers. But the very weakness of Kitty's character makes her, like Lady Bertram or her daughter Julia in *Mansfield Park*, amenable to improvement when in a sphere of good influence. Once Lydia and Wickham are out of the way and Jane and Elizabeth have established married households of their own, Kitty is reported, if not directly shown, to improve: "She was not of so ungovernable a temper as Lydia, and, removed from the influence of Lydia's example, she became, by proper attention and management, less irritable, less ignorant, and less insipid. From the farther disadvantage of Lydia's society she was of course carefully kept, and though Mrs Wickham frequently invited her to come and stay with her, with the promise of balls and young men, her father would never consent to her going" (*PP* 385–6).

From the Darwinian vantage point it seems right that Lydia, whose place as fifth makes her more emphatically laterborn than any other character accorded much attention in Austen's novels, should turn out to be the most openly transgressive female Austen depicts, a bolter more brazen, if less guilty, than Maria Bertram Rushworth:

> Lydia was a stout, well-grown girl of fifteen, with a fine complexion and good-humoured countenance; a favorite with her mother, whose affection had brought her into public at an early age. She had high animal spirits, and a sort of natural self-consequence, which the attentions of the officers, to whom her uncle's good dinners and her own easy manners recommended her, had increased into assurance. (*PP* 45)

Fully as shallow, self-centered, and unable to understand principles as her mother, Lydia either disregards conventions, as when asking Mr Bingley for a ball—or understands them only superficially, as when after Darcy's purchased Wickham as her husband and Mr Bennet's grudgingly allowed the couple a wedding visit to Longbourn she insists, as a married woman, on her right to take precedence at table over her eldest but unmarried sister Jane. Lydia's ungoverned, impulsive nature variously leads her to buy a bonnet she knows is ugly, to order a meal she and Kitty can't pay for, or to throw herself at Wickham, who has no intention of making an honest woman of the girl who's run off with him. Her rule-breaking spirit may appeal to some latter-day readers who take umbrage at the social restrictions hemming in gentlewomen of Austen's time—but when Lydia's youth, fine complexion, and apparent good humour fade with the onset of years and the experience of disappointments, she will be the image of her mother, an irrational, amoral, selfish woman saved from monstrosity only to the extent that her misplaced confidence and noisy pronouncements make her a figure of fun. Even while young, Lydia is a danger to the marital fortunes of all her sisters—except perhaps Mary, who needs no help in repelling men.

The linked nature of the sisters' fortunes is clearest at the Netherfield ball. Here, the indecorous behavior of Lydia and her satellite Kitty, joined with Mary's totally different form of exhibitionism, Mrs Bennet's vulgar, imprudent pronouncements (on Jane's beauty and her fine prospects with Bingley) and transparent scheming to linger longest at the ball, and Mr Bennet's remote, irresponsible amusement at his family's follies, make Elizabeth recognize, long before Darcy's arrogant proposal and blunt follow-up letter underline the point, "that had her family made an agreement to expose themselves as much as they could during the evening, it would have been impossible for them to play their parts with more spirit, or finer success" (*PP* 101). The Bennet family's assorted defects would alone be enough to encourage Darcy and the Bingley sisters' stealth campaign against Jane, though Caroline Bingley also has a totally sufficient motive for thwarting Jane's interests in her hopes that her brother will marry Miss Darcy and thereby increase her own chances with the Pemberley heir. Elizabeth's consciousness of the Bennets' numerous deficiencies heightens when she's reconsidered Darcy's letter with its justification for parting Bingley and Jane. Elizabeth comes to see the defects of her family as

> hopeless of remedy. Her father, contented with laughing at them, would never exert himself to restrain the wild giddiness of his youngest daughters; and her mother, with manners so far from right herself, was entirely insensible of the evil. Elizabeth had frequently united with Jane in an endeavour to check the imprudence of Catherine and Lydia; but while they were supported by their mother's indulgence, what chance could there be of improvement? Catherine, weak-spirited, irritable, and completely under Lydia's guidance, had always been affronted by their advice; and Lydia, self-willed and careless, would scarcely give them a hearing. (*PP* 213)

The prospect of such sisters-in-law—and such a mother-in-law, a specter Miss Bingley delights in conjuring up—would be enough to make a man with even less pride than Darcy's try to resist falling in love with Elizabeth. Similar prospects would go far towards explaining how he could try to detach his friend Bingley from Jane, however worthy and delightful she might be in her own right. But once Lydia's thrown herself into Wickham's power, the damage she can do to her sisters' marital chances is immeasurably greater than the family's collective absurdities combined. On receiving the bad news of Lydia's elopement, Elizabeth has just been noticing the evidence of Darcy's continued, even enhanced, regard for her. But in spite of his dramatically improved manners and his demonstrable personal regard, she can't believe that his love could survive in light of the Bennets' dishonor. His preoccupied look on hearing the news of Lydia and Wickham makes Elizabeth believe "Her power was sinking; every thing *must* sink under such a proof of family weakness, such an assurance of the deepest disgrace. She could neither wonder nor condemn" (*PP* 278). Elizabeth's reading of Darcy is eventually proved wrong, as has been the case before—but the impression she's formed is reasonable if erroneous. It testifies to how, for unmarried sisters at least, the fates of individuals sharply distinguished from one another nonetheless remain connected in the family ecosystem. Only an uprooting as drastic as Elizabeth's and Jane's respective escapes from Longbourn to Pemberley and the estate Bingley eventually acquires some thirty miles away can save the best Bennet sisters from continued mortifications—and offer an environment, healthier than the entangled bank of Longbourn had been, in which to improve the sister who can be salvaged.

Chapter 3
"Marry—Mary—Marry"

This third of the four interlocking essays complements the one just before, which considered the personality development of siblings. The forces that shape personality also help determine marital choices and prospects; and decisions about marriage, as we've already seen through the example of the three Ward sisters in *Mansfield Park*, have significant impact on evolving personalities. In Austen's novels, marriage is the defining moment for character.[1] The choice of marital partner says much about who a man is. The acceptance of a proposal says everything about who a woman has become and what her future status and character will be. Once yoked, the two individuals will continue to influence one another, though in most Austenworld cases the post-marital evolution of character takes place beyond the frame of the fiction. What Austen imagined about marriage in her novels was true to the realities of early nineteenth-century British culture, so we'll consider actual ideas about marriage too—notably those of Austen herself and those of Charles Darwin and the woman who would become his wife, his first cousin Emma Wedgwood. Despite the veneer of romantic sentiment that surrounded and mystified marriage in nineteenth-century British fiction and culture alike, some stark truths related to the struggle for existence lay at the heart of the institution. The marriage market was an important arena in

---

1   See, for instance, Julia Prewitt Brown, *Jane Austen's Novels: Social Change and Literary Form* (Cambridge, MA: Harvard University Press, 1979), 6–24: "In Jane Austen, the choice of a husband is bound up in all sorts of actual difficulties: in the heroine's decisions about herself and her future and her adult posture. The first encounters with her future husband mark the beginning of the heroine's moral growth, and her marriage is a stage in this growth" (7). Prewitt contends that because "the present generation unwittingly inherits the temperamental and moral deficiencies of its parents ... in the choice of spouse the men and women of the present either comprehend the lessons of the past or perpetuate its defects" (8). In a different way, Claudia L. Johnson, writing in *Jane Austen: Women, Politics, and the Novel* (Chicago, IL: University of Chicago, 1988), also sees marriage in Austen's novels functioning as an important signal of moral development: "To most readers, Austen's allegiance to conservative social values is proven by the inevitability of marriage in her novels," marriage being, for many conservative writers of the time, "the sole arrangement by which we can nurture precious moral affections" (89). Citing *Pride and Prejudice* as a refutation of this commonplace, Johnson instead claims that Austen's novels treat marriage as less a prerequisite for personal virtue than as an outcome of improved character: family affections are so far from being considered sufficient and essential to the development of rectitude "that Darcy cannot be an acceptable husband until his moral imagination has been broadened enough to respect the dignity of those outside his family circle" (90). Following this line of argument, we might observe that although against his better judgment Darcy finds himself willing to marry Elizabeth as she is in mid-novel, her deepening moral sensibility makes her a much better candidate for matrimony by the time she accepts his renewed offer.

which civilized humans competed to thrive and survive. Marrying was the only respectable way a man could pass on his biological heritage; for many women, it was the only respectable way to stay alive. Men and women alike found that a marriage partner could promote or impede the personal quest for comfort, prestige, power, wealth, and success. Recognizing the high stakes and many hazards attendant on marriage, both Austen and Darwin are coldly clear about the importance of choosing or accepting a mate wisely. But however practical their theories, both saw marriage as something far more than a socioeconomic convenience. Both understood it to be a relationship that should be grounded in mutual respect and love—an understanding implicitly demonstrated in Darwin's marriage and Jane Austen's spinsterhood.

Austen's preferred fictive formula of a few genteel rural families within visiting distance of one another necessarily limits the pool of suitable prospective mates—unless and until outsiders enter the community or young people are uprooted from home, spend the social season in London, or mingle at Bath and the other fashionable watering-places. The real-life Darwins and Wedgwoods, despite the increased mobility brought by trains and better roads, lived circumscribed existences by standards of our day, when distances and class differences pose less formidable obstacles. In nineteenth-century England's landowning classes, the principles of inheritance called entailment and primogeniture crucially shaped individuals' marriage prospects, so it will be worth seeing what both Austen and Darwin observe about these institutions. In propertied circles, there were economic, practical, and social advantages to marriages between cousins or between neighbors who had grown up together. These advantages might include shared, deeply rooted values and tastes or childhood memories, or they might involve consolidating rather than distributing a family's assets and thereby sustaining its dynastic prestige. We'll scrutinize marriages between principals already connected by blood or bond—in Austen's fiction, the unions of first cousins Fanny Price and Edmund Bertram and of lifelong neighbors (and in-laws) Emma Woodhouse and George Knightley; in life, Charles Darwin's marriage to his first cousin Emma Wedgwood. But even before scientific and popular understanding of genetic inheritance showed the potential dangers of close relations marrying, people realized that there could be reasons against doing so. We'll consider the notable countercases in Austen, Elizabeth Bennet's rejection of her cousin William Collins and Anne Elliot's rebuffing her cousin William Elliot. Darwin's uneasiness about the consequences of intermarriage deserves some attention here too—as do his observations on mating rituals in the animal world, where the elaborate dance of sexual selection is comparable to the social rituals circumscribing and facilitating mutual attraction in the polished human world Austen describes.

What do Mrs Bennet and Charles Darwin have in common? More than one might initially think, given that one's a clueless, vulgar, volatile, financially precarious fictional female and the other a discerning, mannerly, stable, securely affluent actual male. Middle age finds both living with large families on small estates in the south of England. Both are nervous, apparently plagued by ill-health, and certainly prone to valetudinarianism. But the shared attribute interesting enough to spur me to start by posing the question is their belief that well-off men should marry. *Pride and Prejudice* begins with a pronouncement that despite its generalized rhetoric turns out, when unpacked, to be not "a truth universally acknowledged" but a highly contingent self-serving belief fondly cherished by a specific interest group, predatory parents of Mrs Bennet's ilk. The fervor with which Mrs Bennet and her kind cherish this article of faith would itself be a sufficient excuse for Mr Darcy's stiffly unavailable stance at the Meryton ball:

> It is a truth universally acknowledged, that a single man in possession of a good fortune, must be in want of a wife.
> However little known the feelings or views of such a man may be on his first entering a neighbourhood, this truth is so well fixed in the minds of the surrounding families, that he is considered as the rightful property of some one or other of their daughters. (*PP* 3)

The "feelings or views" of financially and socially eligible males—beings referred to by Darwin's youthful friend Fanny Owen as "shootables," a whimsical term simultaneously veiling serious import and revealing the rich bachelors' status as flightless grouse or biped stags to be brought down by unmarried huntresses—may be "little known," but that doesn't matter. These feelings or views are irrelevant from the vantage point of mothers like Mrs Bennet, concerned above all else to marry off female progeny in the grim game of socioeconomic survival.

When the bachelor Darwin returned from his five-years' voyage with an all-male crew and settled down to coping with his collections and the zoological, botanical, and geological ideas they'd inspired, he lost little time in coming to the matrimonial conclusion that Mrs Bennet might hope all financially comfortable bachelors to reach. Back on dry land he first set up in Cambridge, where he worked on a natural history of the *Beagle* voyage for the multi-volume publication that partnered him with Captain Fitzroy and Captain King, Fitzroy's predecessor. In 1837 he moved to London, more convenient for attending events at such institutions as the Zoological and Geological Societies that had welcomed him as a fellow, staying in touch with the experts to whom he'd farmed out particular subsets of his collection, and cultivating his personal and professional relationships with the distinguished naturalists, the geologist Charles Lyell prominent among them, who had welcomed the returned traveler as a friend and equal. Darwin worked and thought hard. He was preoccupied in a scientific way with a matter that also loomed large in his personal life: sexual reproduction, nature's driving force for transmutation. Was Darwin's dauntless industry a refuge from his feelings or a way of exploring them? Whichever, he consciously connected his naturalist projects and his personal situation, as is evidenced by a whimsical epistolary observation to C. T. Whitley on May 8, 1838: "As for a wife, that most interesting specimen in the whole series of vertebrate animals, Providence only knows whether I shall ever capture one or be able to feed her if caught" (*CCD* VII, 469).

The just-quoted passage, which echoes Fanny Owen in facetiously reducing a marriage partner to a collectible animal, shows that Darwin agrees with Mrs Bennet in seeing the man as chief financer of a marriage even though at the time he was unduly pessimistic about ever possessing substantial enough resources to support a wife himself, perhaps because he felt unwilling to be further beholden to the father who had been so generous in subsidizing his five years on the *Beagle* voyage.

But unlike Mrs Bennet or Fanny Owen, Darwin sees man as the hunter, woman as the quarry. This perspective was only natural; young Darwin resembled Mr Bennet and most country gentlemen of his time in being a keen sportsman. In 1837, however, Darwin was a "shootable" being stalked by a female hunting party headed by a mother far more intelligent and agreeable than Mrs Bennet, though similarly provided with five unmarried daughters.

The lady was Anne Susan Horner, whose husband Darwin had known at Edinburgh. Darwin's second cousin Leonard Horner was a distinguished intellectual: a founder of the *Edinburgh Review*, member of Parliament, pillar of the Geological Society, and progressive educator who established and served as first warden of London University, Britain's first secular institution of higher learning. Darwin probably renewed his acquaintance with the Horners through their eldest daughter Mary, Mrs Charles Lyell. The younger sisters Frances (23), Susan (21), Katherine (20), Leonora (19), and Joanna (15) were, like their eldest sister Mary and unlike the Bennet sisters, all intellectually accomplished young ladies—and again unlike the Bennets, whose ages they closely approximate, the five unmarried Horners were not all simultaneously "out." The Horneritas, as Darwin called them, were remarkable young women—botanists, collectors, watercolorists, linguists, travelers, translators. When they thanked Darwin for the gift of a botanical book and indirectly invited him to visit them more often, they were able to toss in a phrase of Maori as tribute to his travels: "*The learned Linguists* feel also grateful for Mr Darwin's generous assistance—Ki te kahore hoki he mahi ['if you have nothing else to do']" (*CCD* II, 12–13). How could a former voyager resist the charms of such bluestocking sirens?

It is richly ironic that Darwin used the back of a note from their father to speculate on his erotic and intellectual future in April 1838. The musings fall into two parts, both centering on the effect marriage would have on the sort of naturalist projects Darwin could pursue. "If *not* marry" imagines a life with travel, to Europe and perhaps America for geological purposes—or, if not traveling, a focus on species work with microscopic observation, some experiments, physiological observation of lower animals, systematizing, and study of affinities. The bachelor life would involve a "small house, near Regents Park—keep horse—take Summer tours." The alternate scenario presents more limitations. "If marry—means limited. Feel duty to work for money. London life, nothing but Society, no country, no tours, no large Zoolog. Collect. No books." A Cambridge professorship would be "better than hybernating in the country." Darwin goes on, "If I were moderately rich, I would live in London, with pretty big house ... but could I act thus with children & poor? No." Realizing that hostages to fortune would cramp his ability to pursue his researches, he reached a grudging tentative hypothesis that involved academic servitude or metropolitan bachelorhood like Erasmus's, though a less affluent younger son's version: "My destiny will be Camb. Prof. Or poor man outskirts of London, some small Square &c., and work as well as I can" (*CCD* II, 443). Despite the Horneritas' allurements, the matrimonial case as Darwin laid it out on the back of their father's letter doesn't look auspicious for them or for any woman.

Then in summer 1838 Darwin again crossed paths with his youngest Wedgwood cousin Emma, whose brother Hensleigh and sister-in-law Fanny had moved next door to Erasmus in Great Marlborough Street. Charles and Emma found one another "remarkably pleasant" in town and again in the country that July, when Charles visited his father at the Mount and his Wedgwood cousins at Maer Hall. During his stay in Shrewsbury, Darwin asked for and received advice—about marriage in general, not about a specific prospective bride—from the paternal voice of wedded experience. Dr Darwin allayed his son's concerns about poverty: a substantial settlement and future inheritance would keep him and any future family from that. But the famously intuitive Robert Darwin probably sensed the direction of his son's feelings and knew all about the possible perils of religiously skeptical men marrying pious women, Darwin men and Wedgwood women in particular. He warned his son accordingly: "Things went on pretty well until the wife or husband became out of health, and then some women suffered miserably by doubting about the salvation of their husbands, thus making them likewise to suffer" (*A* 95).

Freed from economic worries about marrying, Darwin redirected his anxieties and laid out a sort of utilitarian calculation of pleasures and pains in a two-column pro-and-con format headed by a phrase, "This is the Question," that nods to *Hamlet* and thereby establishes a self-consciously literary tone that might warn us not to take all the ideas at face value. Besides its barding title, Darwin's list echoes in its column headings, *To Marry or Not to Marry*, a comedy by Elizabeth Inchbald, the actress and playwright best known to readers of Jane Austen as the translator of the German melodrama *Lovers' Vows* chosen for Mansfield Park's imprudent amateur theatricals. In fact, it is likelier that Austen knew *To Marry or Not to Marry* than that Darwin did. The play is published just before *Lovers' Vows* in Volume XXIII of the 25-volume *British Theatre*, a collection edited from prompters' copies by Mrs Inchbald. The title phrase *To Marry or Not to Marry* certainly sounds the thematic keynote of *Pride and Prejudice*. Mrs Inchbald's play features a spirited young lady who blends traits of the liveliest Bennets Elizabeth and Lydia, a proud aristocrat who spurns the ladies and then changes his tune like Darcy, a fool who resembles Collins in not much caring who his eventual matrimonial object may be, an elopement, a mysterious past quarrel between gentlemen, misunderstandings clarified... But enough of digression, or too much. Readers interested in a more extensive account of the parallels between Inchbald's text and Austen's can find a fuller treatment appended.[2] For now, as Darwin doublemindedly soliloquizes,

---

2 Elizabeth Inchbald wrote the biographical and critical remarks for the multi-volume publication called *The British Theatre, or a Collection of Plays Which Are Acted at the Theatres Royal, Drury-Lane, Covent Garden, and Haymarket* (London: Longman, Hurst, Rees, and Orme, 1808). The next to the last play in Volume XXIII is *Lovers' Vows*, notorious to readers of *Mansfield Park*. The last is Mrs Inchbald's *To Marry or Not to Marry*. Thus the play's position in the collection could not be better for attracting the notice of Austen, a known reader of *Lovers' Vows*. A series of intriguing parallels to *Pride and Prejudice* make me wonder if Austen read and drew upon *To Marry or Not to Marry*. Below are some parallels supplementing those mentioned in the main text.

To Marry or Not to Marry opens at the country house of Sir Oswin Morland, whose sister has extended a vague invitation to Hester, a young lady who's been given up by her father (whose reputation is ruined) and has run away from her guardian Ashdale (who along with his wife has wanted her to marry a man she doesn't love). Afraid of their peevishness and lacking "sense, skill, argument" to answer what they'd said—and also believing that "It was, beside,

This is the Question

Marry	*Not Marry*
Children—(if it Please God) —Constant companion, (& friend in old age) who will feel interested in one,—object to be loved & played with.—better than a dog anyhow.—Home, & someone to take care of house—Charms of music & female chit-chat.—These things good for one's health.—*but terrible loss of time.*— My God, it is intolerable to think of spending ones whole life, like a neuter bee, working, working, & nothing after all.— No, no won't do.—Imagine	Freedom to go where one liked—choice of Society & *little of it.*—Conversation of clever men at clubs—Not forced to visit relatives, & to bend in every trifle.—to have the expense & anxiety of children —perhaps quarrelling—**Loss of time.**—cannot read in the Evenings—fatness & idleness— Anxiety & responsibility—less money for books &c—if many children forced to gain one's bread.—(But then it is very bad for ones health to work too much)

so ill-bred to tell a gentleman that I could not love him—that I could not bear to live with him—that he was disagreeable to me"—Hester has said yes, then run off. In this matter, she's a polar contrast to Elizabeth refusing Collins's offer.

Old Lord Danberry tries to convince Sir Oswin to marry with arguments not unlike Austen's "truth universally acknowledged" and Collins's reasons alike: "Consider, Sir Oswin, marriage, as I have often told you, is a duty every man in your situation owes to his family, to society". But Sir Oswin thinks that "Marriage will interfere with my pursuits, my studies" and that it will "progressively destroy every comfort of my life." Sir Oswin's sister can't get him to enjoy the society of new people. In this social reserve he's like Darcy—and, like Darcy, he has a mysterious quarrel in his past. Sir Oswin's quarrel, with challenge included, involved a man called Lavensforth who was ruined as a consequence of the matter.

Willowear, the silly ass Hester turned down, has come to the country to retrieve her. He complains that she accepted "trinkets in abundance, and a diamond ring of great value—In a word, I myself am the only gift she ever refused." Willowear turns out to resemble Mr Collins in being far from particular about whom he weds: "My lord, I am of an easy, complying disposition. I am willing to marry Hester; or Lady Susan; or the unknown female you propose; or, if she does not like me, some other. I am not one of those who think 'great care must be taken in the choice of a wife, that she may prove a blessing.'"

Hester, like Lydia Bennet, may have run away under the protection of a man—but she did so because an "honourable man was on the point of marrying" her. Hester observes, "I thought it was better to run away before marriage rather than after," a deed like Lydia's but very differently motivated and justified. Explaining herself to Lord Oswin, she says of the man who helped her, "I did not know him for a lover; but trusted him only as a friend to procure me a chaise; when, on a sudden, thinking me in his power, he wanted to come away with me. So, I feigned illness, to leave him behind, too. Any more reproaches?" Sir Oswin, like Darcy, admires a spirited, resourceful woman. When he expresses his regard, Hester softens: "While you were proud, I could treat you lightly;—while you were angry, I did not regard you;—while you were severe, I could laugh at you;—but now you are generous, humble, mild, I cannot impose on you—cannot deceive you any longer." Hester's deceit has involved concealing that she's the daughter of Sir Oswin's sworn enemy "the unfortunate Lavensforth"—and that she loves the man who was her father's foe and the inadvertent cause of his ruin.

living all one's day solitarily in smoky dirty London House.— Only picture to yourself a nice soft wife on a sofa with good fire, & books & music perhaps —Compare this vision with the dingy reality of Grt. Marlbro' St.

Perhaps my wife wont like London; then the sentence is banishment & degradation into indolent, idle fool—

Marry—Mary—Marry Q.E.D.

Beneath his semi-facetious Q.E.D., the customary termination of a formal proof in logic, Darwin moves on to a new phase of the problem:

> It being proved necessary to Marry
> When? Soon or Late
>
> The Governor says soon for otherwise bad if one has children—one's character is more flexible—one's feelings more lively & if one does not marry soon, one misses so much good pure happiness.—
> But then if I married tomorrow: there would be an infinity of trouble & expense in getting & furnishing a house,—fighting about no Society—morning calls—awkwardness—loss of time every day. (without one's wife was an angel, & made one keep industrious). Then how should I manage all my business if I were obliged to go every day walking with my wife.—Eheu!! I never should know French,—or see the Continent—or go to America, or go up in a Balloon, or take solitary trip in Wales—poor slave.—you will be worse than a negro—And then horrid poverty, (without one's wife was better than an angel & had money)—Never mind my boy—Cheer up—One cannot live this solitary life, with groggy old age, friendless & cold, & childless staring one in ones face, already beginning to wrinkle.—Never mind, trust to chance—keep a sharp look out—There is many a happy slave— (*CCD* II, 444–5)

If the economic assumption underlying the first sentences of *Pride and Prejudice* connects Darwin with the unlikely Mrs Bennet, his meditation "This is the Question" shows his equally surprising agreement with another ridiculous *Pride and Prejudice* character's views on marriage. Strange though it seems, Darwin's premarital meditations resemble the Rev. William Collins's laughably ineffective proposal to Elizabeth Bennet, quoted in full below:

> "My reasons for marrying are, first, that I think it a right thing for every clergyman in easy circumstances (like myself) to set the example of matrimony in his parish. Secondly, that I am convinced it will add very greatly to my happiness; and thirdly—which perhaps I ought to have mentioned earlier, that it is the particular advice and recommendation of the very noble lady whom I have the honour of calling patroness. Twice has she condescended to give me her opinion (unasked too!) on this subject; and it was but the very Saturday night before I left Hunsford—between our pools at quadrille, while Mrs Jenkinson was arranging Miss De Bourgh's foot-stool, that she said, 'Mr Collins, you must marry. A clergyman like you must marry.—Chuse properly, chuse a gentlewoman for *my* sake; and for your *own*, let her be an active, useful sort of person, not brought up high, but able to make a small income go a good way. This is my advice. Find such a woman as soon as

you can, bring her to Hunsford, and I will visit her.' Allow me, by the way, to observe, my fair cousin, that I do not reckon the notice and kindness of Lady Catherine De Bourgh as among the least of the advantages in my power to offer. You will find her manners beyond any thing I can describe; and your wit and vivacity I think must be acceptable to her, especially when tempered with the silence and respect which her rank will inevitably excite. Thus much for my general intention in favour of matrimony; it remains to be told why my views were directed to Longbourn instead of my own neighbourhood, where I assure you there are many amiable young women. But the fact is, that being, as I am, to inherit this estate after the death of your honoured father, (who, however, may live many years longer,) I could not satisfy myself without resolving to chuse a wife from among his daughters, that the loss to them might be as little as possible, when the melancholy event takes place—which, however, as I have already said, may not be for several years. This has been my motive, my fair cousin, and I flatter myself it will not sink me in your esteem. And now nothing remains for me but to assure you in the most animated language of the violence of my affection. To fortune I am perfectly indifferent, and shall make no demand of that nature on your father, since I am well aware that it could not be complied with; and that one thousand pounds in the 4 per cents. which will not be yours till after your mother's decease, is all that you may ever be entitled to. On that head, therefore, I shall be uniformly silent; and you may assure yourself that no ungenerous reproach shall ever pass my lips when we are married." (*PP* 105–6)

Before considering and comparing the ideas behind the two bachelors' respective ruminations on marrying, we should address the relationship of tone to meaning. Austen is of course widely acknowledged as a brilliant deployer of irony; and her strategic manipulations of ironic distance make or modify meaning in both passages from *Pride and Prejudice*. The narrator who opens the novel by stating a "truth universally acknowledged" uses the flat, uninflected voice of philosophical generalization with confidence that it will be heard by the discerning as ironic. The narrator's diction insists on absolute certainty: "truth," not "conjecture"—"universally acknowledged," not "cherished by some hopeful parents"—"must," not "might." A tone-sensitive, rational reader will conclude that a declaration so extreme is not meant to be taken at face value and will see that the statement is actually, if indirectly, announcing something limited about the typical mindset of parents with needy daughters, not something absolute about rich men without wives. But taking detached pleasure in this rhetorical and intellectual irony distracts a reader from the often cold, harsh, unromantically practical realities of ruling-class marriage in early nineteenth-century England. Fanny Owen's facetious term "shootables" does the same thing in a less sophisticated way. Metaphor and whimsy lend a playful air to the female pursuit of a mate; but what's said playfully is practiced seriously. Stalking a marriageable man is competitive and self-serving on the part of the huntress who reifies the hunted—and, as Fanny Owen was to learn in her own troubled marriage, the quarry, once bagged, can still wound the woman who's won him.[3]

---

3 Fanny Owen married Robert Middleton Biddulph of Chirk Castle, an MP and a man of good family—thus eminently a "shootable," despite the disadvantage of being a younger son and having "something of a reputation as a rake and a gambler" (Brent, 138). The light, gossipy letters Darwin's loyal sisters dispatched to him on the *Beagle* suggest that Fanny

Collins's dramatically rendered proposal works in a different way. Although his rhetoric is purposeful, even highly contrived, the bumbling bachelor speaks without humor, irony, self-knowledge, or an accurate awareness of the effects his words might have on their immediate audience. His follies are manifold. To the ironic community constituted by narrator and readers, they are delightful—though they may be almost as painful as they are laughable to Elizabeth, another ironist. But the errors and absurdities revealed in Collins's proposal are mainly rhetorical and psychological miscalculations. His offer contains prosaic details that are either digressive (what's Miss De Bourgh's footstool doing in a proposal?) or tactless (why report Lady Catherine's exact words as to what his future wife should be like or specify the meagerness of Elizabeth's eventual portion, "one thousand pounds in the 4 per cents"?). He displays long-windedness, pompous artifice in a situation calling for sincere feeling, attempts at flattery ("fair cousin," "your honoured father") so clumsy as to be insulting. There's a marvelous blend of doltish obtuseness and dogged accuracy in his inclusion of the parenthetical phrase regarding Mr Bennet, "(who, however, may live many years longer)." Mr Collins may present his ideas in a manner amazingly ill-calculated for pleasing or winning his prospective bride, but the ideas themselves are far from foolish. Rather, they're selfish, worldly, and calculating, though no more so than the term "shootable" is. Wooing Elizabeth, Collins nakedly lays out the results of his self-centered reflections on what benefits marriage can offer him. To do him justice, Collins at least recognizes that Elizabeth is a person with her own interests to pursue. His mistake lies in failing to understand that her values and tastes are very different from his own—that, and presenting his observations and offer alike with no veil of charm, wit, or tact.

The features of the Collins proposal that make good sense according to the values of his culture are its assumptions about practical self-interest, which closely resemble the conclusions Darwin reaches in "This is the Question." Collins assumes it right for a man in his position, a clergyman "in easy circumstances," to set the example of matrimony in his community. But in this case, being an exemplar involves no personal sacrifices. Rather, Collins has determined, as does the utilitarian calculus of Darwin's "Marry" and "Not Marry" columns, that marriage will add greatly to his happiness. In marrying he'll also be acting according to the "particular advice" of his patroness Lady Catherine, just as Darwin's decision in favor of matrimony depends on the approval and sponsorship of "the Governor," Dr Robert Darwin. In one respect, however, Collins is acting altruistically or justly rather than interestedly— unless we assume that salving one's conscience is an act of self-interest. Because he'll eventually succeed to Longbourn, he's resolved to select his wife from among his cousins, the Bennet daughters he'll otherwise displace, even though a beneficed clergyman who's heir to a country estate could very likely command something more than a mere thousand-pounder on the marriage market. This last detail offers an interesting contrast with Darwin, whose financial situation would be significantly improved by choosing, as he did, a cousin for his wife.

Biddulph was not completely contented with her husband, but perhaps the Darwin ladies would be unwilling to see her totally happy with anyone but Charles.

Whether or not Darwin had that cousin in view when he wrote "This is the Question" is one of several uncertainties surrounding the document. The date assigned it by the editors of the Darwin Correspondence Project, July 1838, is conjectural, based on the reference to what "the Governor says." This father–son conversation could only have happened during the July visit to Shrewsbury, when Charles stayed at the Mount and also spent time at nearby Maer Hall, Emma's home. When Darwin wrote in November to tell Charles Lyell of his engagement to Emma—news that must have given something of a blow to Lyell's sisters-in-law the Horneritas—he says, "I determined, when last at Maer [in July], to try my chance" (*CCD* II, 114). The cousins' growing attachment is further suggested by the fact that Darwin's first dateable letter on returning to London is a fond, teasing missive sent to Emma, recalling their good times at Maer, and lamenting that in contrast "This Marlborough St is a forlorn place" (*CCD* II, 95). The parenthetical characterizations of Darwin's ideal wife in "This is the Question"—as the "angel" who would keep him industrious and the "better than an angel" who would have money of her own—suit Emma. Emma would not be the sort of woman to pose problems of the kind identified in the "Not Marry" column: she didn't dislike London (when they left for Down it was Darwin's choice, not "banishment"), didn't push him into uncongenial socializing or oblige him to go walking daily with her, didn't force him "to bend in every trifle." Being a Wedgwood, she didn't even supply him with a distracting new pool of relatives to visit: her family was already his. To a great extent, then, it's possible to imagine Emma as the perceived or unconscious focus of Darwin's matrimonial intentions when he constructed his arguments for and against. Even though the next to the last phrase of "This is the Question" is "Never mind, trust to chance—keep a sharp look out," those words may have meant "keep your eyes fixed on Emma and her reactions" rather than "scout out likely prospects." The Darwins' granddaughter Nora Barlow, who published the marital meditation as an appended note to her edition of Charles Darwin's autobiography, speculates that perhaps these "youthful questionings ... fell into the hands of Emma herself" (*A* 231). It's uncertain whether Emma saw the document at all, if she read it before marrying Charles, or after, or heard about it, or merely heard him echo some of its phrases. Whichever, the "many a happy slave" conclusion, like the earlier words "poor slave" and "worse than a negro," clearly anticipates Emma's future marital pet name for Charles, "Nigger."

This epithet and Charles's metaphors are likely to make twenty-first-century readers profoundly uncomfortable. Such discomfort adds to the difficulty of determining, almost a century-and-a-half after the fact, the tone of Darwin's references to slaves. Is he being facetious, as Emma certainly was in so addressing him? In many ways the language seems like conscious self-dramatization along the lines of the facetious "Eheu!!," a rhetorical gesture typical of those who, like Darwin, had received classical educations. Darwin, a keenly sensitive humanitarian, must have been fully aware of the vast difference in the restrictions marriage imposed on a financially solvent ruling-class male and the cruel deprivations slavery inflicted. Including the missed chance of hot-air ballooning among the disadvantages of marriage (a touch of absurd particularity worthy of Mr Collins himself), Darwin must have been indulging in some self-mockery, perhaps exaggerating the egocentricity of bourgeois bachelorhood so that he could imagine his self-serving tone a pose rather than a reality. Yet making light metaphorical use of slavery, even in a document meant for himself alone, seems uncharacteristic of Darwin. Like Emma, he shared the blood and progressive attitudes of Josiah Wedgwood, whose abolitionist medallion "Am I not a man and a brother?" had become an icon of high-minded reformers (and a highly profitable item for the Wedgwood pottery) at the end of the eighteenth century. Slavery lay at the heart of two of the extremely rare outbursts of Darwin's even-tempered life—one with Captain Fitzroy aboard the *Beagle* and one in 1866 with his grown son William, who had made what Darwin considered an inappropriately cynical and flippant remark about the Jamaica Committee formed to raise funds to prosecute Governor Eyre for brutality against the black population. (Desmond and Moore, 540–41).

If it's hard to know how seriously or lightly to take the comparisons of marriage to slavery, other phrases of "This is the Question" are similarly slippery. Can a man of independent, if currently moderate, means be serious in speaking of "horrid poverty"? Is the objectification that, taken straight, sounds so blatant in "nice soft wife on a sofa" meant to be humorous? Or is it flatly insensitive along the Collins line? Heard by an ear accustomed to Darwin's tone of epistolary levity, the words seem comparable to the jocular "shootables"; but the uninflected self-centeredness of the surrounding argument makes it just possible that Darwin is serious in what he says—or unconsciously serious beneath the mask of conscious levity. Similar uncertainties complicate a reader's attempt to understand the presence or absence of humor or irony in "better than a dog anyhow." Unless a man used the blunt phrase to a woman with utter confidence that he was addressing someone possessing a like-mindedly humorous sensibility, this phrase would be perceived as highly insulting in most cultures; though used between men it would be likelier to sound jocular and less potentially offensive, and employed in private musings there would be no need to respect anyone else's sensibilities. But "better than a dog anyhow" offends more against cant than against values. However ungallant acknowledging this comparative ranking might be, the feeling itself would not be outrageously unfamiliar to the English landed gentry of both sexes. If anything, members of the country-house class, accustomed to valuing their dogs highly (remember Lady Bertram and Pug) and sometimes more comfortable expressing emotion to them than to fellow humans, might think the phrase undervalued the canine companion. Still, to characterize a wife as an "object to be loved and played with" is undeniably condescending, whether consciously or not. To think of her as the provider of children and of companionship and care in old age is utilitarian. Whether Darwin is being serious or facetious or mixing the two attitudes in a way that need not be clarified because he's writing only for himself, the main point here is that his text's approach to the question of marriage is just as squarely centered on self and just as little concerned with the personhood of the prospective female as is Mr Collins's spurned offer. The important difference, however, is that Darwin's ungallant rhetoric is for himself alone (unless it's a joke to be shared with Emma, who both knew his tone and shared his sense of humor), not directed towards someone whose independent feelings, needs, and goals must to be taken into account.

Darwin's pro-and-con marital meditations show him typical of his class and time in seeing marriage's central concerns as more than just the relationship of man and wife. Money and children, both alluded to in his lists, were just as important. As mentioned in the last essay, throughout the nineteenth century the income minimally adequate for supporting a family in gentility, according to F. M. L. Thompson's calculations, was 1000 pounds a year (112). This sum could, by way of reference, result from the annual interest on 25,000 pounds invested in "four-per-cent funds" mentioned by Mr Collins—or 20,000 pounds in the "Navy Fives" favored by Jane Austen herself for the accumulated profits on her novels.[4] Thompson claims that annual incomes of the grand gentry could range up to 10,000 pounds a year, which is just the sum that rumor attributes to Mr Darcy (*PP* 10). At the end of the eighteenth century, Jane Austen and her siblings grew up in a household that had to scrape and economize to meet the demands of genteel existence. Besides the use of two clerical residences and their associated land, the Rev. George Austen received a 210-pound annual income from his appointments to the parishes of Deane and Steventon; and throughout his working life he supplemented this sum with the sale of farm produce from the rectory fields and with the fees of the pupils who studied and boarded with him. This combined income, which required occasional supplementary loans from his sister Philadelphia Hancock and other relatives when the large family was growing up, later sufficed for himself, his wife, and their unmarried daughters. On George Austen's death and the consequent end of his church annuity, the widow and her daughters Cassandra and Jane lived on a narrower annual income: 50 pounds each contributed annually by James, Henry, and Frank, about 100 provided by Edward, and about 200 more generated by the interest on Cassandra's 1000-pound legacy from her dead fiancé Tom Fowle and on Mrs Austen's modest fortune. By contrast, the assets on which Charles and Emma Darwin started married life in 1839 were a bit above the minimum needed to maintain the lifestyle of gentry: 5000 pounds in trust for Emma plus an annual income of 400 (the interest on capital later to be settled on her children) from Josiah Wedgwood, 10,000 pounds of stock generating roughly 600 pounds annually from Robert Darwin (*CDV* 393). The fortune the Darwins eventually inherited from their fathers—51,712 pounds over and above the marriage settlement was Charles's share of Robert Darwin's estate, and Emma received over 25,000 in trust from Josiah Wedgwood's (*CDV* 490; Desmond and Moore, 396)—combined with Darwin's financial astuteness and their subsequent inheritances from siblings to make them much richer later in life.

The prevailing practice in landed families with at least some other assets was to settle money on daughters to help them find well-born husbands with their own estates or with gentlemanly professions (which usually meant the church, the bar, the army, or the navy) generating adequate incomes. Austen, financially calculating for a novelist sometimes dismissed as dealing in romance, generally lets her readers know the size of the fortune that will come along with a woman's hand in marriage. In the case of Augusta Hawkins, the narrator teases the reader and mocks pretentious exaggerators by coyly stating that the future Mrs Elton possesses "in addition to all

---

[4] Claire Tomalin, *Jane Austen: A Life* (New York: Knopf, 1997), 262–3. Subsequent citations will be parenthetical.

the usual advantages of perfect beauty and merit ... an independent fortune, of so many thousands as would always be called ten" (*E* 181)—an amount I've always approximated at 8500 pounds. But Austen usually states the size of a woman's dowry more straightforwardly. There are some apparently portionless unfortunates such as Jane Fairfax and Fanny Price. Some young ladies' assets remain undisclosed, though we have evidence enough to speculate about them. Charlotte Lucas's dowry is probably modest. The Bertram sisters and Eleanor Tilney probably receive fairly sizeable paternal contributions to supplement what in such cases each young lady should be able to count on: her eventual share of her mother's fortune, 7000 pounds to be divided four ways from Lady Bertram, 20,000 pounds to be divided three ways from Mrs Tilney. Specified fortunes attached to the females of Austen novels range from the Dashwood sisters' 1000 pounds each to the 9000 pounds the Bennet sisters would eventually divide by five (their mother's 4000 pounds, if she's not eventually obliged to live on this capital, plus 5000 pounds secured on her and her children by Mr Bennet) to Catherine Morland's 3000 pounds, 10,000 pounds each for the Elliot sisters and Fanny Ferrars Dashwood, Miss Campbell's 12,000 pounds, Mary Crawford's 20,000 pounds, 30,000 pounds apiece for the Woodhouse sisters and Georgiana Darcy, and Sophia Grey's 50,000-pound nest egg that buys Willoughby. Best funded of all must be Miss De Bourgh. Besides whatever money is settled on her through Lady Catherine's own fortune, she is heiress to Rosings, an estate not entailed on the male line.

Entailment, in essence an optional intergenerational legal gambit for keeping an estate intact and in the hands of someone bearing the family surname, favored the dynasty at the expense of the individual.[5] Bequeathing an estate in tail male granted the incumbent (or tenant in tail) nothing more than a life-interest in an inherited property that was settled on the heir in tail, his eldest son or, in default of a son, his closest male relation. Thereby the entailment legally prevented the estate's incumbent from dividing his property, or selling it, or bequeathing it according to his personal wishes. Mr Bennet of entailed Longbourn, lacking a son, cannot leave the estate to his daughters; instead Mr Collins will succeed to it. The detail of Miss De Bourgh being heiress to Rosings means that it, unlike Longbourn, was settled in tail general, which meant that in default of a son an estate would be divided equally among daughters (coparceners) or left to one heiress (Rossdale, 503–4). Rosings' settlement in tail general—the legal situation Lady Catherine would prefer—when combined with the

---

5 For an overview of the history of entailment and its appearances in literature, see Zouheir Jamoussi, *Primogeniture and Entail in England: A Survey of Their History and Representation in Literature* (n.p.: Centre de Publication Universitaire, 1999) and Susan Staves, *Married Women's Separate Property in England, 1660–1833* (London and Cambridge, MA: Harvard, 1990), 59–76. Although primarily a historical study, Staves's extremely useful account contains a brief allusion to *Pride and Prejudice* (60) and also offers a clear and informative glossary (233–41) explaining the arcane legal terminology of property ownership and entailment current during Austen's lifetime. For works specifically engaging the issue of entailment in *Pride and Prejudice*, see Sandra Macpherson, "Rent to Own; or, What's Entailed in *Pride and Prejudice*," *Representations* LXXXII (Spring 2003), 1–23; and P. S. A. Rossdale, "What Caused the Quarrel Between Mr Collins and Mr Bennet? Observations on the Entail of Longbourn," *Notes and Queries* XXVII (1980), 503–4.

fact that the house is "a handsome modern building," might lead us to suspect that despite their venerable Norman name the De Bourghs have not been long settled on the estate, though the newness of the house might merely mean that Lady Catherine and her husband were "improvers," a subspecies of the country-house class on which Austen looked with some suspicion, at least in her novels. Or again Sir Lewis and his father, or any paired tenant in tail and heir in tail from generations farther back, could have joined in a fictitious lawsuit to "Suffer Recovery" and break the entail. As is obvious in *Sense and Sensibility*, *Pride and Prejudice*, and *Persuasion* in the respective cases of the Dashwoods, Bennets, and Elliots, entailment could and often did work against the economic interests and marital prospects of daughters.

Primogeniture, the related practice of leaving the landed property of an estate intact to the eldest son of a family rather than dividing it among all the sons or all the children, similarly handicapped the prospects of daughters and younger brothers alike. It did so to protect the dynastic interests of important landowning families in a country where, unlike the nineteenth-century United States with its vast frontier, agricultural property was limited and the countryside was heavily populated. Charles Darwin, being himself a younger son in a rich bourgeois family with a father who bequeathed his largely self-gained wealth somewhat more equitably, recognized certain advantages to the accumulation and inheritance of wealth within families. In *The Descent of Man* he notes that "No doubt wealth when very great tends to convert men into useless drones, but their number is never large; and some degree of elimination here occurs, for we daily see rich men, who happen to be fools or profligate, squandering away their wealth."[6] Despite the drawback of drones, Darwin saw the accumulation of capital through inheritance and other means as a mainly positive means of advancing civilization and the arts. He was more negative about primogeniture and entailment: "Primogeniture with entailed estates is a more direct evil, though it may have been a great advantage by the creation of a dominant class, and any government is better than none" (*DM* I, 140). The problem for Darwin is that primogeniture can unfairly handicap the struggle for existence by enabling eldest sons to marry at the expense of younger brothers with superior qualities and abilities: "Most eldest sons, though they may be weak in body or mind, marry, whilst the younger sons, however superior in these aspects, do not so generally marry" (*DM* I, 140).

Captain Fitzwilliam of *Pride and Prejudice* acknowledges just this situation when he responds to Elizabeth, who doubts that he, an earl's son, can justify his claim that "A younger son, you know, must be inured to self-denial and dependence." Even if Fitzwilliam has spending-money and a far greater power to do as he chooses than is available to Elizabeth, a woman without money, he's right that "Younger sons cannot marry where they like" (*PP* 163). If he is like his cousin Darcy in having the sense and taste to admire Elizabeth's mind and character and in feeling a physical attraction to her, he is not in an economic position to pursue her. Holding out for a

---

6   Charles Darwin, *The Works of Charles Darwin*, eds Paul H. Barrett and R. B. Freeman, vols XXI–XXII: *The Descent of Man* (New York: New York University Press, 1989), I, 140. This is a reprint of the second edition (London: John Murray, 1877). Subsequent citations will refer to this edition, abbreviated *DM*, and will be parenthetical.

fortune in a marriage partner may not be the best way for a man like Fitzwilliam to find happiness—or to beget the best possible children. Hence Sulloway's observation that "Natural selection is the ultimate scientific justification for the abolition of primogeniture" (242), a point that becomes even more compelling if sexual, rather than natural, selection is given this status. But whatever the potential evils of primogeniture, Darwin's generalizations recognize some practical ways that individual choices tend to check the evils:

> The men who are rich through primogeniture are able to select generation after generation the more beautiful and charming women; and these must generally be healthy in body and active in mind. The evil consequences, such as they may be, of the continued preservation of the same line of descent, without any selection, are checked by men of rank always wishing to increase their wealth and power, and this they do by marrying heiresses. (*DM* I, 140)

Similarly, entailment did not always attain its goal of keeping landed property intact—or intact and uncontested. Jane Austen, Cassandra, and their mother owed their tenure at Chawton Cottage to the Chawton estate's having been disentailed at the start of the century and bequeathed to Edward Austen Knight by his adoptive parents the Knights. The deed of disentail was challenged by the Hintons of Chawton Lodge, who claimed themselves the rightful heirs by entail. From 1814 until Edward settled by paying the Hintons 15,000 pounds to drop their claim, the Austen women suffered uncertainty about their tenure at Chawton Cottage.[7]

We've already seen something of how primogeniture influences the development of brothers' personalities in Austenworld. It also affects marital prospects by handicapping a trio of younger brothers who are better men than their elders (young Brandon, Edmund Bertram, Henry Tilney) and giving the inferior heirs a consequence they don't deserve by dint of character. Similarly, Mr Collins, Mr Rushworth, and William Elliot have higher value than their personal qualities would command because they are beneficiaries of the system. But Austen recognizes that individual circumstances complicate any attempt at seeing patterns. Some beneficiaries of primogeniture have virtues, charms, or both that would in their own right attract superior mates (Darcy, Crawford, Knightley). Some landed men known or presumed to be "rich through primogeniture" select "the more beautiful and charming women" (Darcy, Knightley, Brandon). But some don't. Mr Dixon fell for the plainer, less talented Miss Campbell rather than for the beautiful, accomplished Jane Fairfax. "Men of rank" can marry heiresses out of necessity or preference (Willoughby does), or out of love (Knightley), or can ignore dowries and follow feelings (Darcy, Brandon). Rank and landed status can come without primogeniture (Frank Churchill), and parental choice can cheat the deserving and reward the unworthy as unfairly as primogeniture can (Edward and Robert Ferrars).

If money complicates idealistic and romantic notions of marriage as a personally fulfilling union of two physically, intellectually, spiritually, and temperamentally

---

[7] Caroline Austen, *Reminiscences of Caroline Austen*, ed. Diedre le Faye (n.p.; Jane Austen Society,1986), 38–9; Deirdre Le Faye *et al.*, *Jane Austen, A Family Record* (Cambridge: Cambridge University Press, 2004), 194–5.

compatible individuals, so do children. Charles Darwin, William Collins, Charlotte Lucas, Elizabeth Bennet, and many other real and fictive members of the nineteenth-century British gentry may ponder marriage as if it's a private matter of uniting with a partner who can be loved and respected or a social arrangement contrived to promote or thwart individual comfort, but there are other ways of looking at it. View marriage with the cool detachment of a natural philosopher observing populations over generations, and it's not personal at all but rather a mechanism for continuing and improving the human species. As Schopenhauer, quoted by Darwin in *The Descent of Man*, observes, "the final aim of all love intrigues, be they comic or tragic, is really of more importance than all other ends in human life. What it all turns upon is nothing less than the composition of the next generation" (qtd in *DM* I, 610). Darwin uses the word "marriage" "in the same sense as when naturalists speak of animals as monogamous, meaning thereby that the male is accepted by or chooses a single female, and lives with her either during the breeding season or for the whole year, keeping possession of her by the law of might; or, as when they speak of a polygamous species, meaning that the male lives with several females" (*DM* II, 612). Marriage understood in this sense is sexual selection, the shaping force of the next generation. And—just as important in a species whose offspring mature slowly—marriage provides an environment that will nurture that next generation and enhance its members' chances of surviving to reproduce in their own turn. To put it another way, marriage is a social means of helping particular traits (and genes) endure in the general population. Balanced against adaptive advantages to the population as a whole, the personal wishes, dreams, and needs of individual brides and grooms are of little consequence.

In an age when mortality rates for infants and children were high and birth control generally meant separate bedrooms, large families were the rule for the amorous and fertile. Jane Austen's parents had eight children in 14 years. Remarkably, all lived into adulthood, and their mother survived. The Austen brothers were similarly potent if not so lucky in the endurance of their wives. James fathered four children by two wives, Edward eleven in 13 years by Elizabeth Bridges, who died after delivering the last. Henry, who married his older, widowed cousin Eliza de Feuillide when she was already a mother and some years after losing her married again in middle age, was the childless exception. The two naval brothers had large families. Frank's eleven children 16 years apart were born to his first wife Mary Gibson; his second, Martha Lloyd, was 63 when they married. Charles had two marriages producing separate families of children, four born to Frances Palmer, and four to her sister Harriet. Similarly, the Darwin and Wedgwood families were large by the standards of later eras: Charles Darwin was one of six, Emma Wedgwood one of eight, and their own marriage produced ten children, seven of whom lived to adulthood.

From knowing her mother's history and closely observing the experience of her sisters-in-law, Jane Austen understood that a likely fate for a married woman would be a string of pregnancies, with a new baby perhaps every eighteen months or so. Incessant reproduction might eventually kill a wife. If she lived it might make her prematurely old and exhausted—and certainly would allow her very little time or energy for mothering the children who survived infancy. Again and again Austen's letters to Cassandra take on a sad or grim tone when relaying news of a sister-in-law's, niece's, or neighbor's pregnancy or delivery. The description of Anna Austen Lefroy's second pregnancy is typical: "Poor Animal, she will be worn out before she is thirty.—I am very sorry for her" (*JAL* 336). Observing the constrained lives of women doomed to relentless childbirth and serving more often than she might wish as nursemaid aunt during the confinements and recoveries of her sisters-in-law, Austen may have come to understand married life, and especially the consequent children, as real threats to a woman's independent interests and talents, health, and even life.

Jane and Cassandra Austen remained single and turned to one another for the sustaining emotional relationship marriage might otherwise have provided, even though doing so condemned them to lifelong financial dependence. Cassandra's beautiful and moving posthumous tribute to Jane expresses feelings that must have been largely reciprocated: "She was the sun of my life, the gilder of every pleasure, the soother of every sorrow, I had not a thought concealed from her" (Tomalin, 269). This is not to say that the sisters rejected out of hand the possibility of marrying. The young Cassandra loved and engaged herself to Tom Fowle, a clergyman who died in the West Indies. Jane's earliest existing letter—written to Cassandra, unsurprisingly—sparkles with romantic possibility as it tells of her meeting and being smitten by Tom LeFroy, handsome, talented, promising (he eventually became a Tory MP and Lord Chief Justice of Ireland), portionless, related to her LeFroy neighbors, and sent packing by them when the ardent attraction between two young people who couldn't afford to fall in love became clear. Family anecdote suggested that Jane's heart was seriously touched a second time—during a summer visit to a Devonshire resort—by a young man who asked to meet her again the following summer but died before the rendezvous could take place.

Although the Austen sisters were capable of romantic attachment, they were apparently not willing to enter into matrimony without love. After Tom Fowle's death, Cassandra, who believed in loving once, embraced middle-aged spinsterhood while still young and handsome. Jane refused the one proposal we know her to have received. It was a December 2, 1802 offer made by a rich neighbor five years her junior: Harris Bigg Wither, the heir to Manydown Hall and brother of her good friends the Bigg sisters. Despite the many practical advantages to such a match, Harris was an awkward youth she'd known and liked from childhood rather than a man to inspire her admiration or romantic feelings—so after accepting his offer in the evening, she rejected it the next morning. This proposal took place during the unsettled years that were also the fallow period of Jane Austen's creative life, so one can't simply say that she renounced the prosperous and stable existence Harris Bigg Wither could offer her to save time and space for nurturing her talent. But it does seem clear that she and Cassandra both recognized that though women might find happiness in a congenial marriage they could also live satisfying unmarried lives. The financially constrained, husbandless but emotionally partnered adult lives of Cassandra and Jane Austen offer us a real-life example of how things might easily have turned out for the eldest two Dashwood and Bennet sisters.

In light of what personal observation had shown her about marriage and especially motherhood, perhaps we should revisit Austen's seemingly satirical assessment of Mrs Morland, that "woman of useful plain sense, with a good temper, and, what is more remarkable, with a good constitution. She had three sons before Catherine was born; and instead of dying in bringing the latter into the world, as any body might expect, she still lived on—lived to have six children more—to see them growing up around her, and to enjoy excellent health herself' (*NA* 13). Perhaps these words that, read one way, seem to mock the readers of Gothic novels for expecting women to perish or at least ruin their health in childbirth are partly, even mostly, something else. Perhaps they straightforwardly mean that readers should be amazed at the resilience and resourcefulness of a woman who, like Mrs Austen, survived producing a numerous brood but, unlike Mrs Austen, also managed to keep her daughters at home and even found time to teach them a few things. In any case, repeated stints of assisting at her brothers' houses during and after their wives' confinements suffices to explain Jane Austen's unsentimental portrayal of marriages with numerous children—and perhaps also to account for her much-noted reluctance to follow her protagonists into their seemingly promising unions. Limited to domesticity and encumbered with stair-step children, Isabella Knightley, Mrs Musgrove, and Mrs Morland seem happy and healthy (notwithstanding Isabella's hypochondria, apparently derived more from her father's example than from her own maternity). But what might a parade of pregnancies do to the vigor, health, and freedom so crucial to the appeal and the happiness of an Emma Woodhouse or an Elizabeth Bennet, to the restored equilibrium of a Marianne Dashwood or the second bloom of an Anne Elliot?

In the world of animal heterosexuality, the word "attachment," much used in previous paragraphs and in Austen's pages alike, has at least three highly pertinent meanings. The first is literal and involves physical connection of one entity to another, a good example being barnacles, a subclass of animal life crucial to Darwin's development as a taxonomist and evolutionary thinker alike. These small crustaceans typically live inside carapaces anchored to a spot—but, in some cases, the two sexes are also physically joined, in a permanent attachment we might refer to as a marriage. Indeed *Arthrobalanus*, the curious barnacle genus that launched Darwin on his eight-years' odyssey through the entire order, consists of adult females and males of radically different scales, the male being reduced to little more than reproductive organs and being housed inside the female's shell. When we ascend to consider the loves of civilized humanity, "attachment" has legal and affective meanings rather than a literal one. According to the *OED*, the legal meaning came first: "attachment" meant to apprehend or seize a person or property and to put him, her, or it under a law court's control. In the eighteenth and nineteenth centuries, the emotive meaning of attachment—being bound by ties of sympathy, not law—became increasingly predominant. The *OED* even cites a line from the third volume of Austen's *Emma* (Harriet's "When I was very much disposed to be attached to him," referring to Mr Knightley) to illustrate the word's affective meaning. "Attachment" and its linguistic variants recur often in Austen's novels. All six texts present and appraise both the legal and the affective aspects of human attachment.

Marriage, ideally, binds its principals both in law and in sympathy—but not all marriages involve emotional attachments, and not all emotional attachments result in marriage. Accordingly, it might be useful to preface a discussion of the marriages in Austen's novels with a book-by-book list of emotive attachments between men and women and how these attachments change over time. In each case a representation of the woman's evolving attachment will precede a counterpart for the man. Needless to say, oversimplification and personal opinion are involved in finding words to characterize any phenomenon as volatile as affective attachment. What one reader might call "playful flirtation" another might see as "sincere admiration"; one reader's "contempt" might be another's "indifference." Quite apart from the subjective and semantic limits on labeling emotions, feelings in and of themselves are seldom unmixed or invariable. For example, attraction, admiration, disapproval, and repulsion certainly coexist in ever-shifting proportions in Fanny Price's convoluted, largely repressed feelings for Henry Crawford—feelings many readers find fascinating precisely because they're so intricately blended and so variable in shape and flavor.

Evolving Attachments, Book by Book

Northanger Abbey

Catherine Morland (love → engagement → marriage)—Henry Tilney (flirtation → love → engagement → marriage)
Catherine Morland (indifference → contempt)—John Thorpe (calculation → spite)
Isabella Thorpe (calculation → engagement → infidelity → broken engagement—James Morland (infatuation or love → engagement → disillusion and broken engagement)
Isabella Thorpe (flirtation → infatuation → being jilted)—Frederick Tilney (flirtation → jilting)
Eleanor Tilney (implicit love → engagement → marriage)—unnamed viscount (implicit love → engagement → marriage)

Sense and Sensibility

Elinor Dashwood (love → engagement → marriage)—Edward Ferrars (love while engaged to another → engagement → marriage)
Marianne Dashwood (love → being jilted)—John Willoughby (flirtation → love → jilting → continued love)
Marianne Dashwood (indifference → friendship → love → engagement → marriage)—Colonel Brandon (love → engagement → marriage)
Lucy Steele (calculation → engagement → broken engagement)—Edward Ferrars (infatuation → engagement → disillusionment → broken engagement)
Sophia Grey (attraction → engagement → marriage)—John Willoughby (calculation → engagement → marriage)
Eliza Williams (infatuation → seduced → abandoned)—John Willoughby (indifference or attraction → seduction → desertion)

Pride and Prejudice

Jane Bennet (love → separation → engagement → marriage)—Charles Bingley (love → separation → engagement → marriage)
Elizabeth Bennet (flirtation → attraction → jilted)—George Wickham (flirtation → attraction → jilts)
Elizabeth Bennet (dislike → rejects marriage offer → respect → love and continued respect → engagement → marriage)—Fitzwilliam Darcy (indifference → attraction → love → marriage offer rejected → respect and continued love → engagement → marriage)
Elizabeth Bennet (contempt → rejects marriage offer)—William Collins (calculation → marriage offer rejected)
Charlotte Lucas (indifference or contempt → calculation → engagement → marriage)—William Collins (calculation → engagement → marriage)
Caroline Bingley (attraction and calculation)—Fitzwilliam Darcy (indifference)
Miss King (attraction → separation)—George Wickham (calculation → separation)
Lydia Bennet (attraction → elopement and cohabitation → marriage)—George Wickham (indifference → elopement and cohabitation → calculation → marriage)
Georgiana Darcy (infatuation → near-elopement → separation)—George Wickham (calculation → near-elopement → separation)

Mansfield Park

Fanny Price (affection → love → engagement → marriage)—Edmund Bertram (affection → love → engagement → marriage)
Fanny Price (dislike → rejects engagement offer → unacknowledged attraction and faint respect → contempt)—Henry Crawford (respect and interest → flirtation → attraction → engagement offer rejected → continued attraction and admiration)
Mary Crawford (attraction → flirtation → unwilling love)—Edmund Bertram (attraction → love → disillusionment)
Maria Bertram (contempt → engagement → marriage → betrayal and elopement → divorce)—Mr Rushworth (attraction → engagement → marriage → cuckolded → divorce)
Maria Bertram (attraction → feigned indifference → seduction → elopement → abandoned)—Henry Crawford (flirtation → seduction → elopement → abandonment)
Julia Bertram (attraction → indifference)—Henry Crawford (indifference)
Julia Bertram (flirtation → elopement → marriage)—Hon. Mr Yates (flirtation → elopement → marriage)

Emma

Actual attachments
Emma Woodhouse (friendship → love → engagement → marriage)—George Knightley (friendship → love → engagement → marriage)
Emma Woodhouse (attraction → flirtation)—Frank Churchill (flirtation

Emma Woodhouse (indifference → rejects marriage offer → dislike)—Philip Elton (calculation → marriage offer rejected → dislike)
Augusta Hawkins (calculation and possible attraction → engagement → marriage)—Philip Elton (calculation and possible attraction → engagement → marriage)
Jane Fairfax (attraction → love → secret engagement → acknowledged engagement → marriage)—Frank Churchill (attraction → love → secret engagement → acknowledged engagement → marriage)
Harriet Smith (attraction → rejects marriage offer → respect → love → engagement → marriage)—Robert Martin (attraction → love → marriage offer rejected → marriage offer renewed → engagement → marriage)
Harriet Smith (awe → respect and admiration)—George Knightley (amiable indifference → friendly concern)

Imagined or constructed attachments
Harriet Smith (infatuation → rebuffed → dislike)—Philip Elton (indifference → rebuffs → dislike)
Harriet Smith (amiable indifference)—Frank Churchill (amiable indifference)
Jane Fairfax (attraction → continued illicit attraction)—Mr Dixon (attraction → continued illicit attraction)

Persuasion

Elizabeth Elliot (attraction → wounded vanity → renewed attraction)—William Elliot (indifference)
Anne Elliot (attraction → love → rejects marriage offer → continued love → engagement → marriage)—Frederick Wentworth (attraction → love → marriage offer rejected → hostility → renewed love plus respect → engagement → marriage)
Anne Elliot (indifference → amiable indifference → contempt)—William Elliot (calculation and attraction)
Henrietta Musgrove (attraction → love → distraction → engagement → marriage)—Charles Hayter (attraction → love → jealousy → engagement → marriage)
Henrietta Musgrove (attraction)—Frederick Wentworth (amiable indifference)
Louisa Musgrove (attraction → infatuation → flirtation → distraction)—Frederick Wentworth (amiable indifference → flirtation → responsibility → relief)
Louisa Musgrove (friendship → love → engagement → marriage)—Captain Benwick (attraction → love → engagement → marriage)
Penelope Clay (calculation → flattery)—Sir Walter Elliot (flattered)
Penelope Clay (calculation or attraction → seduced → cohabitation → marriage or abandonment)—William Elliot (calculation → seduction → cohabitation → abandons or marries)

Many observations—original or repeated, very clever, moderately clever, or very dull indeed—could be made about these individual attachments. The problem here, like Miss Bates's on Box Hill, is limiting the commentary; and I aim to do that by a bit of preliminary generalizing and grouping. It's important, if self-evident, that not all affective attachments are of equal value in Austen's fictive world. Some of the changing emotional relationships she explores exist mainly for comparative or competitive purposes—or for both. The Bertram sisters, one engaged and one free, vie for the attention of Henry Crawford; but their respective legal attachments to Rushworth and Yates stand in subtle contrast to one another's (Maria's culpability versus Julia's mere imprudence) and in more dramatic opposition to their cousin Fanny's virtuous and prudent attachment to Edmund. Certain other emotional relationships, particularly those involving subsidiary characters, exist mainly to lend the illusion of reality to what otherwise would be the province of romantic fantasy, the only realm where star-crossed or heaven-favored lovers can exist in isolation from other people's attachments. Or, as in the case of Eleanor Tilney's abruptly announced engagement to the anonymous viscount or Lucy Steele's dropping Edward Ferrars for his brother Robert, the subsidiary attachments serve plot needs

As for the significant attachments: each of Austen's novels is a bit different from all the others as far as focus goes, but it's safe to say that every one of them contains one attachment of primary interest that will furnish all or part of the matrimonial conclusion demanded by the genre. In three works—*Northanger Abbey, Mansfield Park,* and *Persuasion*—there's only one attachment both significant to the ongoing story and featured in its matrimonial denouement. In the novels containing more than one such attachment—*Sense and Sensibility, Pride and Prejudice,* and *Emma*— Austen follows a pattern that's familiar to anyone who knows Shakespeare's comedies. The evolution of one attachment—and it's always the most complex and emotionally interesting one—is of primary importance, self-evidently to the narrative but also to the community-building conclusion. (Think of the Marianne Dashwood—Brandon, Elizabeth Bennet—Darcy, and Emma Woodhouse—Knightley alliances.) The secondary attachment is simpler (Elinor Dashwood—Edward Ferrars, Jane Bennet—Bingley, Jane Fairfax—Frank Churchill). Even if the secondary lovers are complicated emotional beings in their own right, their feelings for one another are straightforward enough. The obstacles between them generally involve external circumstances rather than emotions, and their eventual union is less crucial to the form of the microcosm taking shape at novel's end than is the primary attachment. If there's a third attachment important to the ongoing story and culminating in a marriage at the conclusion, it either differs from the others in that it involves characters who, like Shakespeare's rustics, come from a social class lower than that of the principal and secondary lovers (Harriet Smith—Robert Martin) or it joins another subsidiary attachment in contrasting the principal union (the Musgrove sisters' marriages to Charles Hayter and Captain Benwick).

Delineating the six novels' attachments clearly shows at least one way in which the simplest of the six books, *Northanger Abbey*, differs from what's arguably the most complex, *Emma*. *Northanger Abbey*'s attachments are fewer and more straightforward than those to be found in *Emma* where, alone among the novels, the actual attachments coexist alongside imaginary ones existing only in Emma's busy mind. *Northanger Abbey*'s heroine, Catherine, grows in her knowledge of the world and of Gothic fiction alike; but her attachment for Henry Tilney, once formed, never changes. He in turn, despite being the only Austen male who's at once playful, witty, and morally reliable, does not give evidence of feelings that are either complicated or directly accessible to readers. The narrator reports that he first became attracted to Catherine simply because she was attracted to him. What's dramatically presented—and interesting—about Henry Tilney is the nature of his mind and sensibility: his clever, high-spirited blend of irony and didacticism rather than his affinity for Catherine. The more complicated later novels differ from the earlier three in displaying characters with more varied attachments (every romantic player in *Mansfield Park* is involved in two attachments, if one grants a certain ephemeral reality to Mary Crawford's early statement that she always fancies the older son)—or with more subtle modulations in an attachment as it evolves over time. Composing in her fifth decade rather than her second, Austen can imagine Anne Elliot and Captain Wentworth having an eight-years' emotional history. Even that is short compared to Emma Woodhouse and George Knightley's 21-year attachment.

Although the period readers spend in her emotional company is little more than a year, Elizabeth Bennet takes the prize for being the Austen character with the most actual attachments in the course of a novel. Unlike Harriet Smith— imaginatively consigned to Frank Churchill by Emma and temporarily distracted by Elton and Knightley, but actually true to Robert Martin even as Emma strives to script romantic scenarios for her—Elizabeth experiences at least three complicated potential attachments, with the hint of a fourth. The incongruities in her being the object of Collins, who has the social and economic standing sufficient to attach a prudent woman in Elizabeth's circumstances but lacks personal qualities that would win her love or respect, are totally opposite to those characterizing her relations with Wickham, who can genuinely attract her (so long as she's ignorant of his character) but can't afford to address her. Colonel Fitzwilliam is another Army officer, plain and virtuous as opposed to Wickham's handsome and vicious, Elizabeth thinks might be inclined to woo her if his financial circumstances were different. She's quicker in discerning and acknowledging her own potential attraction to him than to his cousin Darcy, equally virtuous but handsome and rich to boot. The intricate yet clearly delineated metamorphosis of Elizabeth's attachment to Darcy is a ballet of retreating and advancing, rebuffing and relenting, repeated sequences of false steps and self-corrections. His progression towards attachment is far simpler: a straight path from disdain on principle to fervent love and increasing respect as he comes to know Elizabeth better. But whatever the difference in their individual movements, the pas de deux proves and broadens the truth of Darcy's early pronouncement to Sir William Lucas—in the ballroom of the heart's attachments, at least. Any savage (or civilized being) who can feel can dance.

That being said, let's turn to the women and men who are paired with permanent partners in the ordering dance of Austen's plots. Below is a list of the marriages that take place in the course of the narratives or at their conclusions:

Marriages, Book by Book

Northanger Abbey

Catherine Morland—Henry Tilney, Eleanor Tilney—unnamed Viscount

Sense and Sensibility

Elinor Dashwood—Edward Ferrars, Marianne Dashwood—Colonel Brandon, Lucy Steele—Robert Ferrars, Sophia Grey—John Willoughby

Pride and Prejudice

Charlotte Lucas—William Collins, Lydia Bennet—George Wickham, Jane Bennet—Charles Bingley, Elizabeth Bennet—Fitzwilliam Darcy

Mansfield Park

Maria Bertram—Mr Rushworth, Fanny Price—Edmund Bertram, Julia Bertram—the Hon. Mr Yates

Emma

Augusta Hawkins—Philip Elton, Harriet Smith—Robert Martin, Jane Fairfax—Frank Churchill, Emma Woodhouse—George Knightley

Persuasion

Henrietta Musgrove—Charles Hayter, Louisa Musgrove—Captain Benwick, Anne Elliot—Frederick Wentworth

Readers' and critics' reactions to these individual marriages are inevitably going to vary according to personal taste, temperament, and circumstances; but it seems to me that Austen intends for us to consider all the marriages that happen while her plots are still unfolding as either problematic or unequivocally bad. Generally speaking, the brides and grooms of these marriages are characters not meant to be liked or admired, and they marry for the wrong reasons—or at least not the reasons meant to be seen as best. Still, in worldly terms the circumstances of their unions may be more auspicious than seems right to readers who believe that fiction means the good end happily and the bad unhappily. It's not necessarily so in Austenworld, where the ruthless fortune-huntress and odious flatterer Lucy Steele gains a degree of security far surpassing worthy Elinor Dashwood's, though her means to that end is marrying the asinine Ferrars brother (who may fritter all they've extracted from his mother) instead of the repressed but responsible one she'd first hooked. Constant "jealousies and ill-will" between herself and Fanny Dashwood and "frequent domestic disagreements" with Robert are costs a woman as mercenary as Lucy can well absorb. Similarly, Willoughby is handsomely provided for thanks to Miss Grey's fortune—and, as we're told by the narrator, "His wife was not always out of humour, nor his home always uncomfortable; and in his breed of horses and dogs, and in sporting of every kind, he found no inconsiderable degree of domestic felicity" (*SS* 379). Intermittent lifelong regret for not choosing Marianne is a high price to pay for horses, hounds, carriages, and comforts—but Willoughby's lot is hardly so bad that the mercenary bargain's merits can't be argued. Likewise, Charlotte Lucas may have to sleep with William Collins and listen to him (which would be worse?), but she has current consolations in the domestic delights of an improved parsonage and future prospects of Longbourn. Unlike Willoughby, Charlotte has no more admirable potential partner to regret losing, and she can manage her spouse rather than being controlled by him. These two advantages further enhance her practical alliance. Another calculation-based alliance that seems even more promising—perhaps partly because there's symmetry of obnoxiousness in its principals—is that of Augusta Hawkins and Philip Elton. The Elton ménage seems to show that two self-serving, coarse-natured individuals can make a reasonably good married team if they hold the right cards. Neither Elton's at all bad-looking—and each is too ill-bred to notice that the other has bad manners. Her bit of money dovetails neatly with his gentlemanly profession and community position. Similarly selfish, they're not too stupid to work together yet not discerning enough to detect the defects that would make people of judgment disgusted with either of them. Like-minded, limited egoists, Mr and Mrs E. have found soulmates, partners with superficial assets sufficient to allow them to bask in the illusion of domestic happiness.

The mid-novel marriages precipitated by foolish passion on one partner's side and calculation on the other have a different feel to them. Although Rushworth proposes to Maria Bertram because he's fallen for a pretty face—a common male fate in Austenworld—she marries the oafish grandee for reasons far worse than any other calculating character displays. Maria will gladly share his wealth and position, but these assets matter little compared to "being prepared for matrimony by an hatred of home, restraint, and tranquility; by the misery of disappointed affection, and contempt of the man she was to marry" (*MP* 202). Even if she weren't toxically disappointed by Henry Crawford's amiable indifference to her charms, Maria's no Charlotte Lucas, able to be philosophical and practical about marriage to a buffoon. Young, handsome, well dowried, a baronet's daughter, and (like Willoughby) keenly aware of the alternate candidate's merits, Maria can't tolerate the lot and the man she's freely if wrongly chosen. Lydia Bennet's circumstances are Maria Bertram's in reverse. Whereas Maria sells herself in marriage to a contemptible husband and then elopes from him, Lydia Bennet first runs away with Wickham, whose manly charms she shamelessly proclaims, then lounges in extramarital bliss until he's bought for her. Lydia's is the only Austenworld marriage involving a woman following her heart or her hormones to ill effect, a form of folly generally reserved for males. Still, her punishment for foolish passion is not that severe compared to Mr Rushworth's humiliating cuckoldry—and her unsettled married life of sponging off richer sisters and exceeding the modest income of an officer in peacetime can't compare to Maria Rushworth's hell of retirement with Mrs Norris. Lydia and Wickham get off comparatively easily: "His affection for her soon sunk into indifference; her's lasted a little longer; and in spite of her youth and her manners, she retained all the claims to reputation which her marriage had given her" (*PP* 387). This mutual disillusionment might describe the even more radically mismatched Mr and Mrs Bennet's marriage with equal truth—but more of that anon.

All problematic but each in a different way, the mid-novel marriages encountered in Austen's novels foreground the gap between successful marriage as defined in worldly or naturalistic terms (self-preservation and reproduction under circumstances allowing the offspring to survive and thrive) and marriage aspiring to a loftier ideal: self-completion, personal fulfillment, and community-building. I believe that Austen always means the two or three marriages that conclude her novels to be seen as unions of the higher sort—though again, readers and critics vary widely in their personal reactions to them. Before examining the novels' marital conclusions individually, we might ask why Austen's novels invariably end in marriage but never in a single marriage. A possible answer: although Austen always offers her readers a female *bildungsroman*—the growth of a maiden's mind and heart—she never fails to embed that personal story within a social comedy. The young lady's personal choices will resonate in a community where other people less central to the *bildungsroman* are also making choices. Critical opinion has long discerned that Austen's often rushed and detached, reportorial rather than dramatic, multi-marriage conclusions can be plausibly viewed as either substantial or hollow—and if hollow as either unintentionally or intentionally (and ironically) so.[8] But however we take the tone of the conclusions, we're obliged to notice that no newlywed couple is an island. Even as the principal heroine and hero we long or lament to see united finally marry, others are doing the same thing. All these end-of-the-story marriages are acts that strengthen an existing community or help make a new one; and whether or not we believe there is ironic distance between Austen and her narrator at a given novel's end, the narrator intends us to see all these marriages as solid attachments in both senses of the world. All are notably free of the two features that blight the mid-novel marriages and many of the already-extant marriages in Austenworld: following head or hormones where the heart doesn't go.

Northanger Abbey offers the simplest but most heavily ironized of the marital conclusions. Eleanor Tilney's marriage to "a man of fortune and consequence" who

---

8   Claudia Johnson suggests that the ending of *Mansfield Park*, for example, displays "a dubious surplus of conventionalized material" that "lurches the novel into fantasies we are not permitted to credit" (114). Johnson has a similar view of the ending of *Northanger Abbey*: "Austen's eleventh-hour fabrication *ex nihilo* of a husband for Eleanor Tilney is a self-conscious repudiation of the verisimilitude of her own ending" (91). In *Jane Austen and the Fiction of Her Time* (London: Cambridge University Press, 1999), Mary Waldron makes a similar diagnosis concerning the ending of *Emma*: "Austen's endings are never conclusive and the language of this one leaves a number of perplexities to the reader not quite prepared to accept the fairy-tale formula" (133). Clara Tuite, writing in *Romantic Austen: Sexual Politics and the Literary Canon* (London: Cambridge University Press, 2002), is similarly skeptical of "the overscripted romance of the standard Austenean marriage-ending" (181). Tuite, like Johnson and Waldron, believes that the compulsively formulaic quality characterizing the conclusions of Austen's six completed novels throws into question the future happiness of the marriages ending the narratives.

has not been present in the novel apart from owning the washing-bills Catherine mistook for a Gothic manuscript is blatantly *ad hoc*. It's contrived to mollify General Tilney and help win his approval of Henry's engagement to Catherine. We are assured that the unnamed viscount "was really deserving of her; independent of his peerage, his wealth, and his attachment, being to a precision the most charming young man in the world" (*NA* 251). The tone here is undeniably ironic, but there's absolutely no evidence to suggest that simply reversing the phrase's import would disclose the ironist's true meaning: as far as one can tell, the literary conventions of a romantic conclusion are being mocked, not the viscount. Similarly, the match between Henry Tilney and Catherine Morland is meant to be seen as a good one. My personal impression is that a man with his assets and excellences could easily find a young woman offering more than Catherine's ordinary qualities. But he loves her for loving him, and her docile ingenuousness suits his benign if sharp didacticism. They should thrive, even if they don't attain what's promised by the narrator's valedictory pronouncements: "to begin perfect happiness at the respective ages of twenty-six and eighteen is to do pretty well." The novel's final irony, though, aims at a different category of domestic relationship: "I leave it to be settled by whomsoever it may concern, whether the tendency of this work be altogether to recommend parental tyranny, or reward filial disobedience" (*NA* 252).

To some extent the matrimonial conclusion of *Mansfield Park* is closest to *Northanger Abbey*'s, in essence and tone alike. Here there's a subsidiary match that's even less important than *Northanger Abbey*'s. Marrying Julia Bertram to the Hon. Mr Yates is simply part of the fiction-subverting narratorial tidying-up that begins, "Let other pens dwell on guilt and misery. I quit such odious subjects as soon as I can, impatient to restore every body, not greatly in fault themselves, to tolerable comfort, and to have done with all the rest" (*MP* 461). The elopement, though rash, comes to seem "a less desperate business" thanks to Julia's being "humble and wishing to be forgiven," Mr Yates being "desirous of being really received into the family" and guided by Sir Thomas and possessing a larger estate and smaller debts than earlier feared. Neither character is sterling, but under the novel's rubric their wishing to be part of the Mansfield Park clan and being accepted there guarantees at least a minimally successful marriage (*MP* 462). The youthful attachment between first cousins Edmund Bertram and Fanny Price starts out even more pedagogically than Henry Tilney and Catherine Morland's, though Fanny's principles are fully formed and indeed firmer than her teacher's once she's reached the age at which Catherine meets Henry. Many readers dislike the Edmund—Fanny match,[9] and to be sure it's announced with an overflowing measure of ironically self-conscious narratorial

---

9   See, for example, Barbara K. Seeber, *General Consent in Jane Austen: A Study in Dialogism* (Montreal: McGill-Queen's, 2000). Seeber argues that the marriage concluding *Mansfield Park* is the sad culmination of the psychological abuse that Fanny has endured throughout the novel. According to Seeber, the Edmund—Fanny match is "the closing example of Fanny's oppression," and "Fanny's love for Edmund is the result of her abuse" (113). In a similar vein, Johanna M. Smith, in "My only sister now: Incest in *Mansfield Park*," *Studies in the Novel* XIX.1 (Spring 1987), 1–15, brands the marriage between Edmund and Fanny as "a dismal failure" (1) and asserts that their relationship is "emblematic of [a] paralyzed retreat within the family" (2).

artifice: "I only intreat every body to believe that exactly at the time when it was quite natural that it should be so, and not a week earlier, Edmund did cease to care about Miss Crawford, and became as anxious to marry Fanny, as Fanny herself could desire" (*MP* 470). It's difficult for many present-day readers to overcome a prejudice (not predominant in Austen's time or Darwin's) against first-cousin marriages; and both Edmund's and Fanny's demonstrated personal attractions pale beside the more sparkling charms of the Crawford siblings who, for all their flaws, have the good taste to love Edmund and Fanny for their excellences—and to attract these two rather cold-blooded paragons, though Fanny never acknowledges or even understands that Henry's persistence would eventually have overcome her reluctance. But despite any readerly resistance, the narratorial endorsement of Fanny and Edmund's marriage is straightforward and unequivocal. "His happiness in knowing himself to have been so long the beloved of such a heart, must have been great enough to warrant any strength of language ...." Her happiness, according to the narrator, cannot or should not be described: "Let no one presume to give the feelings of a young woman on receiving the assurance of that affection of which she has scarcely allowed herself to entertain a hope" (*MP* 471). The final summing-up: "With so much true merit and true love, and no want of fortune or friends, the happiness of the married cousins must appear as secure as earthly happiness can be.—Equally formed for domestic life, and attached to country pleasures, their home was the home of affection and comfort" (*MP* 473). Admittedly, Dr Grant has to be killed off by *deus ex machina* gluttony "just after they had been married long enough to begin to want an increase of income, and feel their distance from the paternal abode an inconvenience" in order to make Fanny and Edmund's "home of affection and comfort" Mansfield's parsonage rather than Thornton Lacey's. This narratorial fiat may make us doubt the credibility of the neatly circular ending in which the humble niece, formerly patronized and fireless in the garret, becomes the guiding presence of the Mansfield Park community. But even without the pluralist addition of Mansfield's parsonage and clerical income, a marriage of minds and hearts described like Fanny's and Edmund's would thrive at Thornton Lacey.

The marriages of eldest and second-eldest sisters conclude both *Sense and Sensibility* and *Pride and Prejudice*. There are other significant ways in which these two conclusions resemble one another. Elinor and Marianne, Jane and Elizabeth, are, like Cassandra and Jane Austen, sisters in the spirit as well as in the flesh. Each loves her sister as much or more than anyone else in the world. Each depends on her sister as on no other family member or friend. Had no acceptable men come for their hands, they would have been to one another what the Austen sisters were. In each book the elder, less lively and more dutiful sister makes the more modest marriage, to a man whose emotional compatibility with her is never in question. The second sister's alliance is relatively grander, and her emotional path in reaching it is much less straightforward. In each novel, the two married sisters move away from the neighborhood where their family is settled and constitute a new community—though Marianne and Elinor at the manor and parsonage of Delaford are far closer to one another than are Elizabeth at Pemberley and Jane "within thirty miles" at the estate Bingley's purchased. But there the similarities end and the contrasts begin.

Although the narrator insists on their married happiness, the Dashwood sisters both make matches some readers regret.[10] On engaging himself to Elinor, Edward is described as "not only in the rapturous profession of the lover, but in the reality of reason and truth, one of the happiest of men." She in turn is said to be "overcome by her own felicity." But the lovers' raptures are reported, not dramatized. Their modest circumstances at Delaford parsonage—a comedown for the elder son who should have had the bulk of the Ferrars fortune—are said, not shown, to be no cause of regret for Edward. If judged "from the ready discharge of his duties in every particular, from an increasing attachment to his wife and his home, and from the regular cheerfulness of his spirits, he might be supposed no less contented with his lot" than his silly brother is with a thousand a year and Lucy Steele (*SS* 377). "Might be supposed" to find as much contentment with Elinor as Robert does with Lucy, his partner in "frequent domestic disagreements"? Never having seen Edward happy in the course of the novel, readers can't be blamed if they find this backhanded assertion of his marital joy uninspiring—and marriage with him a mighty small reward for Elinor, unselfish nurturer though she may be.

Marianne's lot provokes some even stronger negative readerly reactions, though other readers think she's fortunate to have won the heart of Brandon, an admirable, competent, strong-minded and tender-hearted man who in fact is more or less what

---

10 Critics who dislike the marriages in *Sense and Sensibility* are variously motivated. Arguing on thematic rather than moral or psychological grounds in "Jane Austen and the Marriage Plot: Questions of Persistence," in *Jane Austen and Discourses of Feminism*, ed. Devoney Looser (New York: St Martin's Press, 1995), Laura Mooneyham White asserts that the marriages of both sisters "have failed to engage the interest of many readers" because the "unions with these heroes fail to enrich our understanding of the novel's chief thematic conflict" (i.e., sense versus sensibility). "Marriage cannot resolve the central clash of ideology represented by Marianne and Elinor, and thus Marianne's capitulation to Elinor's values at the novel's close cannot satisfy" (78). A commoner reason for disapproval of one or both the Dashwood sisters' marriages centers on the men they marry. In *The Politics of Jane Austen* (New York: Macmillan, 1999), Edward Neill finds both marriages suspect because "[T]here is something questionable" about both Edward and Brandon (49).

Johnson, perceptively noticing the "insistent redundancy" of the backstory's two Elizas and the comparable ways Brandon's elder brother and Willoughby idly trifle with women, extends the parallel to include Edward Ferrars, another idle but financially insecure elder or only son of the landed class. The distinct differences in personalities, motivations, and outcomes (the elder Brandon's marriage being coldly calculated for financial reasons, the more emotionally involved Willoughby being the manipulative principal in a seduce-and-abandon liaison, and the naïve Edward Ferrars being lured into a clandestine engagement that does not, as far as we know, involve sexual intimacy) may complicate or qualify Johnson's generalization more than she acknowledges; but her point that Edward Ferrars's previous history marks him, like Willoughby, as "weak, duplicitous, and selfish, entirely lacking in that rectitude and forthrightness with which Austen is capable of endowing exemplary gentlemen" (57–8) stands as plausible.

George Knightley would be if he'd been born a younger son and star-crossed in young love.[11] True, Marianne's almost pushed into the engagement by gratitude to Brandon and by the strong wishes of her mother and Elinor, the two women whose opinions she's finally learned to value appropriately: "With such a confederacy against her—with a knowledge so intimate of his goodness—with a conviction of his fond attachment to herself, which at last, though long after it was observable to everybody else—burst on her—what could she do?" (*SS* 378). Well, a deep-dyed sensibility heroine would pursue other options. Speaking as if from sensibility's perspective, the narrator offers a heavily ironical account of Marianne's progress towards legal and emotional attachment to Brandon:

> Marianne Dashwood was born to an extraordinary fate. She was born to discover the falsehood of her own opinions, and to counteract, by her conduct, her most favourite maxims. She was born to overcome an affection formed so late in life as at seventeen, and with no sentiment superior to strong esteem and lively friendship, voluntarily to give her hand to another!—and *that* other, a man who had suffered no less than herself under the event of a former attachment, whom, two years before, she had considered too old to be married,—and who still sought the constitutional safeguard of a flannel waistcoat! (*SS* 378)

But such language notwithstanding, I think that the narrator means us finally to understand that Marianne accomplishes an emotional task far more difficult than Elizabeth Bennett's of learning the truths of her own heart—and that she can give her 19-year-old heart, as such other youthful literary heroines as 20-year-old Emma Woodhouse and Charlotte Brontë's 19-year-old Jane Eyre do, to a mature lord of the manor roughly twice her age (which means a gap of 19 years in Marianne's case,

---

11   An inclination to continue seeing Brandon as the Willoughby-infatuated Marianne once saw him gives a melancholy tone to Mary Poovey's description of Marianne's marriage in *The Proper Lady and the Woman Writer* (Chicago and London: University of Chicago Press, 1984), 189: "Austen ushers Marianne into Brandon's world of diminished desires in such a way as to make Marianne herself negate everything she has previously wanted to have and to be." There is more vehemence but (for me) less force in Barbara K. Seeber's hostility to Brandon. She sees his character and actions as morally questionable in the context of the backstory involving the two Elizas and argues, "Colonel Brandon's nervousness is the result not just of pain and delicacy but also of his attempt to cover up his own guilt. When Eliza is married against her will, Brandon is conveniently absent, as he is for all of the second Eliza's misfortunes." Seeber sees Brandon's failure to warn the Dashwoods concerning Willoughby as stemming from a desire "to protect his own secret rather than Marianne's happiness." Suggesting that "[b]oth Brandon and Willoughby know when to be conveniently absent," Seeber effectively collapses the moral distinction between the seducer and the rescuer and concludes that the tale of the unfortunate Elizas "destabilizes the main narrative's construction of Colonel Brandon as the noble and patient hero" (72). A few pages later, she laments the Marianne—Brandon match on account of "the violence and coercion that is used to transform Marianne" prior to her marriage to Brandon, the courtship "not so much an educative process in which she learns to see the errors of her ways as a process of oppression that forces her to capitulate" (74). There's a similarly strong but subjective anti-Brandon feeling discernible in Edward Neill's claim that "it's surely a far from eccentric reader who finds him more than a little off-putting, with a Humbert-and-Lolita touch underlying [his] sternly ethical ambience", *The Politics of Jane Austen* (New York: Macmillan, 1999). 49.

17 or 18 in Emma's, and about 20 in Jane's). The narrator reports that Marianne, having truly loved one man, truly comes to love another and to find success and self-fulfillment in her new lot as wife, mother, and patroness of a village:

> Colonel Brandon was now as happy, as all those who best loved him, believed he deserved to be;—in Marianne he was consoled for every past affliction;—her regard and her society restored his mind to animation, and his spirits to cheerfulness; and that Marianne found her own happiness in forming his, was equally the persuasion and delight of each observing friend. Marianne could never love by halves; and her whole heart became, in time, as much devoted to her husband, as it had once been to Willoughby. (*SS* 379)

No authorial signals or ironies seem to cast doubt on the straightforward accuracy of any claim made in this paragraph—until we reach the mention of Marianne's heart eventually becoming "as much devoted to her husband, as it had once been to Willoughby." Here lies a potential ambiguity. If we believe that Marianne never wholeheartedly loved Willoughby, then we should conclude that she doesn't wholeheartedly love her husband Brandon. But if we assume that Marianne once gave her whole heart to Willoughby—and those who dislike her marriage to Brandon would usually grant that assumption—then we should also acknowledge that she ends up ardently in love with Brandon. If we trust the narrator's phrase "as much devoted to her husband, as it had once been to Willoughby," our only logical basis for considering Marianne doomed to a cool marriage of convenience with Brandon is to doubt the strength and reality of her previous passion for Willoughby.

In contrast to pockets of readerly rebellion at the marital fates of the Dashwood sisters, the rightness of *Pride and Prejudice*'s ending as it does isn't contested. No one thinks the amiable Bingley, even if easily duped by his sisters and Darcy, is an unworthy husband for Jane—and though Elizabeth when speaking to her aunt Gardiner facetiously dates her love for Darcy "from my first seeing his beautiful grounds at Pemberley" (*PP* 373), no reader seriously believes that she's adopting Charlotte Lucas's mindset and marrying for convenience or fears that Darcy, laden as he is with patriarchal gravitas, will crush her lively spirit. What accounts for the different degrees of acceptance? First, the Bennets would eventually be much worse off than the Dashwoods if both sister pairs failed to marry, and they are far better off than the Dashwoods when both pairs do so. Idealistically speaking, a husband she respects and loves or at least respects and will come to love may be all a single woman should ask for, but from the practical vantage point and the romantic one alike Bingley's a bigger prize than Edward Ferrars—just as Darcy's a bigger prize than Brandon. Also there's the fact that *Pride and Prejudice* is in various ways the more polished and reliable narrative. Skepticism and self-subversion appear often, but always as attributes of a particular character's sensibility—or as narratorial ironies, such as the "must be in want of a wife" opener, that can easily be interpreted. The narrator's own comments never cause us to doubt that Jane and Bingley belong together—as do Elizabeth and Darcy. Indeed, one considerable pleasure for first-time readers of *Pride and Prejudice* is joining the narrator in discerning the latter pair's true compatibility long before either is aware of it. Further, where *Sense and Sensibility* relies on reported transformations of character, *Pride and Prejudice* offers dramatized evolution: readers actually see Darcy and Elizabeth learning from one another and from their own mistakes of judgment and conduct, becoming better people for love long before they acknowledge their feelings to one another. Finally, the concluding chapter of *Pride and Prejudice* offers no reason to doubt the future felicity of the sister-brides. "Happy for all her maternal feelings was the day on which Mrs Bennet got rid of her two most deserving daughters" (*PP* 385). So the chapter begins, but readers will think the day happier still for the deserving young women who exchange their status as daughters of so mortifying a mother to that of wives to easy-tempered Bingley and a loosened-up Darcy who, his sister Georgiana learns with astonishment, can be "the object of open pleasantry." No need to fear that he'll extinguish Elizabeth's "lively sportive manner"—or that a high-born husband or remote country estate will detach her from deserving relations, for the novel's last sentence is reserved for the excellent Gardiners: "Darcy, as well as Elizabeth, really loved them; and they were both ever sensible of the warmest gratitude towards the persons who, by bringing her into Derbyshire, had been the means of uniting them" (*PP* 388).

Emma and *Persuasion* both offer a trio of concluding marriages, and they do so in ways as provocatively distinct as are the differences in the sisterly matches ending *Sense and Sensibility* and *Pride and Prejudice*. In Austen's last two novels, as in *Mansfield Park*, the sense of how matrimony influences community is particularly strong. *Emma*'s marital conclusion is mainly a conservative reinforcement of the status quo in a Highbury that throughout the novel has weathered threats (some generated by Emma) of what might be called social upheaval. Harriet Smith, that naturally unassuming "natural daughter of somebody" who seemed to be surging up into the ranks of gentility under Emma's patronage, subsides to an appropriate level. At the Abbey Mill Farm the admirably loyal and patient Robert Martin will offer her "security, stability, and improvement. She would be placed in the midst of those who loved her, and who had better sense than herself; retired enough for safety, and occupied enough for cheerfulness" (*E* 482). This passage, Emma's indirectly conveyed appraisal of the match, sells Harriet a bit short (a close look at Harriet's speeches shows that though she's by no means decisive or keen in judgment, she's honest, observant, and able to report with clarity what she sees); but Harriet is still, as Emma admits, "the luckiest creature in the world to have created so steady and persevering an affection in such a man" (*E* 482)—or second only to Emma herself in such good luck. Yet another candidate for being fortune's most favored child is Frank Churchill. The clandestine engagement between him and Jane Fairfax, who's exemplary in everything except agreeing to the secret understanding, serves as analogue to the secondary matches of Bingley and Jane Bennet, Edward Ferrars and Elinor Dashwood insofar as it's an attachment formed early (though hidden from other characters and readers alike) between characters who undergo no personal transformation or evolution, even though their worldly circumstances change. But there's less sense of Churchill deserving his Jane than of Bingley being worthy of his. In each case, the man has the money and position to offer, though Frank Churchill has more money than Bingley and Jane Bennet has more than Jane Fairfax. In both, the woman possesses more intelligence and clearer moral sense, though Bingley's easily misled through his own modesty while Churchill's a playful and artful misleader. The Fairfax—Churchill union, which takes them to distant Enscombe, serves both principals well but also stands to benefit Highbury. Frank's marriage to so sound a wife will ease the Westons' minds and hearts; Jane's attachment to so solvent a husband will ensure future provision for Mrs and Miss Bates. As for Emma and Mr Knightley: there's no question that she doesn't "deserve" him, though how small or great a gap exists between them depends on whether the reader tolerates or deplores Emma's youthful sins of snobbery, "imaginism," and misplaced self-confidence. But whatever her peccadilloes, Emma's a magnificently marriageable young woman: "handsome, clever, rich," improved by a year's experiences of distress and vexation, generous, solid in her basic principles if capricious in her pronouncements, unremittingly healthy. When she and Mr Knightley are able to leave Hartfield for Donwell Abbey, she'll bring an infusion of capital and female energy to the substantial country estate he can offer her. However tall and authoritative Mr Knightley may loom in Highbury, she'll always be able to tease him, as Elizabeth does Darcy. Like her sister Isabella is to his brother John, she'll probably be a fine mother to a succession of Knightley children.

Biologically speaking, Emma and Knightley's marriage, like Elizabeth and Darcy's, is just the sort of salubrious outcrossing Darwin would endorse. Anne Elliot and Frederick Wentworth of *Persuasion* comprise another such married couple, though here the match is socially progressive rather than generally conservative. This is not to say that progressive elements aren't to be found in the first two marriages: in choosing Elizabeth, Darcy shows himself a romantic rather than practical suitor inclined to value individual merit far more than station and to follow his feelings rather than his social principles. Knightley need not condescend in rank in marrying Emma, but his willingness to live with her at Hartfield while Mr Woodhouse survives bespeaks unusual flexibility for a lord of the manor. But despite their progressive elements, the practical import of both of these marriages is to strengthen the established, landed order. In contrast, by marrying Captain Wentworth, Anne Elliot turns her back on the hereditary landed class into which she's born and allies herself with the rising meritocracy—notably the landless navy. Similarly, the secondary marriages in the making at the novel's conclusion—Henrietta Musgrove's to her cousin Charles Hayter and Louisa Musgrove's to Captain Benwick—affirm personal merit rather than family position. Beautifully symmetrical, the Musgrove sisters' attachments are litmus tests by which other characters reveal their values. Louisa's to Captain Benwick—previously engaged to and bereft of "a very superior creature," the late Fanny Harville—spurs Captain Wentworth to utter the words that give Anne reason to hope Wentworth's own feelings for her are not dead: "'A man does not recover from such a devotion of the heart to such a woman!—He ought not—he does not'" (*P* 183). Henrietta's match is a sort of amalgam of Fanny Price's (to a cousin in holy orders) and Elinor Dashwood's (a friend's generous offer of a clerical living makes possible the engagement) with Charlotte Lucas's (because Charles Hayter, like Mr Collins, is now a clergyman but will inherit an estate, if only the modest Winthrop). Anne takes delight in the fortunes "of two sisters, who both deserve equally well, and who have always been such good friends" (*P* 217). Whereas Anne's snobbish sister Mary "does not above half like Henrietta's match," her good-hearted husband Charles approves of both his sisters' attachments, though as a short-of-cash heir he wishes the prospective husbands were richer so that the marriage portions wouldn't be so immediately needed: "'two daughters at once—... However, I do not mean to say they have not a right to it. It is very fit they should have daughters' shares; and I am sure he has always been a very kind, liberal father to me'" (*P* 218). And directly afterward, Charles's report of the senior Musgroves' happiness in their daughters' future marriages causes Anne to confer on them the highest compliment given to a parental pair in Austenworld: "'What a blessing to young people to be in such hands! Your father and mother seem so totally free from all those ambitious feelings which have led to so much misconduct and misery, both in young and old!'" (*P* 218).

Equally free from "all those ambitious feelings," the engagement of Anne Elliot to Frederick Wentworth is arguably the most satisfying in the Austen canon. It's a long time coming, eight years after they first fell in love:

> He was, at that time, a remarkably fine young man, with a great deal of intelligence, spirit and brilliancy; and Anne an extremely pretty girl, with gentleness, modesty, taste, and feeling.—Half the sum of attraction, on either side, might have been enough, for he had nothing to do, and she had hardly any body to love; but the encounter of such lavish recommendations could not fail. They were gradually acquainted, and when acquainted, rapidly and deeply in love. It would be difficult to say which had seen highest perfection in the other, or which had been the happiest; she, in receiving his declarations and proposals, or he in having them accepted. (*P* 26)

This attachment, as sound as any in Austenworld, is thwarted by a variant on a theme announced in *Emma*. Lady Russell plays an older, more accurately rank-conscious version of Emma, Anne a far more intelligent if equally compliant Harriet, Wentworth a more bitter and resentful Robert Martin. Getting the separated lovers back together is the gradual and keenly gratifying business of the novel as a whole, and particularly of the revised conclusion, the most leisurely and dramatically rendered in the Austen canon. It's impossible to read the final four chapters without sharing Anne's mounting impatience at the obstacles—Mr Elliot's unwelcome attentions, Bath's trivial pastimes, the sheer press of flesh and talk even in friendly domestic situations—that prevent her and Frederick Wentworth from reaching an understanding. When at last they do, one's as sure of the marriage's rightness as it's possible to be. If there's a shadow on the sunny conclusion it's the uncertainty of fortune—greater in wartime than at peace—that will be Anne's tax for being a sailor's wife: "Anne was tenderness itself, and she had the full worth of it in Captain Wentworth's affection. His profession was all that could ever make her friends wish that tenderness less; the dread of a future war all that could dim her sunshine" (*P* 252). This union of worthy hearts takes Anne out of her ancestral landed community and establishes her in the floating world of naval dependents. Although Wentworth's fortune gives Anne ample provision and his rank guarantees her adequate social consequence, we never see her settled in the way that all other Austen heroines are. We never know if she and Wentworth will have children or an establishment of their own, or if, like Admiral and Mrs Croft, they will form a mobile community of two, all in all to one another. And for once such uncertainty doesn't seem to matter. Jane Austen as novelist, like Anne Elliot as heroine, seems to have begun with prudence in her youth and learned romance as she grew older.

If, as I have argued, Austen means her readers to consider all the marriages that end her novels as positive acts that will lead both to personal fulfillment and strengthening of the community, the uniformly promising nature of these unions makes them stand out sharply against the extant marriages presented in the novels. A census of married couples populating the six novels appears below:

Married Couples, Book by Book

(Partners dead before the narrative begins appear in parentheses.)

Northanger Abbey

Mr and Mrs Morland, Mr and Mrs Allen, General and (Mrs) Tilney, (Mr) and Mrs Thorpe.

Sense and Sensibility

(Mr) and Mrs Dashwood, Mr and Mrs Dashwood the younger, Sir John and Lady Middleton, (Mr) and Mrs Jennings, Mr and Mrs Palmer.

Pride and Prejudice

Mr and Mrs Bennet, Sir William and Lady Lucas, Mr and Mrs Gardiner, Mr and Mrs Phillips, (Sir Lewis) and Lady Catherine De Bourgh, (Mr and Lady Anne Darcy), Colonel and Mrs Forster.

Mansfield Park

Sir Thomas and Lady Bertram, Mr and Mrs Norris, Lieutenant and Mrs Price, Dr and Mrs Grant, (Mr) and Mrs Rushworth, Lord and Lady Stornaway, Mr and Mrs Fraser, Admiral and (Mrs) Crawford.

Emma

Mr and (Mrs) Woodhouse, Mr and Mrs John Knightley, Mr and Mrs Weston (his two marriages, first to Miss Churchill, second to Miss Taylor), Mr and Mrs Churchill, Colonel and Mrs Campbell, Mr and Mrs Dixon, Mr and Mrs Suckling, Mr and Mrs Perry, Mr and Mrs Cole, (Lieutenant and Mrs Fairfax), (Mr) and Mrs Bates.

Persuasion

Sir Walter and (Lady) Elliot, (Unnamed knight) and Lady Russell, (Mr) and Mrs Clay, Admiral and Mrs Croft, Mr and Mrs Musgrove, Mr and Mrs Musgrove the younger, Mr and (Mrs) Elliot, (Mr) and Mrs Smith, Captain and Mrs Harville.

Take this list as a whole, and it's much easier to find a dysfunctional marriage or one that consists of at least one deeply flawed partner than to point out a solid union of two admirable and compatible individuals, though the proportions of at least minimally successful marriages rises in the last two books.

Northanger Abbey has the sparsest population of already married people. Of these, only the Morlands, despite the ironized introduction considered earlier, seem to be a solid couple comprised of two sound partners. Otherwise, Mr Allen's married to a mindless clothes-horse, the late Mrs Tilney was tyrannized by the General, and the Thorpes at best proved improvident and apparently unable to raise children with decent values. *Sense and Sensibility* pays more serious attention to married couples, but its view is even darker than *Northanger Abbey*'s. The senior Dashwoods were a loving couple and good parents, but the widow lacks sufficient adult sense to run a household. The younger Dashwoods are generally opposite to them. John and Fanny are prosperous and apparently happy with one another; but to love, rely on, and agree with someone as hatefully selfish as Fanny reflects badly rather than well on John. Sir John and Lady Middleton are silly in their different, incompatible, fashions—he, at least, in a hospitable, warm way. Likewise the Palmers: Charlotte is a mouth without a brain, her husband, not surprisingly, surly or silent and grumpily distant—though he's a character who improves on acquaintance and looks better in adversity, like Mrs Jennings herself. Having produced such notably foolish daughters, the Jennings marriage cannot have been a total success; but Mrs Jennings, for all her heavy-handed, privacy-invading ways, eventually wins the respect of Elinor, Marianne, and readers alike for her kind heart and generosity. Again, *Pride and Prejudice* suggests that a well-matched pair of individuals who are admirable in their own right is a rarity. Besides the disastrously incompatible Bennets, there's at least one limited or downright foolish person in the Lucas, Phillips, and Forster marriages. Lady Catherine is both foolish and overbearing, whatever the late Sir Lewis must have been. If her dead sister Lady Anne was anything like her, the late Mr Darcy must have found his wife a trial, though their son fondly recalls both as admirable if rank-conscious. Among the married couples in *Pride and Prejudice* only the Gardiners offer a mature example of the sort of loving, prudent, mutually sustaining relationship one hopes and imagines the Bingleys and Darcys will achieve.

Austen's way of presenting married couples in the earliest three novels tends to follow a pattern of either describing or allowing them to strike the keynotes of their relationship and their individual characters early on, and then for the most part returning to that familiar pitch whenever they're on display. Thus readers seldom need to revise their first opinions of married couples. A typical example: after allowing Mr and Mrs Bennet dramatically to reveal their distinctive natures and the essence of their relationship in a dazzlingly funny dialogue that fills the first chapter, Austen's narrator offers a thumbnail appraisal of each as the final paragraph:

> Mr Bennet was so odd a mixture of quick parts, sarcastic humour, reserve, and caprice, that the experience of three and twenty years had been insufficient to make his wife understand his character. *Her* mind was less difficult to develope. She was a woman of mean understanding, little information, and uncertain temper. When she was discontented

she fancied herself nervous. The business of her life was to get her daughters married; its solace was visiting and news. (*PP* 5)

A relationship manifestly formed because of youthful sexual attraction and nothing more, the Bennet marriage is bad, though it could be much worse if the disappointed husband had not been inclined to take refuge in books, field sports, cynicism, and teasing—extramarital pleasures that would be harmless did they not increase his distance from daughters who desperately need guidance:

> [Mr Bennet] captivated by youth and beauty, and that appearance of good humour, which youth and beauty generally give, had married a woman whose weak understanding and illiberal mind, had very early in their marriage put an end to all real affection for her. Respect, esteem, and confidence, had vanished for ever; and all his views of domestic happiness were overthrown ... To his wife he was very little otherwise indebted, than as her ignorance and folly had contributed to his amusement. (*PP* 236)

Mrs Bennet believes she can raise daughters, but her competence extends no farther than material concerns such as planning a good meal and knowing which London ware-houses are the best. She's not even a practical housewife. Her tastes and expenditures are those of a lady of the manor whose long-term financial position is secure, not in dire need of shoring up through daily economies that might gradually add to the capital that one day may have to sustain her and her daughters—and her blatant strategies for flaunting her daughters hurt rather than help the cause of getting them engaged. Even the potential shame of a daughter living in sin with a scoundrel can't really shake the Bennets from their habitual ways; and they end the novel more or less as they began it, apart from there being three fewer daughters for Mrs Bennet to dispose of and two more estates (presumably well stocked with books and game) for Mr Bennet to escape to.

Austen manifests a more complicated and adult attitude towards marriage in the three novels composed in her maturity. In *Mansfield Park*, extant married relationships no benevolent reader would wish on anyone are the unvarying rule. Yet we are bound to recognize that, without being exemplary and without containing two people who can be admired or who even seem compatible, a union can be functional and perhaps minimally or intermittently satisfying. It's hard to imagine Sir Thomas taking much pleasure in the company of his phlegmatic wife—he makes a point of maneuvering her to another card table at the Grants' entertainment—but he never shows dissatisfaction and disappointment of the sort Mr Bennet demonstrates. Similarly, Mrs Grant has to cope with the Doctor's gourmand expectations and his irritable temper, but there's no sign that his behavior disturbs her equanimity. *Emma* goes farther still in offering what one might call realistic marriages—enduring unions of less-than-perfect people who have built reasonably good lives together—but here the emphasis is much more positive than in *Mansfield Park*. Enduring and presumably functional marriages constitute the social fabric of Highbury. There's no reason for us to assume that the characters beyond its environs—the Campbells, Dixons, Churchills, and Sucklings—are ill suited, though we might not be disposed to esteem all the individuals equally. The couples whose marriages are most carefully presented—the John Knightleys, the Westons, and the newlywed Eltons—all seem to be compatible unions. While recognizing John Knightley's less-than-perfect temper, Isabella's limited understanding, Weston's overly sanguine nature, and the manifold flaws of the two Eltons, we must nonetheless acknowledge that the marriages work well enough. At once realistic and romantic, *Persuasion* too offers a realistic but essentially optimistic view of the institution. The senior Musgroves, the Harvilles, and above all the Crofts should give the novel's three engaged couples ample grounds to hope for the best in a carefully nuanced world where even Charles Musgrove, who had the sense and taste to propose to Anne but the indolence or impatience to settle for Mary rather than seeking farther, can find marriage not incompatible with a reasonably gratifying life.

Viewing the match between Charles Darwin and Emma Wedgwood in light of their families' previous intermarriages, their longstanding acquaintance as cousins and neighbors, and the socioeconomic and personal compatibility that various relatives had recognized long before Charles did, Emma's friend Georgina Tollet observed on learning of the engagement, "'It is very like a marriage of Miss Austen's'" (qtd in *CDV* 392). She's not the only one to strike or discern the Jane Austen note. Darwin's dream of what awaited him when the *Beagle* would finally return to England was a sweet wife and a rural parsonage. His shipboard fantasy—often expressed in his letters home, reinforced by his sisters' correspondence, and wryly mocked by his urban bachelor brother Erasmus—is the essence of an Austen denouement. And when Emma Wedgwood saw her fiancé looking unwell and over-tired, she facetiously viewed life through Austen's art and wrote to Charles on December 23, 1838, "when *I* come & look after you I shall scold you into health like Lady Cath. De Burgh used to do to the poor people" *(CCD* II, 144*)*.

These Austen echoes ring true. The Darwins' four decades of married life seem to have been a real-world union of the sort one might expect to find several Austen pairs settled into with the passage of years: Elinor and Edward Ferrars, Catherine and Henry Tilney, or Fanny and Edmund Bertram, if only the last two ladies were closer to their husband's ages. And, though Emma was actually a few months older than Charles, the early-established, long-enduring nurse—patient relationship mockingly but accurately prophesied in her reference to Lady Catherine also resembled what Hartfield life might have been while Emma Woodhouse was ministering to her valetudinarian father. The available evidence seems to suggest that practical, dutiful Darwin married because he concluded marriage would serve his interests, then prudently chose an appropriate partner and, having chosen, bestowed on her the feelings that were her due—true love and respect that, to be sure, Emma fully earned and truly inspired by being the best of wives to him. The Darwin marriage may not have been precipitated by the fervent passionate attraction some readers demand in fiction and many prefer in life, but it brought enduring happiness and fulfillment to both parties: mutual love and comradeship, a brood of children they loved and were loved by, a comfortable, affluent home, a respected place in their secluded country village—all blessings one imagines Austen's end-of-the-story marriages eventually entailing. These blessings were probably everything that Emma, unselfish, domestic, and equipped with a strong but generally conventional mind, required or desired. For Charles, marriage offered a further reward that one doesn't imagine Austen's heroes needing. Emma constructed and maintained a domestic fortress that the naturalist and thinker knew he needed, a soft yet stable buffer between him and the outside world's clamor and distractions. No person on business from Porlock would interrupt Darwin's visionary projects. The specters of ungratified desires or unmet emotional needs would not haunt him. The vampire demands of a socially or materially ambitious, egocentric wife would not bleed him. Married to patient, practical, motherly Emma, he could leave the details of his ostensibly traditional, eminently respectable bourgeois life in capable, benevolent hands—and get on with his endlessly engrossing and ultimately subversive vocation.

Among the sacred or conventional things undermined or demystified by his cold-eyed curiosity was the institution of marriage itself. Darwin treats marriage mainly in *The Descent of Man, and Selection in Relation to Sex* (1871), a book whose last section interweaves the twin subjects of the book's double title as it treats sexual selection in relation to humans. These chapters, full of innovative discussions bearing on anthropology, biology, ethology, philosophy, psychology, sociology, and other fields, point out physical, mental, emotional, and social characteristics humans share with other animals, especially the great apes. Writing when Victorian imperialism and the British Empire's "dominion over palm and pine" were at optimistic full tide, Darwin presents anecdotes and evidence garnered from correspondents on mating conventions among diverse peoples and other primates. Darwin, who saw no unbridgeable gulfs between humanity and the lower animals, ranges over a continuum extending through the Quadrumana, from baboons, mandrills, and gorillas to "savages" to "civilization." Whereas his refusal to posit a gap between apes and humankind troubled some readers in his day, his Eurocentric yardstick for judging human societies—and the resultant implication of vast ethical and moral gaps between one culture and another—can disturb some readers in our own time. Indeed, a famous passage from the conclusion to *Descent* suggests that Darwin was actually more comfortable with the radical conclusion he imagines will be "distasteful to many" of his contemporary readers—"that man is descended from some lowly organized form"—than with the more moderate acknowledgment of his own brotherhood with "savage" Fuegians as he beheld them: naked, bedaubed with paint, looking like wild animals to his English eyes and behaving in a way that disturbed his English conscience:

> He who has seen a savage in his native land will not feel much shame, if forced to acknowledge that the blood of some more humble creature flows in his veins. For my own part I would as soon be descended from that heroic little monkey, who braved his dreaded enemy in order to save the life of his keeper, or from that old baboon, who descending from the mountains, carried away in triumph his young comrade from a crowd of astonished dogs—as from a savage who delights to torture his enemies, offers up bloody sacrifices, practices infanticide without remorse, treats his wives like slaves, knows no decency, and is haunted by the grossest superstitions. (*DM* II, 644)

These words, powerful emotional opinion rather than rigorous rational observation, accurately express the complicated essence of Darwin's sensibility. True, he is a progressive naturalist who conceives of human races as having few and merely superficial differences separating them and the human species as having perceptible connections with other members of the animal kingdom. But he is also a fairly conventional person of his own time, place, and class, someone for whom the Wedgwood catchphrase "Am I Not a Man and a Brother?" implies basic human equality but does not suggest cultural relativism.

For the most part, however, *The Descent of Man* studies humanity with more detachment than is evident in this passage. Darwin acknowledges that his views of marriage and the place of sexual selection in human history, though far from mere speculation, "want scientific precision" (*DM* II, 630)—and, to be sure, his standards for empirical data and intellectual rigor are significantly lower when dealing with humanity than they are when he considers other species. But even if Darwin can't aspire to the comprehensive understanding he attained after years of anatomizing the loves of the barnacles, he tries to ground his claims as best he can in observations, his own or those made by fellow naturalists. He begins by noting that in humans the differences between the sexes are greater than they are in most, though not all, other primates. Darwin attributes physiological differences in male and female size, weight, musculature, body hair, voice, and in some races skin color to sexual selection, choices made one-by-one but incrementally reflected in overall changes to a general population of varying individuals. Over many generations, secondary physical characteristics deemed attractive in one sex by the other would be favored in the competition to reproduce, so males and females would gradually become more distinct from one another. Similarly, Darwin sees racial characteristics as the slow and gradual consequence of sexual selection acting in isolated populations. Over time, a trait that members of a breeding population considered beautiful or desirable would intensify. Indeed, Darwin hypothesizes, among humans this power of selection might even promote the greater beauty of those classes most favored in the marital competition for mates:

> Many persons are convinced, as it appears to me with justice, that our aristocracy, including under this term all wealthy families in which primogeniture has long prevailed, from having chosen during many generations from all classes the more beautiful women as their wives, have become handsomer, according to the European standard, than the middle classes; yet the middle classes are placed under equally favourable conditions of life for the perfect development of the body. (*DM* II, 610)

But, Darwin acknowledges, among civilized beings and "savages" alike many causes compete with sexual selection. "Civilized men are largely attracted by the mental charms of women, by their wealth, and especially by their social position; for men rarely marry into a much lower rank" (*DM* II, 609). Women living in civilized societies with "free or almost free choice" of marriage partners may ignore physical attractiveness in favor of social position and wealth, attributes that depend "much on their intellectual powers and energy, or on the fruits of these same powers in their forefathers" (*DM* II, 610). Among "savages," such practices as "so-called communal marriages or promiscuous intercourse," female infanticide, early betrothals, and the quasi-enslavement of women could be potential obstacles to sexual selection (*DM* II, 611). Darwin downplays the first of these, despite what his sources present as strong indirect evidence of its existence, because he believes that human males have from earliest times resembled their fellow animals in being extremely jealous of rivals in love: "The pairing may not last for life, but only for each birth; yet if the males which are the strongest and best able to defend or otherwise assist their females and young, were to select the more attractive females, this would suffice for sexual selection" (*DM* II, 615). But in other ways Darwin believes that human societies, civilized and "savage" alike, have evolved means of checking the open competition that would have existed in an earlier state of development, where

> Both sexes, if the females as well as the males were permitted to exert any choice, would choose their partners not for mental charms, or property, or social position, but almost solely from external appearance. All the adults would marry or pair, and all the offspring, as far as that was possible, would be reared; so that the struggle for existence would be periodically excessively severe. Thus during these times all the conditions for sexual selection would have been more favourable than at a later period, when man had advanced in his intellectual powers but had retrograded in his instincts. (*DM* II, 619)

The consequence as Darwin saw it: sexual selection, the force that differentiated human races from one another and men from women, was a more potent force in the remote past, though its influence probably lingers on in a weakened form. Marriage for reasons of social or economic advantage or compatibility of mind and temperament, then, might lead to the greater happiness and comfort of individuals but also interfere with the natural processes that sustain the vigor of the human species. Thus Darwin speculates that civilization, despite all its improvements to human life, could have a degenerative effect on the strength and viability of the species itself. The possibility is far more likely and obvious today, when science and technology are capable of keeping individuals with devastating hereditary physical problems alive and able to reproduce, than it was in Darwin's time. This idea leads in a paradoxical direction. Humanity cannot return to the state of nature that prevailed earlier in its development, when sexual selection would have had stronger play. But an opposite force could have analogous—and eugenic—results. Humanity could theoretically exert over its own reproduction the sort of conscious control that has long shaped breeds of domestic animals:

> Man scans with scrupulous care the character and pedigree of his horses, cattle, and dogs before he matches them; but when he comes to his own marriage he rarely, or never, takes any such care. He is impelled by nearly the same motives as the lower animals, when they are left to their own free choice, though he is in so far superior to them that he highly values mental charms and virtues. On the other hand he is strongly attracted by mere wealth or rank. Yet he might by selection do something not only for the bodily constitution and frame of his offspring, but for their intellectual and moral qualities. Both sexes ought to refrain from marriage if they are in any marked degree inferior in body or mind; but such hopes are Utopian and will never be even partially realized until the laws of inheritance are thoroughly known. Everyone does good service, who aids towards this end. When the principles of breeding and inheritance are better understood, we shall not hear ignorant members of our legislature rejecting with scorn a plan for ascertaining whether or not consanguineous marriages are injurious to man. (*DM* II, 642–3)

The last sentence in particular demands to be set in historical and personal context. Although Darwin knew nothing of the genetic experiments of his near contemporary Gregor Mendel, he had a longstanding, empirically achieved understanding of the possible negative effects of "consanguineous marriages"—and both personal and dynastic reasons to worry about such alliances, his and Emma's being the fourth first-cousin marriage between Darwins and Wedgwoods. *Origin of Species* pays close attention to the degenerative potential of inbreeding and the beneficial consequences of crossing. Darwin's experiments in breeding pigeons and his extensive study of cross- and self-fertilization in plants both showed diminished vigor to be a potential danger to the progeny of an inbred match.[12] While Darwin was working on the first edition of *The Descent of Man*, his friend, neighbor, fellow naturalist, data source, and local MP Sir John Lubbock had raised a parliamentary question about inbreeding during the second reading of the Census Bill on July 22, 1870. Lubbock argued that because "consanguineous marriages were injurious throughout the whole vegetable and animal kingdoms" it would be prudent to find out whether the same was true of humanity, and to further that goal he moved that parliament gather data about first-cousin marriages in the census. Lubbock's line of reasoning was widely decried as cruel and intrusive, and his amendment defeated by a two to one margin. This parliamentary incident provoked Darwin's contemptuous allusion in *Descent* to "ignorant members of our legislature."

Darwin's sickly, widowed son George, who spent much time with his parents at Down House and served as his father's research associate during the time when Darwin was writing *Descent*, picked up his father's interest in the dangers of consanguineous marriage—an interest shared and more boldly speculated upon by the Darwins' cousin Francis Galton, another bourgeois heir whose independent fortune had bought him the economic freedom for a naturalist's life. Galton's early work on hereditary talent and character had influenced Darwin's thinking in *Descent*. Galton claimed that positive and negative moral and mental traits are, like physical characteristics, inheritable and that social classes' and races' collective characters come from the traits of the individuals constituting them. He concluded that conscious, scientifically directed breeding could improve humanity, just as desirable traits had long been enhanced by the careful work of livestock breeders. Following his cousin's and his father's lead, George Darwin amassed statistical research on first-cousin marriages, which he found three times likelier in the ruling class than among the lower orders, and wrote an article recommending "beneficial restrictions to marriage" and arguing that criminality and vice should be allowable

---

12 Darwin's longstanding interest in outcrossing and inbreeding manifested itself in experimentation as well as observation followed by theory-spinning. He was particularly persistent in working on cross-fertilization versus self-fertilization in plants, a topic that he began studying in 1839 and that resulted in a book, *The Effects of Cross and Self-Fertilization in the Vegetable Kingdom*, in 1876. Darwin's observations showed that the overwhelming majority of flowering plants cross-pollinate, that self-pollination probably evolved as a secondary phenomenon, and that self-pollinators are likelier to become extinct than are cross-pollinating species. He did not, however, understand the genetic basis for this last phenomenon—namely, that cross-pollinators' far greater genetic variation would allow for individuals of a species to evolve characteristics potentially desirable in a wider range of environmental circumstances. His botanical experiments further revealed that diminished reproductive vigor is associated with inbreeding. The inbred plants produced fewer seeds than did outcrossed plants.

grounds for divorce (Desmond and Moore, 610–13). On reading this article, the turncoat Darwinian St George Mivart attacked the son and impugned the father in an anonymous *Quarterly Review* piece that precipitated a bitter quarrel and even threatened Darwin's relationship with his longstanding publisher John Murray, who also published the *Quarterly* (*CDPP* 353–6).

The sweeping consequences of what happens when self-styled masterminds take seriously the notion of implementing eugenic marriage are frightening whether played out in the realm of social policy or that of literary thought-experiment: Hitler's dreams of Aryan beauty and vigor, the in-vitro-predestined caste system of Aldous Huxley's *Brave New World*, and the genetically designed superpeople of the 1997 Andrew Niccol film *Gattaca* are a few of many examples. But Darwin's goal in the eugenic matter most important to him—recognition of the potential hereditary risks of intermarriage between close blood relations—has prevailed in most societies and is reflected in their marriage laws. Furthermore, it is interesting that eugenic choices made freely, on an individual basis, in a microcosm, can seem much more palatable—especially when what's good for society at large coincides with personal preference. I'm stepping into the realm of subjective opinion to make this claim, but it seems that of all the principal marriages concluding Jane Austen's novels, by far the likeliest to trouble readers is the *Mansfield Park* union of first cousins Edmund Bertram and Fanny Price. In contrast, the principal marriages readers are likeliest to regard as highly positive all involve rejection of consanguineous alliance in favor of what might be characterized as a "beneficial cross." When at Emma's initiative George Knightley asks her to dance—their first moves in what has hitherto been and for a while will still remain an unconscious mutual sexual attraction—the language is that of marriage and of repudiated consanguinity:

"Will you?" said he, offering his hand.
"Indeed I will. You have shown that you can dance, and you know we are not really so much brother and sister as to make it at all improper."
"Brother and sister! no, indeed!" (*E* 331)

In *Persuasion*'s deeply satisfying conclusion Anne Elliot turns from the attentions of her cousin William Elliot and reaffirms what her 19-year-old self had sensed, that Frederick Wentworth is the man for her. Probably the most widely appreciated of all Austen marriages is that of Elizabeth Bennet and Fitzwilliam Darcy, each of whom rejects (or ignores) the pragmatically advantageous possibility of marrying a cousin. Read in light of Darwin's thoughts on inbreeding and outcrossing, Lady Catherine's indignant question "'Are the shades of Pemberley to be thus polluted?'" (*PP* 357) takes on a fresh meaning totally unintended by its speaker and assumes a richer irony. Lady Catherine's snobbish notions of good and bad blood are one thing, nature's rules are another. In proposing to Elizabeth, Darcy has clearly followed the imperatives of sexual selection, which in this case felicitously correspond with rather than fight against civilization's cultivated tastes. First struck by Eliza's fine eyes, healthy body, and abundant vitality, he later comes to value her mental powers, temperament, and moral principles. Elizabeth is not quite so explicitly motivated by sexual selection—and even if she were, one would be hard pressed to prove it, seeing that public knowledge of Darcy's worldly assets precedes his virile presence into the ballroom where they meet. In the courtship rituals of their species, nation, class, and time, Darcy's is the power of choice, Elizabeth's only the power of refusal—and as a civilized woman of the new, best sort she avails herself of that power until convinced that his qualities of mind and heart make him as worthy as his physical, social, and economic endowments make him desirable. Nature and culture combine to smile on this union. When one imagines ensuing generations of Darcys, which woman's genetic contribution to the bloodline would be likelier to pollute Pemberley's shades: Anne de Bourgh's or Eliza Bennet's?

And did consanguineous marriage stain the shady Sandwalk, Down's meditative refuge where the mischievous Darwin children delighted in replacing the stones their father would knock off a small cairn with his walking-stick as a way of keeping track of his laps? Despite all Darwin's anxieties, it would be hard to say so. True, he and Emma lost three of ten children in infancy or childhood.[13] Most of the surviving children were, like their father and numerous Wedgwoods of Emma's and the previous generation, sickly or hypochondriacal, though as a group they amassed prodigious achievements and lived to ripe old ages. Accounting for Darwin's ill-health or that of his progeny is a fascinating exercise—but one whose answer is bound to stay hypothetical or over-determined. Psychic or somatic? Hereditary or environmental? One factor or several? If the latter, in what proportions? Given the complex circumstances, Nora Barlow's comments on her grandfather's ill-health and that of his and Emma's children are as penetrating as it seems possible to be: " ... health anxieties did trouble Charles Darwin even in the early days before the voyage, so that his marriage to a deeply sympathetic wife can hardly have done more than increase a deep-seated tendency. Her over-solicitude helped to cast that faint aura of glory on the Symptom, an attitude that was carried on into adult life by several of their children" (*A* 240–41).

Who could say that the first cousins Charles Darwin and Emma Wedgwood should not have married? On the one hand, Darwin's much-invoked contention that inbreeding diminishes vigor may have held true, and having first cousins for parents may perhaps have handicapped the Darwin progeny. But the practical advantages of a considerable, consolidated family fortune plus the emotional advantages of being raised in stability and comfort by attentive, loving parents who also truly loved one another certainly offered the children powerful compensations. In terms of what it offered its two principals and the next generation alike, Charles and Emma Darwins' marriage is not adequately characterized by the collected and scrutinized biological, historical, social, and anthropological evidence in *The Descent of Man*, or the general

---

13 The three Darwin children who died young were Mary Eleanor (1842), Anne Elizabeth (1841–51), and Charles Waring (1856–58). Mary Eleanor lived only three weeks. Annie, Darwin's dearly beloved favorite, most likely died of typhoid. Her death certificate declared the cause to be "bilious fever with typhoid character," though the grief-stricken Darwin feared that she had inherited his tendency to gastrointestinal illness and fretted that "the worst of my bugbears, is hereditary weakness" (*CCD*, V, 100). Emma was 48 when Charles Waring, the Darwins' youngest child, was born, probably with Down's Syndrome. He died of scarlet fever in a virulent epidemic that swept through England in 1858.

truths suggested by the unions that conclude Austen's novels. Their marriage, like all such partnerships, was unique, only partially comprehensible from the outside and only partially explainable by generalizations. In the autobiography he wrote for his children, Darwin's own appraisal of Emma's success as his wife offers unreserved praise and unrelieved superlatives:

> She has been my greatest blessing, and I can declare that in my whole life I have never heard her utter one word which I had rather have been unsaid. She has never failed in the kindest sympathy towards me, and has borne with the utmost patience my frequent complaints from ill-health and discomfort. I do not believe she has ever missed an opportunity of doing a kind action to anyone near her. I marvel at my good fortune that she, so infinitely my superior in every single moral quality, consented to be my wife. She has been my wise adviser and cheerful comforter throughout life, which without her would have been during a very long period a miserable one from ill-health. She has earned the love and admiration of every soul near her. (*A* 96-97)

Emma, a shrewd realist, must have smiled wryly but fondly at being styled such a paragon; but the effusive language accurately expresses Charles's affection for and appreciation of her.

The fact that he could feel that way and write those things is a real testimony of mutual love; for although Charles and Emma Darwin were kindred, they were not kindred spirits. They were similar or complementary as far as the matters of ordinary life went, but at heart they were different. Emma's feelings seem to have been deep and strong; his, apparently weaker but more accessible. She was generally reticent; he, habitually expressive. Especially in her younger and middle years, Emma was sustained by an abiding and largely unquestioning Christian faith. Charles, who began as an unreflective, fairly conventional Anglican, progressively lost whatever faith he might have had and became increasingly materialist as his belief in natural selection as the formative principle of life grew. Emma conquered both personal reserve and conventional feminine deference to strongly but tactfully argue against Charles's creeping skepticism on the grounds that his "interesting subjects & thoughts of the most absorbing kind" distracted him from giving his whole attention to religious questions and that Erasmus's agnostic example had paved the way for his own doubt (a keen understanding of the fraternal relationship). "May not the habit in scientific pursuits of believing nothing till it is proved, influence your mind too much in other things which cannot be proved in the same way?" she asked (*A* 236). Emma's "beautiful letter" profoundly moved Charles, who wrote upon it, "When I am dead, know that many times, I have kissed & cryed over this. C. D." (*A* 237). But C. D. would not deceive Emma, even to be kind; and he would not break faith with his principle of seeking to see things as they are and to say what he saw. In 1844, Darwin had finished a draft of his ideas on species theory. Unwilling or unable to publish his iconoclastic ideas without even more evidence to support his claims, he was also determined that his thoughts not be lost. In a gesture that some might see as insensitive but that actually constitutes the highest tribute to Emma's strength, love, intelligence, and magnanimity and testifies to Charles's absolute confidence in her, he wrote a letter instructing Emma that in the event of his sudden death it was his "most solemn & last request" that she devote 400 pounds to the book's publication, find "some competent person" to edit the work with help from her and from his notes and marked natural history texts, and "take trouble in promoting" the resulting book (*CCD* III, 43–4). It's obvious that however much Darwin doubted the existence of God or the immortal soul he had a deep and abiding faith in both the woman he married and the union they had built.

Chapter 4

Variations on Variation

If, as I claimed at the start of this series of interlocking essays, Jane Austen and Charles Darwin are intellectual and spiritual kindred in their reliance on empiricism and serendipity, their ways of pursuing the distinct but not-unrelated goals of novelist and naturalist, and their need to live and work rooted in the domestic stability of a country village, they are alike in other important ways as well. A great consequence of the grounded, closely observant approach Austen and Darwin share is their common appreciation of the power and subtlety of the pervasive natural phenomenon that philosophers and poets have long called mutability but Darwin called variation. This concluding phase of the book will consider several instances of how, in Austen and Darwin alike, variation's minute distinctions and gradual but constant changes are the way of the world, whether the world under consideration is geological, biological, social, or literary. Here, admittedly, the differences between naturalist and novelist can be seen as at least as important as are the similarities. Darwin, whether working on a geological timescale or a zoological one, whether pondering the changes in coral islands or fancy breeds of pigeons, interprets found details he does not control. Austen, who's chosen to specialize in short-term rather than long-term case studies of human relationships, may anchor her novels in precise observation; but as a maker of fiction she devises the details she interprets.

Despite these differences in spheres of observation and control over data, a crucial part of Austen and Darwin's shared awareness that gradual changes are ever remaking the world is their understanding that this change happens on all scales and that the great and small changes are linked. What distinguishes Austen and Darwin from some other similarly sharp-eyed observers who, like them, have grasped the paradox that change is constant and that the natural world's constant is change is their remarkable ability to intuit the complex connections linking the minute and the vast, the microcosmic and the cosmic. From Austen's and Darwin's vantage points, a gathering of Box Hill picnickers can be a metonym for English society, or an entangled bank can be the natural world in miniature. In Austen's and Darwin's eras uniformitarianism and catastrophism were competing explanations for changes in the earth and its life forms. Uniformitarians argued that change came progressively and continually from ongoing processes, whereas catastrophists believed in periods of stasis punctuated by apocalyptic events such as Noah's Flood. Similarly, political, economic, geological, biological, and meteorological events—phenomena that might in the short view be called catastrophes, but that a longer view shows to have occurred over the ages in a uniformitarian way—change the fortunes of individuals and families, even in works as famously devoid of explicit political and historical content as Austen's novels are. Turning the question of scale in the other direction, small, repeated individual acts have great incremental consequences in both the evolving social world described by Austen and the ever-varying natural world observed by Darwin.

"Variation" is a word distinguished by its own variations of significance in different contexts and disciplines. The word conveys special, precise, and indeed *varying* meanings when it's used as a formal term in algebra, astronomy, ballet, biology, mathematics, music, or physics. But the common foundation of all meanings of variation is change and difference. Underlying each narrower sense of "variation" is a still-discernible vestige of the word's oldest usages: emphasis on discrepancy between two or more things generally alike, divergence of things that begin close together, departure from a type, alteration over time. In biology, "variation" indicates both a member of a distinctly recognizable subgroup (variety) of organisms within a species and the process by which those subgroups diverge from one another to form species. In evolutionary biology, categories are actually more dynamic than they look in a taxonomic classification: varieties are incipient species, and species are strongly marked varieties.

Biological variation was a lifelong interest to Darwin, from his beetle-collecting boyhood to his plant-breeding old age. He rang the changes on this concept throughout his career and especially in projects that resulted in the books that immediately preceded or followed *Origin of Species*. Darwin's preoccupation with variation is embodied most exhaustively in his still-definitive multi-volume taxonomy of barnacles and in *The Variation of Animals and Plants under Domestication*, but also in his sometimes charming and always groundbreaking botanical monographs on orchids, insectivorous plants, climbing plants, and different forms of flowers. Jane Austen, viewed a certain way, can also be said to take a biologist's view of variation. As we have already seen, like a breeder concerned to make the most of her stock's potential she habitually mates the male and female possessing the traits she's most inclined to admire and implicitly endorse in the matrimonial conclusion that ends all her books—though unlike those fanciers of pigeons or poultry who ruthlessly cull inferior specimens to improve the breed as a whole, she does not deny the potential pleasures of partnership and the possibility of reproduction to lesser individuals. But the Austen-as-breeder analogy is relatively superficial. In a deeper and more complex sense, variation might be said to work musically in her novels. Shifting from music to biology might seem like changing muses mid-invocation, but the two realms do overlap: some features of musical variation are amenable to scientific explanation. And in an essay that's suggestive rather than definitive, eclectic rather than rigorous, one might lay claim to using the varying word "variation" in various senses.

Musical variation involves modifying a strain or theme (usually first presented in its simplest form) by changing the pace, meter, melody, or harmony so that on repetition the theme becomes a new thing. Despite its novelty, the variation remains recognizable as a version of the original theme. Taken from music to literature, this sort of variation might describe a writer's practice of adapting and altering a motif, situation, pattern, or character type that recurs from work to work. For instance, Austen repackages the complacent, good-natured, dim-witted, indolent selfishness of *Mansfield Park*'s Lady Bertram in male widower form when, for her next novel, she imagines *Emma*'s Mr Woodhouse. She places female wit, physical vigor, charm, and mental quickness in three subtly varied contexts to produce in the cases of Elizabeth

Bennet, Mary Crawford, and Emma Woodhouse three varying personalities whose contingent interactions in their respective communities have three very different effects in three successively published novels. Each of the six completed Austen novels offers a distinctive variation of unexamined, self-contradicting loquacity that, depending on what other qualities combine with it, stamps its possessor as a bore, an ingénue, or a hypocrite. The variable lineage of self-refuting chatterers extends from John and Isabella Thorpe in *Northanger Abbey* to Nancy and Lucy Steele and Mrs Palmer in *Sense and Sensibility*, Mr Collins, Mrs Bennet, and Lydia in *Pride and Prejudice*, Mr Rushworth in *Mansfield Park* (he doesn't speak often, but everything he says is inane and extraneous), Mrs Elton, Harriet Smith, and Miss Bates in *Emma*, and Mary Musgrove in *Persuasion*. In a certain way *Persuasion*, where in the backstory a younger Anne Elliott yielded to over-prudent advice and rejected Wentworth and where Louisa Musgrove rashly hurls herself into his arms and is knocked unconscious on the Cobb as consequence of her rashness, can be seen as a less schematic variation on the duality central to *Sense and Sensibility*, Austen revisiting and varying the problem of how to strike a healthy balance between thinking and feeling. Most significantly, Austen's plots—all of which can be said to involve a single situation (the need of unmarried female protagonists to define and establish themselves through the ordering act of matrimony) but each of which poses fresh moral problems in distinctive circumstances—are clearly but subtly marked variations on a theme, or within a literary species.

An eye for variation is what, above all, allowed Darwin to make his first steps towards understanding the complex process he anthropomorphically called natural selection—and birds played key roles in his progressive enlightenment on this score. Observing the small Patagonian rhea later named *Rhea darwinii* first spurred Darwin to think seriously about the complex matters of variation and speciation as a challenge to divine design: why would God separately create two distinct forms of a South American bird so markedly similar to, and yet clearly distinct from, African ostriches?[1] As we've already seen, once the Galápagos mockingbirds and finches had been identified by the ornithological specialist John Gould they gave Darwin a sense of the mutability of living species. Domestic pigeons provided the most extensively documented example in *The Variation of Animals and Plants under Domestication* (1868), the hefty remnant of a still vaster projected work called *Natural Selection* in which Darwin intended to provide evidence backing up the evolutionary claims made in his earlier "abstract of an argument," *The Origin of Species*.

Variation is almost certainly Darwin's least read and cited book. It's also his longest and one that he, in keeping with his empirical bent, considered among his

---

1   First alerted to the existence of this rhea by the Patagonian gauchos, who referred to an extremely rare bird called "Avestruz Petise," Darwin examined his first specimen at Port Desire but unfortunately didn't realize the significance of his find until after the bird had already been cooked and eaten. Nonetheless, the head, neck, wings, bones, many feathers, and a large part of the skin remained for preservation and eventual identification back in England by Gould, who gave Darwin's name to this distinctive rhea that is smaller, with shorter legs, and feathered lower down than the more common *Rhea americanii*. See *CCD* I, 370–71, n. 4; *The Collected Papers of Charles Darwin*, ed. Paul H. Barrett (Chicago, IL: University of Chicago Press, 1977), I, 38–40.

most important. After completing *The Origin of Species*, Darwin had planned to mine the draft of *Natural Selection*—on which he'd labored between 1856 and 1858, when the arrival of Wallace's letter and evolutionary manuscript made him drop the long project and outline its argument in what became *Origin of Species*—for three books that would provide the data and citations not included in *Origin*. Darwin envisioned one book on the principle of natural selection, one on how organic beings vary in a state of nature, and one on variation under domestication. Only the last, a two-volume behemoth that ran to 899 pages in its first edition and was even longer in the much-revised second edition of 1875, actually came into being. *The Variation of Plants and Animals under Domestication* was the result of exhaustive observation and fact-gathering from far-flung correspondents, initially agriculturists who had responded to Darwin's 1839 questionnaire on the breeding of animals. It contains Darwin's speculations on heredity, which he recognized as the key to understanding how changes in plants and animals take place in nature and in agriculture alike—speculations that included his now disproved hypothesis of "pangenesis." But the bulk of the book is a richly detailed collection, assimilation, and interpretation of specific data on how plants and animals vary through intentional and unconscious choices made by human breeders. Darwin's own research on this topic centered on domestic pigeons, to which he devotes two full chapters.

The introduction to *Variation* usefully recapitulates the essential points of Darwin's evolutionary theory of varieties of plants or animals diverging into the more strongly distinguished groups called species as a result of incremental changes in a population over time. In nature, such changes preserve individual differences that prove advantageous in the perennial struggle for existence, but under domestication they embody the intentions of human breeders. Darwin usefully reflects on his choice of terms in the introduction. For him, "natural selection" means what Herbert Spencer called "survival of the fittest."[2] Darwin sees the term "natural selection" as having the disadvantage of seeming "to imply conscious choice," which he did not intend it to do—but he recognizes that "after a little familiarity" users of the new term will disregard its figurative features, as is the case when chemists say "elective affinity" or "astronomers speak of the attraction of gravity as ruling the movements of the planets" (*V* I, 6–7). What's good about the term "natural selection," claims Darwin, is that it linguistically connects linked activities, human production of domestic varieties through breeders' power of selection with the way varieties and species arise in the natural state. Further, says Darwin, it is important to realize that human breeding of domestic plants and animals is not really a matter of tampering with nature. "If organic beings had not possessed an inherent tendency to vary, man could have done nothing. He unintentionally exposes his animals and plants to various conditions of life, and variability supervenes, which he cannot even prevent or check" (*V* I, 2). Breeders may choose among varying individuals, sow the selected seeds or mate preferred animals, and again select seed stock or sire and dam from

---

2   Charles Darwin, *The Variation of Animals and Plants under Domestication*, ed. Harriet Ritvo (Baltimore, MD: Johns Hopkins, 1998), I, 6. Subsequent citations will refer to this reprint of the revised second edition of 1883 with citations appearing parenthetically and using the abbreviation *V*.

among the varying individuals of the next generation; but "the initial variation on which man works, and without which he can do nothing, is caused by slight changes in the conditions of life, which must often have occurred under nature" (*V* I, 3). In other words, human breeders are engaged in the same experimental project that nature, anthropomorphically speaking, has pursued from time immemorial. Thus breeders, whether working intentionally or unconsciously, methodically enhancing particular traits or following the vague dictates of preference, slowly but surely will produce marked changes in their stocks of plants and animals. But selection as exerted by domestic breeders cannot cause or prevent variability. Rather, breeders merely "can select, preserve, and accumulate" the variations afforded by nature. This relationship being as it is, Darwin recognized that understanding how varieties arise under domestication allows us also to perceive how they come about in nature and how they further diverge into species.

While he was still envisioning a big book on natural selection in the years before the arrival of Wallace's manuscript precipitated the rapid drafting of *Origin of Species*, Darwin had settled on domestic pigeons as good potential subjects for the observation and experimentation necessary for supporting though not proving his conjectures on the transmutation of life forms. The embryological and neonatal similarities among domestic breeds that on reaching adulthood developed physical features that gave them radically divergent appearances would, he hoped, provide an analogue to the workings of nature. On March 19, 1855 Darwin described his project to and enlisted aid from his second cousin and former Cambridge companion in beetle-hunting William Darwin Fox, who had continued to pursue his own naturalist interests in Delamere, Cheshire, while practicing the vocation Darwin had once considered, that of country clergyman:

> As you have a noah's ark, I do not doubt that you have pigeons; (how I wish by any chance they were fantails!) Now what I want to know is, at what age nestling pigeons have their tail feathers sufficiently developed to be counted. I do not think I ever even saw a young pigeon. I am hard at work on my notes, collating & comparing them, in order in some 2 or 3 years to write a book with all the facts & arguments, which I can collect, *for & versus* the immutability of species.—I want to get the young of our domestic breeds to see how young, & to what degree, the differences appear. I must either breed myself (which is no amusement, but a horrid bore to me) the pigeons or buy them young, & before I go to a seller whom I have heard of from Yarrell, I am really anxious to know something about their development not to expose my excessive ignorance, & therefore be excessively liable to be cheated & gulled—With respect to the *one* point of the tail feathers, it is, of course, in relation to the wonderful development of tail feathers in the adult fantail. (*CCD* V, 288)

Darwin's request to Fox reveals several important sides of his distinctive mindset in pursuing the big project on species. Although Darwin had been wrestling with transmutation in his thoughts and notebooks since 1837, when John Gould had informed him that his four Galápagos mockingbirds were not mere varieties but distinct species related to similar mainland birds, he continued patiently and cautiously to amass supporting evidence. In 1855 he still saw himself some years away from laying out the pros and cons of species mutability or immutability and connecting the facts with his hypothesis in book form. Besides showing Darwin's habitual patience and caution, the letter to Fox displays his remarkable ability to think on both minute and vast scales and to intuit how the two scales are connected: Darwin's mind sees how tail feathers might play a role in supporting a world-changing idea.

The letter to Fox contains mixed signals of engagement with pigeons and resigned acceptance of the "horrid bore" of breeding them. But as had been the case with barnacles, which had only just ceased to preoccupy him at the end of 1854, Darwin serendipitously found himself much more involved in the arcane world of domestic pigeons and their fanciers than he had initially imagined he would be. Pigeons never became quite as exclusive an obsession as barnacles had been; for even as he bred, observed, experimented with, and collected anecdotes about pigeons, he was gathering similar data about agricultural plants, poultry, horses, pigs, cattle, bulldogs, greyhounds—any life forms modified by the selective eye and will of human breeders. Still, by October 14, 1855 Darwin could proudly feature a catalogue of his pigeon acquisitions in a postscript to a letter written to Fox:

> I have now
> >   Fan-tails
> >   Pouters
> >   Runts
> >   !!! Jacobins !!!
> >   Barbs
> >   Dragons
> >   Swallows
> >   !!! Almond Tumblers !!!
> >   !!! (*CCD* V, 482)

The pigeons had become a "decided amusement" to Darwin and a "delight" to his daughter Henrietta (*CCD* V, 337); and though he had to kill the birds to dissect and skeletonize them for his meticulous measurements, he lamented the necessity to Fox with a depth of feeling that the levity of hyperbole fails to conceal: "I am getting quite 'a chamber of horrors'. I appreciate your kindness [in providing already killed specimens] even more than before; for I have done the black deed & murdered an angelic little Fan-tail & Pouter at 10 days old.—" (*CCD* V, 386). Darwin aimed for the most humane means of killing the birds needed for his measurements and observations by experimenting with chloroform, ether, and finally cyanide of potassium—but kill them he did. Still, though Darwin's quest for knowledge may have trumped his tenderheartedness in his pigeon research, the emotional cost of working with animals may have influenced his turn in later life to experimental work focused on plants and finally to his observing the behavior more than the morphology of earthworms.

Pigeons, however beloved they became, were worth sacrifice because they proved a particularly rich source of scientific information. Recognizing that they would do so required the maverick quality that was a key part of Darwin's empirical brilliance. Fanciers knew first-hand that domestic stocks could be manipulated over generations to shape plants or animals as the will of the breeder dictated.

But natural philosophers were not inclined to look to the farmyard and the poultry coop for evidence supporting theories about creation. Least of all, perhaps, would a gentlemanly naturalist interest himself in pigeon-breeding, a hobby within the reach of working-class urbanites interested in animals but lacking acreage to support prize quadrapeds or woodlands to be stocked with gamebirds. Though Darwin, contrary to his own expectations and to class convention, came to relish breeding pigeons, his first-hand experience with this avian equivalent to Austen's "3 or 4 families in a country neighborhood" didn't satisfy him. His pigeon work also entailed gathering facts from far-flung correspondents, a particular stalwart being Edward Blyth, curator of the Asiatic Society of Bengal—and venturing beyond rural Kent to the readership of the *Poultry Chronicle* and the London world of "odd little men" who bred pigeons. Darwin gathered data at the Freemason's Tavern where the comparatively genteel pigeon fanciers of the Philoperisteron met. But he also visited the gin palaces where the more plebian enthusiasts of the Borough and City clubs convened and where, he reported to the American geologist and zoologist James Dwight Dana, "I am hand & glove with ... all sorts of odd specimens of the Human species, who fancy Pigeons" (*CCD* VI, 236). It is easy, impressed by Darwin's thorough and meticulous approach to domestic pigeons, to forget that he was equally keen-eyed and careful in studying their human fanciers of the past and present, at home and abroad. Darwin remained the squire of Down House on his fact-finding missions to the metropolis; but though he retained his gentlemanly detachment he was able to recognize the merits of pigeon enthusiasts from other classes, sincerely value their contributions to his study, and perceive that one can't understand domestic breeds without understanding breeders. Darwin respected the expertise of some of the London fanciers much as George Knightley of Donwell Abbey might appreciate the talents, practical training, and commitment of William Larkins or Robert Martin—and Darwin's work with pigeons was the richer for his broadmindedness.

Darwin begins Chapter V of *Variation*, the first of the two devoted to pigeons, with a straightforward indication of several reasons why he chose them for particular attention and of what the precise nature of his study's "particular care" has involved:

> I have been led to study domestic pigeons with particular care, because the evidence that all the domestic races are descended from one known source is far clearer than with any other anciently domesticated animal. Secondly, because many treatises in several languages, some of them old, have been written on the pigeon, so that we are enabled to trace the history of several breeds. And lastly, because, from causes which we can partly understand, the amount of variation has been extraordinarily great. The details will often be tediously minute; but no one who really wants to understand the progress of change in domestic animals, and especially no one who has kept pigeons and has marked the great difference between the breeds and the trueness with which most of them propagate their kind, will doubt that this minuteness is worth while. Notwithstanding the clear evidence that all the breeds are the descendants of a single species, I could not persuade myself until some years had passed that the whole amount of difference between them, had arisen since man first domesticated the wild rock-pigeon.

I have kept alive all the most distinct breeds, which I could procure in England or from the Continent; and have prepared skeletons of all. I have received skins from Persia, and a large number from India and other quarters of the world. Since my admission into two of the London pigeon-clubs, I have received the kindest assistance from many of the most eminent amateurs. (*V* I, 137–8)

A footnote to the first sentence of the second paragraph acknowledges by name those who have assisted him from abroad: the Hon. C. Murray, Mr Keith Abbott, Sir Walter Elliot (who unlike his two "t" namesake in *Persuasion* was willing to risk his British complexion in Madras), Mr Blyth, Sir James Brooke, Mr Swinhoe, and Dr Daniell. A comparable footnote to the second sentence thanks Messrs. B. P. Brent, William Tegetmeier (a suburban London editor and naturalist who might, in the studies of pigeons and barnyard fowl, vie with Fox for the title of Darwin's most faithful domestic collaborator), Bult, Wicking, Haynes, Corker, Harrison Weir, J. M. Eaton, Baker, Evans, and J. Baily, jun., for their help on the homefront.

The worthwhile minuteness then begins. Darwin enumerates and describes the several breeds of domestic pigeons, which he arranges into four groups containing a total of eleven races. Group I consists exclusively of Pouter pigeons. Group II contains Carriers, Runts, and Barbs, all manifestly allied to one another, with the first two distinguished "by such insensible gradations that an arbitrary line has to be drawn between them" (*V* I, 145). Darwin terms the heterogeneous Group III, where the common ground is a beak shorter than the ancestral rock-pigeon's and little development of the skin around the eyes, "artificial." Into this category he puts Fantails, Turbits, Owls, Tumblers, Indian Frill-backs, and Jacobins. Group IV contains Trumpeters and several subraces only minimally distinguished from their wild ancestor: Laughers, Common Frill-backs, Nuns, Spots, and Swallows. These domestic pigeons vary remarkably, not just from breed to breed but from individual to individual, with regard to many structural features, some correlated to one another. Darwin considered weight and size; measurements and shapes of skulls, lower jaws, and vertebrae; the correlated variation of tongues and beaks; eyelids, nostrils, and the wattled surrounding skin that differs widely from variety to variety; the number of tail feathers or wing feathers and length of wing; the color and nature of plumage and down; feet, calls, and other specific features.

Darwin noted two especially intriguing oddities in the matter of how particular characteristics vary in domestic pigeons. In each domestic breed, the distinctive traits for which fanciers value that breed are highly variable. These include the number and direction of tail feathers, carriage, and trembling of fantails, the degree and nature of crop inflation in pouters, the length, narrowness, and curvature of the beak and the amount of wattle in carriers, the manner of tumbling in tumblers, and so on. Darwin also observed that in many domestic breeds of pigeon, the distinguishing features become ever more distinctive with increasing age and are more pronounced (or exclusively present) in males, though in the ancestral rock-pigeon there are no conspicuous differences between the sexes at any age.

Relying solely on empirical observation, it would seem impossible to conclude that the short-faced, tiny-beaked tumblers with their bizarre trajectory and the beaky, wattled, carbunculated carriers, the fantails with roughly three times as many tail feathers as ordinarily found in the genus *Columba* and the pouters with their balloon-like crops and their upright posture all descend from a common ancestor. These dramatically different kinds of domestic pigeon have been established and have bred truly for centuries. Indeed, as Darwin observes of the humans devoted to pigeons, "Fanciers almost unanimously believe that the different races are descended from several wild stocks, whereas most naturalists believe that all are descended from the *Columba livia* or rock pigeon" (*V* I, 189). How to show that the fanciers were wrong and the naturalists right on this score? If Darwin had possessed our current understanding of genetics and had had access to DNA testing, proof would have been easy. In his time and with his information, Darwin had bolstered his meticulous observations by drawing upon logic, history, and human psychology—the last because he had shrewdly realized that to understand artificial selection it would be necessary to consider the breeder as well as the bred.

Darwin's sixth chapter, the second of the two on pigeons, begins with the matter of parentage. The domestic breeds of pigeon are all social birds, and all of them nest on the ground rather than building or habitually roosting in trees. Domestic animals are known to retain atavistic traits long after the need for them has vanished—the domestic ass displaying a dislike of crossing streams that's a vestige of its wild desert ancestry, or a house dog's turning round and round on a carpet before lying down to sleep as if shaping a bed in tall grass—and thus it seems evident that all pigeons must descend from a social, ground-dwelling ancestor or ancestors. Darwin enumerates the five or six wild pigeons with these habits, all variants of the rock pigeon *Columba livia* living in different parts of the world. This bird has a vast range on continents and islands, from Norway to the Mediterranean, Africa to India and Japan. Rock-pigeons can be easily domesticated. Texts from around the world record the presence of semi-domesticated dovecote pigeons in ancient civilizations. The still-extant dovecote pigeons, which take shelter in human constructions but don't require special care or feeding, can both interbreed with wild rock-pigeons and revert to surviving in the wild. Dovecote pigeons show greater variation in color, markings, and size of beak or body than do wild rock-pigeons, but they display nothing close to the variability of the established domestic breeds So how might the domestic pigeon's variations so dramatic that they could be called monstrosities—the fantail's fan, the pouter's pout, the tumbler's tumble—come about?

The answer for Darwin lies in the difference between existence in nature and life in the pigeon-coop—and also, though Darwin doesn't spell this out, between life in the dovecote and life in the pigeon coop. At some point, certain humans grew interested in doing more than just building shelters that would guarantee them a ready supply of pigeons; they wanted to "improve" the stock of birds available to them. The variations valued by fanciers don't necessarily operate to the advantage of the bird and sometimes do quite the contrary; instead, they please the human eye and judgment. Natural selection would not perpetuate the remarkable adaptations that have come to characterize some strains of domestic pigeons. Nor would human breeders, at first, deliberately set out to create these dramatic features. But Darwin points out that fanciers devote close attention to their stock and use great care in choosing which specimens to mate and which to cull. Unconscious preferences might, over time, shape one fancier's stock of birds according to one peculiar taste, another fancier's stock in quite another direction. Over generations, the variable features in one strain could be made ever more distinct, until at some point in its history the breed's distinguishing qualities would be explicitly described and consciously valued.

Besides observing the behavior of his fellow fanciers, Darwin consulted breeders' records going back many years—artificial selection's analogues to natural selection's fossil record—to confirm such selective behaviors. The fancier's habitual mindset likewise explains why, apart from some cases such as the almost indistinguishable gradations between the most strongly marked carriers and the most distinct runts, intermediate forms don't generally exist. Fanciers typically favor extremes so that, for example, some admire the longest bills and some the shortest but few prefer bills of intermediate lengths. Accordingly, over time fanciers constantly trying to breed new stock from what they consider their best birds will cull offspring resembling parental stock that they see as inferior with regard to the valued traits. The intermediate forms from generations back that, if still extant, could be seen as links between two widely divergent stocks would thus be likely to vanish. But that's not to say that the ancestral qualities themselves are gone. One of Darwin's strongest supports for the case of common ancestry is that all domestic breeds of pigeon are fertile when crossbred and that after successive generations of crossbreeding all combinations will produce some throwbacks displaying a few or all of the traits characteristic of the rock-pigeon, with its slate-blue color, double black wing bars, and white-edged, black-banded tail. Although Darwin did not have Mendelian genetics to explain the cause of this phenomenon, he rightly interpreted its significance and recognized it as confirming evidence that tumblers and carriers, barbs and pouters, all descend from a common wild ancestor.

The attentive, even exhaustive specificity of Darwin's research on domestic breeds of plants and animals, epitomized in the chapters on pigeons but evident throughout *Variation*, was something of a refuge for a man whose heart loathed controversy but whose head knew that eventually he'd have to provoke it by going public with his transformationist theory. Although the need to abstract and publish his evolutionary ideas in *Origin* sidetracked and partly pre-empted the envisioned big book on natural selection, once *Origin* had made its way into the hands of readers, reviewers, and disputants, Darwin again needed the solace he always found in empirical minutiae. He turned to the field of botany and preoccupied himself, among other things, with insectivorous plants such as sundews and with the various structures promoting self- or cross-pollination in flowers, both topics that eventually resulted in books. But his most compelling botanic interest, and the one that most immediately resulted in a monograph, was orchids. Darwin's part of rural Kent was home to many species of indigenous orchids he could observe on excursions or at home, and to obtain information on exotic orchids and specimens of these delicate plants he resorted to strategies perfected in his pigeon and barnacle work. He approached readers of the *Gardeners Chronicle* for information (his letter seeking information on "Fertilisation of Orchids by Insect Agency" appeared June 9, 1860) and cultivated a network of fellow orchid specialists and enthusiasts. Among others, Darwin relied on his friend and staunch ally J. D. Hooker of the Royal Botanical Gardens at Kew for access to the empire-spanning collection of exotics and to Hooker's far-flung botanical contacts in British colonies, on Alexander Moore for native orchids, on the society hostess Lady Dorothy Nevill for rare exotics, and on his Downe neighbor George Turnbull of the Rookery for use of a hothouse and frequent aid from his skilled, knowledgeable gardener John Horwood.[3]

Always aware of potential connections between small things and great, Darwin understood that his fascination with the wonderful specificities of orchids would by no means distract him from major long-term goals. He shrewdly suspected, months before *On the Contrivances by Which British and Foreign Orchids are Fertilised by Insects, and on the Good Effects of Intercrossing* was published in May 1862, that the monograph would serve his larger purposes. Darwin's introduction to the monograph explicitly makes the point to readers: "In my volume 'On the Origin of Species' I have given only general reasons for my belief that it is apparently a universal law of nature that organic beings require an occasional cross with another individual; or, which is almost the same thing, that no hermaphrodite fertilizes itself for a perpetuity of generations. Having been blamed for propounding this doctrine without giving ample facts, for which I had not, in that work, sufficient space, I wish to show that I have not spoken without having gone into details."[4]

The monograph comes close to the exhaustive meticulousness of Darwin's multi-volume taxonomy of barnacles as it anatomizes different species and genera of the family *Orchidaceae*—sexually peculiar plants that are, as Janet Browne points out, a botanical equivalent to barnacles, "anatomically hermaphroditic but functionally male and female" (*CDPP* 182). It also pays close attention to symbiotic matters, the wonderful details of how insect pollinators interact with the exquisite and sometimes bizarre reproductive structures of orchids in much the same way that Darwin's pigeon work takes account of the interplay between the fancier and the breed fancied. It offers occasional glimpses of Darwin waxing almost as lyrical about the reproductive anatomy of plants as his paternal grandfather did in *Loves of the Plants*. Unlike Erasmus, however, Charles Darwin grounded his flights of imagination in close observation and in anatomizing so scrupulously effective that the techniques he developed are still practiced by botanical taxonomists. Concluding his remarks on the genus *Orphrys*, Darwin speculates in playful language that simultaneously expresses his fancy and distances him from it: "A poet might imagine, that whilst the pollinia are borne from flower to flower through the air, adhering to a moth's body, they voluntarily and eagerly place themselves, in each case, in that exact position in which alone they can hope to gain their wish and perpetuate their race" (*FO* 92).

But Darwin's relentless empirical attention to just what happens as insects visit and pollinate orchids is a more characteristic feature of the monograph. The following paragraph, an account of a Darwinian half-hour spent first watching, then capturing and scrutinizing three humble-bees of two kinds visiting a patch

---

3 Janet Browne, *Charles Darwin: The Power of Place* (Princeton, NJ: Princeton University Press, 2002), 171–2, 512, nn. 7, 8, 9. Subsequent citations will be parenthetical and will use the abbreviation *CDPP*.

4 Charles Darwin, *Fertilization of Orchids by Insects* (Stanfordville, NY: Earl M. Coleman, 1979), 1–2. Subsequent citations will refer to this text, a reprint of the 1862 John Murray first edition, and will appear parenthetically with the abbreviation *FO*.

of *Spiranthes autumnalis* near Torquay, proves typical in its way of describing the smallest features and circumstances, then establishing their significance in a larger natural pattern:

> The bees always alighted at the bottom of the spike, and, crawling spirally up it, sucked one flower after the other. I believe humble-bees generally act thus when visiting a dense spike of flowers, as it is most convenient for them; in the same manner as a woodpecker always climbs up a tree in search of insects. This seems a most insignificant observation; but see the result. In the early morning, when the bee starts on her rounds, let us suppose that she alighted on the summit of the spike; she would surely extract the pollinia from the uppermost and last opened flowers; but when visiting the next succeeding flower, of which the labellum in all probability would not as yet have moved from the column (for this is slowly and very gradually effected), the pollen-masses would often be brushed off her proboscis and be wasted. But nature suffers no such waste. The bee goes first to the lowest flower, and, crawling spirally up the spike, effects nothing on the first spike which she visits till she reaches the upper flowers, then she withdraws the pollinia: she soon flies to another plant, and, alighting on the lowest and oldest flower, into which there will be a wide passage from the greater reflexion of the labellum, the pollinia will strike the protuberant stigma: if the stigma of the lowest flower has already been fully fertilised, little or no pollen will be left on its dried surface; but on the next succeeding flower, of which the stigma is viscid, large sheets of pollen will be left. Then as soon as the bee arrives near the summit of the spike she will again withdraw fresh pollinia, will fly to the lower flowers on another plant, and fertilise them; and thus, as she goes her rounds and adds to her store of honey, she will continually fertilise fresh flowers and perpetuate the race of our autumnal Spiranthes, which will yield honey to future generations of bees. (*FO* 127–9)

According to Francis Darwin in a footnote to his father's *Life and Letters*, Darwin's American ally and friend Asa Gray, who offered strong support for Darwin's evolutionary theory while still retaining his belief in divine creation, "pointed out that if the Orchid-book (with a few trifling omissions) had appeared before the 'Origin', the author would have been canonised rather than anathematised by the natural theologians."[5] Perhaps Gray is right that the meticulous observations would, if unallied with Darwin's conclusion-drawing, have edified old-school readers in the Design camp; but the passages that would have to be omitted to make possible this effect are anything but "trifling." Darwin both understands the stakes of his specific anatomizings and observations and insists that his reader understand them. Concluding his exhaustive discussion of the homologies of orchid flowers, Darwin asks,

> Can we, in truth, feel satisfied by saying that each Orchid was created, exactly as we now see it, on a certain "ideal type;" that the Omnipotent Creator, having fixed on one plan for the whole Order, did not please to depart from this plan; that He, therefore, made the same organ to perform diverse functions—often of trifling importance compared with their proper function—converted other organs into mere purposeless rudiments, and arranged all as if they had to stand separate, and then made them cohere? Is it not a more simple and intelligible view that all Orchids owe what they have in common to

---

[5] Francis Darwin (ed.), *Life and Letters of Charles Darwin, Including an Autobiographical Chapter* (London: John Murray, 1888), III, 274, n.

descent from some monocotyledonous plant, which, like so many other plants of the same division, possessed fifteen organs, arranged alternately three within three in five whorls; and that the now wonderfully changed structure of the flower is due to a long course of slow modification,—each modification having been preserved which was useful to each plant, during the incessant changes to which the organic and the inorganic world has been exposed? (*FO* 306–7)

These questions, full of detail supporting one of the two opposed potential answers and positioned at the end of a summarizing section, are clearly rhetorical. Darwin the casemaker skillfully leads his readers, who are at once witnesses able to observe the minute workings of the natural world as he does and jurors judging his larger argument about the origins of these marvelous particularities.

Orchids had become trendy among botanical enthusiasts in the 1860s much as tulips had fueled a more general mania in the seventeenth century (*CDPP* 173), so Darwin's study adds to the knowledge contemporary naturalists were accumulating about the overarching homologies uniting diverse orchid species. Each species within each genus of the family displays different features of what, built up incrementally and theoretically through homology, can be seen as the general pattern or ideal type to which all individuals conform in some ways but from which they vary in others. The importance of homology, says Darwin, "rests on its giving us the key-note of possible difference in plan within any group" (*FO* 287). The study of homology reveals subtly graduated relationships that might otherwise have passed unnoticed, explains apparent monstrosities, leads to the detection of hidden parts, and shows the significance of rudimentary features. Homology thus serves as a link between the minute and the vast. Concluding his section treating the particular homologies of orchid flowers, Darwin generalizes on a point of broad significance to natural science, addressing the reader in his own voice:

> The more I study nature, the more I become impressed with ever-increasing force with the conclusion, that the contrivances and beautiful adaptations slowly acquired through each part occasionally varying in a slight degree but in many ways, with the preservation or natural selection of those variations which are beneficial to the organism under the complex and ever-varying conditions of life, transcend in an incomparable degree the contrivances and adaptations which the most fertile imagination of the most imaginative man could suggest with unlimited time at his disposal.
>
> The use of each trifling detail of structure is far from a barren search to those who believe in natural selection. (*FO* 351–2)

Darwin, the apostle of natural selection, had the practical patience and the visionary spirit to embark on such far-from-barren searches wherever they led. Resorting to the first person pronoun, this passage offers, in the rhetorical form of a profession of faith rather than a pronouncement of truth, the same expansive yet minutely particular view of life so eloquently expressed in the "entangled bank" conclusion of *Origin*. Here as there, variation in its various senses is crucial. The word "variation" is thrice invoked in two of its variant forms, but the concept of variation is pervasive. As this credo reveals, progressive development of ideas through the continual accumulation and interpretation of evidence is the defining character of Darwin's mind. That mind sees change as the uniform condition of existence, difference from one another in diverse ways as the state of being for individual organisms, and incremental evolution over generations as the practical consequence for populations.

Biological variation occurs on a timescale that allows human observers to detect its occurrences. Although the gradual evolution of today's genera and species that diverged from common ancestors can be studied only through the imperfect fossil record, we are able to watch over years and decades as a fancier's prize-winning pigeons or the Grant research team's finches on Daphne Major vary, and in a matter of months we can see generations of viruses permute.[6] But variation—and here I am using the word in its loose sense of "change"—also happens on other scales and at other rates.

Variation in the earth itself occurs too slowly and on too large a scale to be easily perceived and empirically understood. In both Austen's and Darwin's eras uniformitarianism and catastrophism were actively competing to explain changes in the earth and its populations of life forms. The Judaeo-Christian viewpoint largely uncontested in the West up until the Enlightenment derived from Genesis and argued that God had created the universe as a whole and the earth in particular a relatively short time ago—in 1654 Bishop James Ussher had specified the date as October 23, 4004 BCE—and that the earth had been populated by life forms individually designed by God. On such a young earth, radical change would have to be the result of catastrophes—destructive acts as sweeping and anomalous as Noah's biblical flood. The French systematist and comparative anatomist Georges Cuvier believed in periods of stasis punctuated by apocalyptic events, with this pattern of successive catastrophes and re-creations explaining why the fossil record contains life forms no longer found on earth and never seen alive by previous generations of humans.[7] In 1788 James Hutton, the Scotsman sometimes called the father of geology, countered the catastrophic model in his book *Uniformitarianism*. He argued that the earth's surface had been shaped, and was still being shaped, progressively and continuously by ongoing natural forces: volcanic activity, earthquake, erosion due to the actions of rain, wind, ice, sedimentation, subsidence, and meteor and asteroid strikes. Seen from the limited vantage point of an individual person's lifetime

---

6   Peter and Rosemary Grant publish results from their decades of research on the Galápagos finch population of Daphne Major in such works as *Ecology and Evolution of Darwin's Finches* (Princeton, NJ: Princeton University Press, 1986; repr. 1999); *Evolutionary Dynamics of a Natural Population: The Large Cactus Finch of the Galápagos* (Chicago, IL: University of Chicago Press, 1989); "Phenotypic and genetic effects of hybridization in Darwin's finches," *Evolution* XVIII (1994), 297–316; "Predicting microevolutionary responses to directional selection on heritable variation," *Evolution* XLIX (1995), 241–51; and "The Calmodular pathway and evolution of elongated beak morphology in Darwin's finches," *Nature* CDXLII (August 2006), 563–7.

7   Cuvier's preferred term for the wholesale extinctions he envisioned was "revolutions" rather than "catastrophes." Although he did not believe in the evolution of life forms, Cuvier's study of fossils first convinced naturalists of the reality of their past extinctions. His important statement of the theory of successive creations and extinctions, *Discours sur les revolutions du globe*, introduced his fossil quadraped study, *Recherches sur les ossemens fossiles des quadrapèdes* (1812), and was first translated into English in 1813.

passed in a particular place, many such natural events might seem "catastrophes"; but in the long, panoramic sweep of geological history such local changes would be recognizable as the ordinary workings of change on a vast scale. Hutton's advocacy of uniformitarianism proved to be somewhat ahead of its time. The uniformitarian argument gained widespread credence only some decades later when, after a series of 1820s religious and geological debates on Noah's flood in light of the dinosaur fossils that had been excavated in the previous decade, Charles Lyell gave it a somewhat different emphasis in his earthshaking three-volume *Principles of Geology: Being an Attempt to Explain the Former Changes of the Earth's Surface, with Reference to Causes Now in Operation*. Lyell's first volume was published in 1830, in time for the young Darwin to include it as part of the small library he took aboard the *Beagle*. Lyell's assumptions that natural law was a constant and thus that the earth-shaping forces at work in 1830 were the same ones that had always been in effect meant that small, cumulative changes could over time produce dramatic effects. But for continuous incremental variations to produce vast changes, they would have to occur over a vast expanse of time, which would make the world much older than Bishop Ussher had calculated. In arguing the uniformitarian case, Lyell stuck to the realm of the physical sciences and remained silent on the development of life forms; but it doesn't take an outrageous leap to extend his assumptions about natural law to the biological sciences and to play out the evolutionary argument that then follows.

Darwin's travels, notably the *Beagle*'s surveying mission along the coast of South America and its subsequent passage to the islands of the Pacific, allowed him to see at first hand specific evidence tending to confirm Lyell's uniformitarian claims. Darwin's earliest published books on variation at work in the world center on geological or geographical change: popularly known by their subtitles, *The Structure and Distribution of Coral Reefs* (1842), *Geological Observations on the Volcanic Islands Visited during the Voyage of HMS* Beagle, *Together with Some Brief Notices of the Geology of Australia and the Cape of Good Hope* (1844), and *Geological Observations on South America* (1846) were written as a three-volume report of Darwin's geological observations from the five-year voyage, *The Geology of the Voyage of HMS* Beagle. Darwin's Lyell-primed mind was able to seize on serendipitously encountered evidence during his travels and to read back from effect to cause. Closely examining Peruvian rockfaces, Darwin understood from patterns of stratification, shell deposits, sedimentation, and disruption that formerly submerged layers now stood hundreds or thousands of feet above water—an elevation that we now understand to be the consequence of the Pacific tectonic plate being forced against and underneath the South American continent. The presence of fossil remains of human art in strata at San Lorenzo proved to him that the process of uplift, sudden or gradual, had persisted into times when humans inhabited South America; and elevations from the earthquake of 1835 showed him that it continued to occur.[8] Though Darwin characteristically moved from observation to theory, from effect to

---

8 Charles Darwin, *The Works of Charles Darwin*, Vol. IX, eds Paul H. Barrett and R. B. Freeman, *The Geology of the Voyage of HMS* Beagle*: Vol. III—Geological Observations on South America* (New York: New York University Press, 1986), 555–66. Barrett and Freeman's edition reprints the 1846 first edition.

suspected cause, his well-furnished, serendipitous mind was also able to reverse the pattern. He speculated on the evolution of coral islands in a thought-experiment that preceded his first on-the-spot observation of a coral reef by some months. Darwin turned out to be correct in his hypothesis that, given the fact that reef-building corals can flourish at only very limited ocean depths, subsidence explains the differing forms reefs can take. Subsidence of land-masses converts coast-hugging fringing reefs to barrier reefs at a greater distance offshore; and "barrier-reefs into atolls, as soon as the last pinnacle of land sinks beneath the surface of the sea."[9]

Do Jane Austen's novels show signs of being written from what might be called a uniformitarian perspective rather than a catastrophic one? I believe they do, though any answer to this question must remain subjective or conjectural and must use the term "uniformitarian" loosely. Austen does not, in either her fiction or her letters, weigh in as a catastrophist or a uniformitarian on matters of geology or biology. She doesn't address the age and nature of the earth, the origins of its life forms, or other allied issues that were controversial among naturalists of her time. She does, however, acknowledge the sway constant change holds in the human world—both in her fiction and in correspondence, as for instance when she muses on mutability in an April 11, 1805 letter from Bath to Cassandra, who was staying at Ibthorpe with the Lloyds: "This morning we have been to see Miss Chamberlayne look hot on horseback.—Seven years & four months ago we went to the same Ridinghouse to see Miss Lefroy's performance!—What a different set we are now moving in! But seven years I suppose are enough to change every pore of one's skin, & every feeling of one's mind" (*JAL* 99). The generalization's non-dogmatic assertion of change, a supposition shadowed by its potential if unvoiced rebuttal, may rise like a ghost out of Jane Austen's romantic past. Just as Miss Chamberlayne on horseback evokes Miss Lefroy similarly engaged on the same spot over seven years back, Miss Lefroy's recollected name and younger image may conjure up the specter of her cousin Tom Lefroy, who flirted with Austen over Christmas in 1795, may well have loved and been loved by her, and in any case was sent packing by Miss Lefroy's pragmatic parents, Tom's uncle and aunt, who knew that these two young people, however promising and congenial, could not at that time afford a mutual attachment. This epistolary acknowledgment of human variability may or may not be the seed from which eventually grew the idea of Anne Elliot, another lover thwarted by the older voice of worldly practicality, an unmarried woman who after eight years manifests an altered skin but an unaltered mind. But the passage certainly shows Austen's mental kinship with Enlightenment empiricists of Hutton's uniformitarian stripe—and with the associational psychologists who, like uniformitarian naturalists, sought constant laws that would explain the mysteries of how one idea led to another in the human mind.[10]

---

9   Charles Darwin, *Works of Charles Darwin*, Vol. VII, eds Paul H. Barrett and R. B. Freeman, *The Geology of the Voyage of HMS* Beagle*: Vol I—The Structure and Distribution of Coral Reefs* (New York: New York University Press, 1987), VII, 122. Barrett and Freeman reprint the 1889 third edition.

10 For Jane Austen's affinity with Enlightenment psychology's ways of understanding personal character and its evolution, see Peter Knox-Shaw's *Jane Austen and the Enlightenment*

The English novel as practiced by Austen's contemporaries and her predecessors was at its most extensive a dynastic affair allowing readers to follow the fortunes of a family through several generations—only later would novels offer the thousands of years chronicled by Edward Rutherfurd's locale-centered *Sarum* or *London* or the even vaster time span of scientific romances such as H. G. Wells's *The Time Machine*. Austen's own preferred pattern is narrowly focused even for an early nineteenth-century British novel of manners. She may concisely sketch a backstory in the opening paragraphs, pages, or chapters of a novel—the birth and 16-year evolution into embryo heroine of Catherine Morland in *Northanger Abbey*, the marital history of Mr Dashwood in *Sense and Sensibility*, and, most overtly genealogical, the beginnings of *Mansfield Park* and *Persuasion*. As we have seen, *Mansfield Park* begins by detailing the marriage choices and divergent socioeconomic fortunes of three sisters in a two-page paragraph, then provides a somewhat lengthier backstory for the next generation, the remainder of the first chapter being devoted to Fanny Price's Portsmouth childhood, the second chapter to her first six years under the Bertrams' roof. *Persuasion* begins with the hand-emended Elliot genealogy in Sir Walter's copy of the baronetage and contains a quick summation of Anne's and Wentworth's aborted courtship eight years back. But Jane Austen's novels are never truly dynastic. She invariably centers on a limited number of months at a crucial point in the life of her heroine. Given this restricted scope, it would not be possible for Austen's novels to show geological variation or biological variation at work. Even the gradual, multi-generational improvement of Charlotte Lucas Collins's poultry stock would be a process too leisurely to fit into the 13- or 14-month chronology of *Pride and Prejudice*.[11]

Working within her novels' limited timeframes, it would not be possible for Austen actually to show an individual's morality, sensibility, mind, or personality developing along uniformitarian rather than catastrophic lines. But I think we can intuit that her view of human nature was essentially uniformitarian. It seems to me that she saw her characters' qualities—personalities diverging in sibling ecosystems, values incrementally defined by years of particular human interactions and behavioral choices, innate talents sometimes nurtured and sometimes neglected—as evolving within specific, limited parameters, intensifying or fading but never drastically changing to something truly new.[12]

(Cambridge: Cambridge University Press, 2004). Sarah Emsley's *Jane Austen's Philosophy of the Virtues* (New York: Palgrave Macmillan, 2005), with an emphasis on self-knowledge, balance, and practical application of the virtues in daily life, shows Austen's philosophical and religious foundations for the developmental view of character I am calling "uniformitarian."

11 R. W. Chapman's edition contains an appended "Chronology of *Pride and Prejudice*," a small masterpiece of empirical research and interpretation that determines in great detail the dates of many of *Pride and Prejudice*'s events. According to Chapman the temporal sequence starts with Mr Collins's letter proposing his Longbourn visit (Tuesday October 18, 1811) and extends to the double wedding of Jane and Elizabeth to Bingley and Darcy, a ceremony that has to be before the Christmas holidays of 1812, seeing that the Gardiners were to spend the holidays at Pemberley with the newlywed Darcys (*PP* 400–408).

12 In this regard, Austen strongly resembles two of the later novelists sometimes seen as her successors, George Eliot and Henry James.

This claim might at first seem unlikely. Given the formal features of the novel of manners as Austen practices it, catastrophe seems to shape events. Sudden, sharp shocks thwart or forward the novels' marriage plots. John Thorpe's misinforming General Tilney about Catherine Morland's station and prospects first garners her an invitation to Northanger, then gets her sent home in disgrace—and that unseemly departure spurs Henry Tilney to propose marriage to Catherine—and the incredibly well-timed union between Elinor Tilney and her unnamed *deus ex machina* viscount mollifies General Tilney enough to acquiesce in the match. Elizabeth Bennet reads, considers, re-reads, and reconsiders Darcy's letter of self-justification, then says, mortified, "'Until now I never knew myself'"; and the letter changes her sense of things just as profoundly as her earlier indignant refusal of his tactless marriage offer changes Darcy's perceptions and conduct. Marianne Dashwood's putrid fever and Colonel Brandon's faithful friendship as she recovers turn her from a scorner of his flannel waistcoats to the lady of his manor. Maria Bertram Rushworth's elopement with Henry Crawford sends out shock waves that shatter three relationships: her own marriage, Henry's growing rapport with Fanny Price, and Edmund Bertram's infatuation with Mary Crawford. Louisa Musgrove's knock on the head at Lyme Regis, a fortunate fall in the long run, shapes the marital plot of *Persuasion* in multiple ways to be considered in detail later on. Quickest of all such seeming catastrophes, Emma Woodhouse hears Harriet Smith's sanely sensible avowal of attachment to Mr Knightley and her surprisingly convincing reasons for thinking he might reciprocate her feelings, then understands her own life's proper direction absolutely and instantly: "It darted through her, with the speed of an arrow, that Mr Knightley must marry no one but herself!" (*E* 408).

These personal catastrophes—or epiphanies, crises, turning points, call them what you will—may seem to be remarkable and momentous events in the timescale of an Austen novel. Seen in a wider frame, whether that of an individual character's entire life as lived so far, or the broader context of life among the Regency gentry in the southern and midland counties of England, or the still broader one of human existence more generally understood, they offer evidence for a uniformitarian view of personal change and development. The characters involved in these seeming catastrophes respond in ways consistent with the traits, values, habits, and temperaments they've partly inherited and partly developed through interaction in their different microenvironments. In Austenworld, hearts or minds change in ways they've given previous evidence of being able to change. Darcy, however proud, has been brought up to cultivate virtue and honor; Elizabeth, however prejudiced, has hitherto shown herself clear-sighted, intelligent, honest, and able to think about other points of view than her own; Emma, however often she's played the imaginist, has shown a capacity for self-knowledge in scenes prior to being pierced first by Harriet's confession and then by love's arrow. Because these characters vary only within what most readers would deem a plausible range of behaviors, the very fact that they alter is supporting evidence for a uniformitarian principle at work on the human scale. Adam Smith claimed that "Man is perpetually changing every particle of his body; and every thought of his mind is in continual flux and sensation." The Byronic narrator of *Don Juan* deems nature and human nature analogously mutable: "The heart is like the sky a part of heaven,/ And changes day and night too like the sky."[13] Intellectual kin to Smith, Byron, and Darwin in her empirical understanding of variation, Austen sees and presents a human world of constant change, a realm where what stays the same is the fact that hearts, minds, bodies, and their natural surroundings are ever varying.

The blush is one particular form of variation involving complex interactions of the human mind and body that both presents itself in an easily visible form and exists in a temporal frame that allows for direct, relatively uncomplicated scrutiny.[14] Not surprisingly, both Austen and Darwin studied it. But the fact that blushing lends itself to observation doesn't mean that it is easy to explain. In fact, the phenomenon still remains enigmatic. Described in the very simplest possible terms, blushing involves a temporary increase in the superficial blood volume of the face and, to much lesser extents, other body parts. Engorged with superficial blood, the face appears redder than normal in fair-skinned individuals, whereas darker complexions intensify without changing color. To this day there is no completely satisfactory explanation of why people blush or how the response started, and the neurophysiological reason for the temporarily increased blood volume remains largely a mystery, although some partial explanations have been proposed.

Though the phenomenon of blushing is only imperfectly understood, it has received comparatively little scientific study in the decades since Darwin—perhaps partly because blushing, unlike many other biomedical phenomena, involves no threats to life or health. Also, in an age of professional subspecialization, it is impossible to single out a discipline where blushing would most profitably be studied. The somatic nature of the response might seem to make it the province of neurophysiology; but its emotional aspects fall under the realm of psychology, particularly ethology. The social features of blushing and its connection with culturally conditioned norms of behavior give anthropology or sociology a claim on the subject. Even linguistics might be seen as necessary for clarifying the phenomenon. As Darwin knew when he cast about for terms and came up with "natural selection," words are things; and our understandings of natural phenomena are at least partly constrained by the limits of terminology.

We can at least begin etymologically. The *New Online OED* states that "blush" is a word obscure in its origins, and that it is uncertain in what order its series of different meanings evolved. But the word seems related to a series of Old Norse and Low German words pointing back to a stem *blusi from a verbal root meaning "burn, glow, be red." The French synonym *"rougir"* conveys the same sense of redness. Yet though not all human complexions display blushing's superficial sign of reddening, all humans share the socially triggered neurophysiological response that constitutes the blush. How far do the specific features of the word define, and thus partly create,

---

13 Adam Smith, "History of the Ancient Logics and Metaphysics," in *Essays on Philosophical Subjects*, eds W. P. D. Wightman and J. C. Bryce (Oxford: Clarendon, 1980), 121; Lord Byron, *Don Juan*, ed. Jerome J. McGann (Oxford: Clarendon Press, 1986), 156, canto II, stanza 214.

14 I say "relatively uncomplicated" because the interactive emotional and somatic process of blushing often means that a scrutinized blush will increase on account of the scrutiny.

the phenomenon it names? Which is unstable or culturally limited, the word "blush" or the phenomenon?

These neuro-physio-psycho-socio-linguistic issues that are so perplexing once articulated did not complicate Jane Austen's empirically based representations of blushing. For her, as for many other English novelists of her generation and the preceding one, the blush, along with the tear, served as one of the chief bodily signs of sensibility. It was a somatic way of registering the emotional sympathy that, for the moral philosopher Lord Shaftesbury and other eighteenth-century proponents of sensibility, is the true source of personal virtue. In placing high value on emotional responsiveness, affirming a wisdom of the heart, and asserting human benevolence, the advocates of sensibility opposed philosophical rationalists such as Thomas Hobbes, who advocated the rule of reason and argued that human virtue rises out of self-interest rather than sympathy. The cult of sensibility could easily be carried to excess in life and especially in mediocre fiction, as the young Jane Austen clearly recognized.

One of her earliest portrayals of sensibility's varying facial color constitutes Chapter 9 of the juvenile "novel in twelve chapters" called *The Beautifull Cassandra*, written some time between 1787 and 1790. Here, the title character and another young woman whom she has just encountered at the corner of Bloomsbury Square run the gamut of bodily response to emotion, as Austen mockingly follows the rubrics of sensibility without supplying any stated or implied motivations or contexts: "Cassandra started & Maria seemed surprised; they trembled, blushed, turned pale & passed each other in a mutual silence."[15] This faithfully observed but totally unexplained incident of sensibility is as hilariously excessive in one way as, in the opposite way, is the over-analyzed sensibility that causes the death of Sophia in the longer juvenile piece *Love and Freindship* [sic], a miniature novel in letters. The letter-writer Laura and her friend Sophia have been wallowing in emotion following what Laura describes as the "horrid Spectacle" of "Two Gentlemen most elegantly attired but weltering in their blood," (*MW* 99), the elegant but bloody gentlemen being their husbands Edward and Augustus. Laura reports that "Sophia shreiked & fainted on the Ground—I screamed and instantly ran mad" (*MW* 99)—but neither woman pays much attention to the suffering husbands. After this exhausting bout of sensibility that demonstrates emotional narcissism rather than Shaftesburian sympathetic benevolence, Sophia perishes, though not before offering deathbed wisdom to Laura. In the insistently rationalist rhetoric of Sophia's dying words, careful and complex grammatical subordination, precise qualifiers, and even a quantifier ("not one quarter so pernicious") ironically undercut the extravagant sensibility her conduct has affirmed:

> "... take warning from my unhappy End & avoid the imprudent conduct which has occasioned it ... beware of fainting-fits.. Though at the time they may be refreshing & Agreable yet beleive me they will in the end, if too often repeated & at improper seasons,

---

15 Jane Austen, *Minor Works*, ed. R. W. Chapman (London and New York: Oxford University Press, 1959, repr. with further revisions by B. C. Southam, 1972), 46. Subsequent quotations from Austen's juvenile pieces and from her fragment *Sanditon* will refer to this edition and appear parenthetically with the abbreviation *MW*.

prove destructive to your constitution ... Beware of swoons Dear Laura ... A frenzy fit is not one quarter so pernicious; it is an exercise to the Body & if not too violent, is I dare say conducive to Health in its consequences—Run mad as often as you chuse; but do not faint." (*MW* 102)

"Run mad as often as you chuse" indeed: after she matured into an adult novelist, Jane Austen's portrayals of sensibility sanely steered a moderate and realistic course between the two deliberately laughable extremes portrayed above. When women or men change color in her novels, the phenomenon is neither inexplicable nor over-analyzed. Austen grounds the varying complexions of her characters both in empirical observation and in literary conventions drawn from the novel of sensibility, a genre she read and cherished as well as mocked. In Austenworld, characters' complexions turn pale or pink for reasons readers can believe or intuit. As in life, a somatic variation might have an overdetermined number of possible causes, some emotional, some physical, with the relative proportions of each potential cause also being impossible to pin down with certainty. A face might go pale from anger or fear (Darcy's complexion becomes pale with anger on his hearing a high-colored Elizabeth stoutly reject his proposal—*PP* 190) or illness (Marianne Dashwood has "lost her colour" and become thin after Willoughby publicly humiliates her—*SS* 227). A face might redden from irritation, social confusion, embarrassment, exertion, heat, wind, the blood rush that comes from bending over, or a combination of two or more factors, this last perhaps being the case in an amusingly described moment from *Emma* that features Knightley, accused by Emma of admiring Jane Fairfax, "hard at work upon the lower button of his thick leather gaiters, and either the exertion of getting them together, or some other cause, brought the colour into his face, as he answered" (*E* 287). Austen's study of her characters' varying complexions takes account of all these phenomena; but the variation of facial color most interesting to her is what's explicitly called, or implicitly discernible as, the blush.[16]

There are many instances in Austen's fiction when rising color is probably or possibly a blush even though it's not explicitly called one, whether because the narrator is simply choosing a different word or because she is allowing attendant details to show that the heightened color is what we'd call a blush. More rarely, the narrator strategically leaves the precise details of a color-varying moment mysterious. Perhaps the most memorable such instance is when Darcy, who's accompanying Bingley, and Wickham, in company with Denny, Jane, Elizabeth, Kitty, and Lydia, unexpectedly encounter one another on the Meryton streets. The narrator characterizes this meeting as cryptically as Cassandra's and Maria's was

---

16 For other perspectives on blushing in Austen's novels, see John Wiltshire's excellent *Jane Austen and the Body* (Cambridge: Cambridge University Press, 1992), with a particular emphasis on blushing in *Mansfield Park* in the second chapter, "'Eloquent Blood': The coming out of Fanny Price," 62–108 but especially 77–83, and Mary Ann O'Farrell's *Telling Complexions: The Nineteenth-Century English Novel and the Blush* (Durham, NC and London: Duke University Press, 1997). O'Farrell theorizes the literary blush from a critical vantage point blending Foucauldian and Barthesian principles on pp. 1–11 and then devotes her book's first two chapters to blushing in Austen, with *Pride and Prejudice* and *Persuasion* as the respective main texts of Chapters 1 and 2.

presented in *The Beautifull Cassandra*: "Both changed color, one looked white, the other red" (*PP* 73). Darcy and Wickham's awkward encounter unfolds under the gaze of Elizabeth—and at the very moment when in the narrator's interesting and precise formulation Darcy, displaying one of the bodily signs of self-consciousness, "was beginning to determine not to fix his eyes on" her. The two gentlemen acknowledge one another with a touch of the hat, Darcy's gesture being minimal. The reader, seeing the event through the lens of Elizabeth's consciousness, wonders with her, "What could be the meaning of it?—It was impossible to imagine; it was impossible not to long to know" (*PP* 73). True enough, but the narrator's selective description of the scene leaves the reader more puzzled than the heroine has to be. Elizabeth at least knows which man turned which color. We're left wondering: did Wickham go white and Darcy red? Or was it the reverse? Being denied the precise somatic details, we are obliged to remain even less able than Elizabeth to interpret the emotional mystery of this encounter between two men whose characters are as yet very imperfectly known by her or us. One man—which?—was apparently pale with anger, fear, or sickening disgust (and which of these alternatives?). The other (again, which?) was red with embarrassment, shame, or rage—and only the first two of these three feelings motivate what we call a blush. But the strategically withholding narrator has prevented our getting beyond this point to make even conjectural sense of a mystery that Elizabeth, who unlike us at least possesses first-hand evidence of Darcy's and Wickham's body language, also wishes in vain to decipher.

Sometimes Austen's narrators and characters speak of a blush without one actually occurring. Occasionally this is a matter of a hypothetical blush—for example, "Anne hoped she had outlived the age of blushing" (*P* 49). But more often the word is being used figuratively. At its simplest, such figurative language is poetic diction, as in the anthropomorphism of Thomas Gray's "'many a flower is born to blush unseen,'" quoted in both *Northanger Abbey* and *Emma* (*NA* 15, *E* 282). More often, the term's figurative use involves a more complicated relationship of word and meaning, such as Sir Thomas Bertram's "'I blush for you, Tom,'" and "I blush for the expedient which I am driven on" (*MP* 23)—utterances giving concrete form to the abstract sentiment "I am ashamed of you and of the corrective actions your follies compel me to implement" and also, especially in the first case, implying, "You, Tom, should blush with shame and guilt." Similarly, when Emma supposes Elton attached to Harriet and declares, "'This, Harriet, is an alliance which can never raise a blush in either of us,'" (*E* 74) she means, "Neither of us could be ashamed of your making this connection; and in fact, for different reasons, we can both be proud of it"—although as circumstances turn out both Emma and Harriet will have ample if different reasons and actual occasions to blush over Emma's wrongheaded perception. In much the same way, Emma's gazing over the Donwell Abbey estate and thinking that, notwithstanding John Knightley's small faults of temper, Isabella "had given them neither men nor names nor places that could raise a blush" (*E* 358) means, "Isabella made a match we Woodhouses can be proud of."

Sometimes the act of naming a blush can replace or supplement the bodily experiencing of it. Emma is almost certainly not blushing when, as Harriet bids farewell to the pencil stub and court-plaister remnant that have been her precious relics of Elton, she recalls her own misguidedly manipulative ways of throwing Harriet and Elton together and hyperbolically declares, "'I deserve to be under a continual blush all the rest of my life'" (*E* 339). This utterance's clearheaded blend of moral recognition and verbal precision strongly suggests that Emma is not physically in thrall to the mind-muddling phenomenon she names. In contrast, when the narrator of *Northanger Abbey* reports of Henry Tilney, "He blushed for the narrow-minded counsel which he was obliged to expose" (*NA* 247), the young man's face may or may not actually be showing the proxy shame he feels for his father the General's mean-spirited rudeness to Catherine: the speeded-up detachment of the novel's conclusion doesn't let the reader stand close enough to discern. Much the same might be said of Elinor Dashwood's vicarious shame for the brazen Lucy Steele, who has just confessed her secret engagement to Edward Ferrars and disingenuously avowed having such a high opinion of Elinor's judgment that on a word from Elinor she'd release Edward from his promise. In these circumstances, "Elinor blushed for the insincerity of Edward's future wife" (*SS* 150) could indicate either a figurative blush or an actual one. Whether or not Elinor's face has reddened, the word "blushed" chiefly serves to mark the contrast between a guiltless girl with the moral sensitivity necessary for this kind of response and a guilty girl too coarse or amoral to display the somatic sign of shame that the conventions of sensibility would assign her in this circumstance. And after a reader has completed the novel, the sentence can take on yet another meaning, a retrospectively ironical one that's truer to the book's final outcome than to the psychological immediacies of the situation: Elinor, who as events turn out is actually "Edward's future wife," might be imagined to blush for her own "insincerity" in bottling up what she feels at Lucy's revelation rather than giving voice to her heartfelt pain.

Most of the time, however, what Austen's narrators call a blush or "colour" indicates the bodily response of a blush. Austen's preferred term for the phenomenon varies from novel to novel, though all six show some internal variation as to whether a blush is called a blush or something else. Austen favors "colour" over "blush" in *Sense and Sensibility* and, to a lesser extent, in *Pride and Prejudice*. *Northanger Abbey* and *Mansfield Park* contain somewhat evener distributions of the terms, with "blush" predominating. In *Emma* and *Persuasion* "blush" is the overwhelmingly preferred word, though it is interesting to notice that *Persuasion* contains relatively little actual blushing in spite of its marked emphasis on the loss and return of Anne Elliot's "bloom" and on the different actual or hypothetical ways complexions can be marred (by illness, sadness, time spent outdoors and especially at sea) or mended (by fresh maritime breezes, a man's approving gaze, regular application of Gowland's lotion). Men and women alike are capable of blushing in Austenworld, but apart from self-proclaimed and generally figurative blushes like Sir Thomas Bertram's discussed above, the grammatical variants of the word "blush" describe only women's responses. Austen's embarrassed or self-conscious male characters "colour," as her females also do some of the time.

This gender-based verbal distinction is evident in both *Pride and Prejudice* and *Sense and Sensibility*, the two Austen novels where varying facial color is most evenly distributed between female and male characters. In the former novel, Darcy repeatedly "colours," as Elizabeth also does. But he is never said to "blush," though she and Jane often do so. *Sense and Sensibility*, as befits both its title and its plot heavy with secrets and reticence, exhibits Austen's broadest distribution of self-conscious color-changing among her characters. Elinor and Marianne Dashwood, each possessing both moral sense and emotional sensibility (if in varying proportions), go pale or redden throughout the novel—mostly in situations involving either self-conscious withholding of information to respect confidences or equally self-conscious awareness of what other people are thinking of them. For instance, Marianne colors at Mrs Jennings's nosy pronouncement that she knows what Willoughby and Marianne have been up to (*SS* 67), when she tells Elinor that "most people" hunt but means that her beloved Willoughby does (*SS* 92), and when after her illness she assures her mother and Elinor that she sees Willoughby's situation as they would wish her to, the blush in this last situation signifying her awareness that her previous conduct has not prepared them to expect such mature sense from her (*SS* 349). Both Marianne and Mrs Dashwood change color when, aware that an approaching male visitor is Edward Ferrars rather than the expected Colonel Brandon, they imagine Elinor's perturbation, blush sympathetically, look at her, and whisper (*SS* 358). Elinor, in spite of being considered by many critics the embodiment of cool sense rather than warm sensibility, blushes as readily and as sympathetically as Marianne: for instance, when Colonel Brandon (little imagining the pain his generosity is causing) asks her to be his agent in offering the Delaford parish living to Edward Ferrars (*SS* 281) and after a tipsy, confessional Willoughby himself blushes as he becomes conscious that Elinor must be aware of his seduction and abandonment of Eliza (*SS* 322).

All three male suitors, each of whom has something to conceal, change color in the course of the novel. Colonel Brandon goes either red or white (more likely the latter) on receiving a letter disclosing his ward Eliza's whereabouts on the morning of the abortive Whitwell excursion (*SS* 63). Willoughby, a libertine who's not indifferent to the opinions of others, reddens and then reddens still further with guilt when forced to admit himself unable to take future advantage of Mrs Dashwood's innocently offered hospitality (*SS* 76)—and later, as just mentioned, he colors at the awareness that Elinor knows him for Eliza's seducer. Edward Ferrars, though guilty of nothing worse than a clandestine engagement, colors when Marianne notices his ring containing the plait of Lucy's hair and thereby obliges him to lie that it's a lock of his sister's (*SS* 98). "White with agitation" when he enters the Dashwood parlor in the sensibility-soaked group scene that follows his brother's elopement with Lucy Steele, Edward "coloured and stammered out an unintelligible reply" to Mrs Dashwood's gracious gesture of offering him her hand and wishing him joy—and then again when Elinor inquires first after "Mrs Ferrars," then after "Mrs *Edward* Ferrars" (*SS* 359–60).

With rare exceptions such as Maria Bertram blushing "in spite of herself" when first admitting that she'll take the part of the unwed mother in *Lovers' Vows* (*MP* 139)—a sign that though bold she's not shameless—most of the female blushes appearing in Austen's novels are ascribed to her heroines: Elinor and Marianne Dashwood, Elizabeth and Jane Bennet, Catherine Morland, Fanny Price, Emma Woodhouse, Anne Elliot. It is interesting to wonder but difficult to determine whether this state of affairs mainly follows literary convention or principally reflects Austen's empirical understanding of blushing as manifested by people she observed.

Did Austen believe young, marriageable women blush more than other people do? Perhaps in her experience this was the case, given that girls out in society and on the marriage market were probably much more intently scrutinized and thus more self-consciously aware of being observed than other categories of people would be (children, old people, married couples, women who had "gone into caps" and taken themselves out of the competition for husbands). But do morally, emotionally, and intellectually superior marriageable women—such as those relative paragons on whom Austen's novels focus and who do most of the feminine blushing reported in those narratives—blush more than other young women do? In the early nineteenth century, it was a commonplace among lay observers and medical experts alike that the blush was a God-given gauge of morality and sensibility, a reliable index more finely calibrated in some beings than in others, with the complexions of young, fair-skinned (thus probably Northern European and leisure-class) women being the most exquisitely tuned and sensitive such instruments. But art is a matter of selections and conventions, elisions and metonyms; so it might also be the case that Austen's heroines display the most frequent blushes simply because she's more involved in reporting the specifics of their moral and emotional lives than those of subordinate characters—or, even more simply, because she's following the customary forms of the novel of sensibility. In Austenworld, it's obvious that marriageable maidens in general, and leading ladies in particular, blush more often than other characters do. But why this should be so is a slippery matter. Perhaps looking at such blushes in their simplest and their most intricate contexts will help us grasp something of the truth.

Blushing in *Northanger Abbey*, which of all the three novels Austen composed in the 1790s was published in the least revised form, is almost exclusively done by Catherine Morland, who's the most unpolished and ingenuous girl to be accorded the status of main Austen heroine. Apart from Henry Tilney's blush for his father and one highly uncharacteristic blush parenthetically attributed to Isabella Tilney (likely to be counterfeiting the feignable features of embarrassment such as downturned eyes and confusion without the actual coloring, because she certainly isn't manifesting the emotional or psychological symptoms), the numerous usages of "blush," "blushed," and "blushing" are all assigned to Catherine. Catherine, a temporary wallflower on account of being stood up by John Thorpe, blushes at the sudden reappearance of Henry Tilney in the Bath assembly-rooms (*NA* 53). Noticed by General Tilney, she blushes with confusion and fear that there may be "something wrong in her appearance" (*NA* 80). She blushes with mortification when, calling at the Tilneys' and fully aware that they're in, she is told by the manservant that they aren't (*NA* 91). Henry Tilney's complimenting Catherine's superiority in "good nature" stimulates a blush (*NA* 133), as does her proxy shame for Isabella Thorpe when he points out that a man never minds other men admiring the woman he loves unless that woman's conduct makes such admiration a torment to him (*NA* 151).

Once the scene shifts to Northanger Abbey, Catherine blushes at each successive blow to her naïve, literature-derived assumptions that life in an abbey follows the conventions of gothic novels. Catherine blushes when Elinor Tilney catches her in the act of opening a curious chest and finding a mere counterpane inside (*NA* 165) and blushes unobserved when, the morning after a nearly sleepless night's fretting over a mysterious manuscript she's found locked in a chinoiserie cabinet, she realizes that the document is only a laundry list and that she herself had initially locked the cabinet's door (*NA* 173). Catherine self-consciously blushes at what she conceives as her own artful subtlety when, imagining that General Tilney has been a stereotypical gothic wife-abuser, she tries to amass supporting evidence by asking Henry Tilney if his mother's portrait hangs in his father's room. Later, as she further tests her hypothesis of the General's guilt, she blushes deeply when Henry Tilney appears up a back staircase just as she's finished sleuthing in the late Mrs Tilney's bedroom (*NA* 194)—and shortly afterward, caught in her suspicions by Henry, she feels that she "must ever blush" to recall her ungrounded suspicions of the General (*NA* 200). Having recovered her equanimity and regained her sense of Henry's goodwill, Catherine must color yet again a few pages later when he reads the last sentence of her brother James's dejected report of Isabella's having jilted him—"'Dearest Catherine, beware how you give your heart" (*NA* 209)—and no sooner has her head cleared than she's condemned to "blushing again that she had blushed before" (*NA* 205). Finally, packed off home in disgrace by the irate General, a sadder and wiser Catherine contemplates rhetorical strategies for avoiding a hypothetical future blush as she faces the epistolary and mannerly challenges of composing a letter to Elinor that will do its author credit should Henry chance to read it (*NA* 235).

In contrast to *Northanger Abbey*, *Emma*, another novel of surveillance but arguably Austen's densest and subtlest construction, distributes blushes more widely among the cast of characters. The reason lies in the nature of observation as differently practiced by the two books' respective narrators and characters. In *Northanger Abbey*, the ingénue protagonist Catherine is the one person trying to make sense of things and the one consciousness of pre-eminent interest to the narrator. In *Emma*, what Henry Tilney claims for England as a whole in *Northanger Abbey* is shown to be true in Highbury: "every man [and woman] is surrounded by a neighborhood of voluntary spies" (*NA* 198). With many complicated if prosaic mysteries being investigated by a squad of Highbury busybodies and with the narrator broadly concerned with the interacting minds of the community as well as the development of the title character's moral sense and sensibility, the varieties of self-consciousness are much more widely distributed.

Even if marriageable young women are the main blushers in *Emma* as in the rest of Austenworld, the spinster Miss Bates is given a "slight blush" of self-consciousness to show that she's capable of understanding Emma's Box Hill insult and being pained by it. The day afterward Mr Knightley, whose possible blush of self-consciousness at hearing Emma say that he's been paired with Jane Fairfax in Highbury gossip has already been cited, has another face-reddening episode. Mature and poised though he may in general be, Knightley displays a sympathetic response to Emma's blush when her doting father's "unjust praise" of Emma's habitual attentiveness to the Bateses reveals what a contrite yet reticent Emma hasn't told him, that she's paid a prompt visit of penance. Knightley's answering glow is but one feature of the body language closely observed by the narrator as the two characters' sensibilities, sometimes so well attuned and sometimes so much at odds, regain accord and then move past it to something momentarily more profound:

Emma's colour was heightened by this unjust praise; and with a smile, and shake of the head, which spoke much, she looked at Mr Knightley.—It seemed as if there were an instantaneous impression in her favour, as if his eyes received the truth from her's, and all that had passed of good in her feelings were at once caught and honoured.—He looked at her with a glow of regard. She was warmly gratified—and in another moment still more so, by a little movement of more than common friendliness on his part.—He took her hand;—whether she had not herself made the first motion, she could not say—she might, perhaps, have rather offered it—but he took her hand, pressed it, and certainly was on the point of carrying it to his lips—when, from some fancy or other, he suddenly let it go.... (*E* 385–6)

The narrator, here as in many other cases filtering precise but conjectural impressions through Emma's consciousness, notices the expression of males' emotions almost as attentively as she does females'—partly, it may be, because the novel's concerned with the collective emotional life of the community and partly because Emma herself, so often deployed as a central consciousness, professes a keen curiosity about many of her neighbors and their emotional lives but also is more deeply interested in Knightley's state of feelings than she admits or knows. Furthermore, uniquely among the Austen novels, repeated blushes are the prerogative of all the unmarried young women, principal and secondary alike. Emma's contemporary Augusta Elton, whether because she's shameless, rouged, or married, never blushes in the course of *Emma*. But Emma, Jane Fairfax, and Harriet Smith do often—if for distinctly different reasons.

Harriet Smith, a 17-year-old who like Catherine Morland has little experience of adult society at the novel's start is, again like Catherine, an ingenuous blusher, a girl not yet accustomed to being object of the amorous or critical gaze. She blushes with the self-consciousness that comes from speaking of one's beloved when informing Emma how Mrs Martin had told her there couldn't be a better son than Robert (*E* 28)—blushes confused when Emma repeats Elton's praise of her (*E* 34)—blushes and smiles when sitting for her portrait, a situation engineered by Emma to allow Elton to gaze with impunity (*E* 46)—blushes at the overload of conflicting feelings as Emma manipulates her into confessing regard for Elton and turning down Robert Martin's offer of marriage (*E* 53). A somewhat more experienced Harriet blushes when recollecting and reliving her now-passed Eltonian infatuation, as she's about to destroy her relics of this crush, the cherished pencil stub and court-plaister—and yet again when Emma reveals that she's mistaken Harriet's unvoiced admiration for Knightley for a silent crush on Frank Churchill. An even wiser Harriet is sure to be blushing in the concluding phase of the novel as she recalls perambulating the Donwell limewalk with Knightley and receiving from him ingratiating attentions she then thought were on his own behalf but now understands rose from his desire to understand if she still cherished feelings for Robert Martin (*E* 408).

Jane Fairfax, 20 years old and a habituée of sophisticated circles in London and at Weymouth, blushes as much as Harriet does, but for very different reasons. Jane is a naturally reserved person, probably inclined by temperament to be sensitive to the spotlight—and, due to her pale complexion, cursed to endure a conspicuous bodily display of her sensitivity. She's also come into the community bearing the guilty burden of a clandestine engagement. She must endure being an object of prurient curiosity to Emma, who's clever enough to detect an air of mystery surrounding Jane but not able to understand it accurately, particularly given that her misunderstanding is rather cruelly encouraged as a red herring by Jane's secret fiancé Frank Churchill. And if all these reasons weren't enough to bring many blushes to the cheeks of Jane Fairfax, she's tied to a laughable social albatross, her tirelessly talkative aunt Hetty Bates.

Jane's blushes, rising as they do out of motivations more mature and complex than any a Catherine Morland or a Harriet Smith might experience, are sometimes pleasant for her, sometimes painful, and often a mixture of the two sensations. Jane colours deeply when thinking of Weymouth (*E* 242) and, similarly, blushes with consciousness of both present delight and recollected pleasure that cannot be publicly acknowledged when the mystery of her pianoforté's provenance comes up or when Frank Churchill brings her music to play on it (*E* 220, 243). These blushes no doubt deepen due to Jane's awareness of prying eyes, those of Emma and the other Highburians. Coming hard on the heels of Mrs Elton's presumptuous attempts to manage the picking-up of Jane's correspondence at the post office, John Knightley's profession of hope that Jane will one day, like him, care less about letters because she'll be settled amidst a domestic circle of those she loves best is the immediate stimulus for an over-determined and self-perpetuating blush that blends embarrassment at being the center of public attention, unvoiced outrage at Mrs Elton's patronizing, gratitude for John Knightley's benevolence, and mingled guilt and pleasure at the secret engagement—a blush that then makes her blush again for having been observed blushing (*E* 293–4). In one of the novel's most intricately layered episodes of surveillance, the narrator watches George Knightley watch Jane Fairfax, Frank Churchill, and Emma playing the anagram game. First Knightley sees the word "blunder," offered by Frank to Jane and enunciated by Harriet after everyone's moved on to other things, rouse "a blush on Jane's cheek which gave it a meaning not otherwise ostensible" (*E* 348). Later, Knightley quickly deciphers the scrambled word "Dixon" put before Jane by Frank, who even as he does so makes laughing league with Emma. Knightley then turns to the enigma of Jane's response, which he watches with an empiricist's precision:

> Jane Fairfax's perception seemed to accompany his; her comprehension was certainly more equal to the covert meaning, the superior intelligence, of those five letters so arranged. She was evidently displeased; looked up, and seeing herself watched, blushed more deeply than he had ever perceived her, and saying only "I did not know that proper names were allowed," pushed away the letters with even an angry spirit, and looked resolved to be engaged by no other word that could be offered. Her face was averted from those who had made the attack, and turned towards her aunt. (*E* 348–9)

Jane's episodes of blushing after her engagement has been made public and her relations with Emma are at last truly amiable rather than courteously inimical become simpler and more enjoyable, the emotional prerogative of a happy girl conscious of her self-preoccupation with pleasant memories and prospects and aware that social circumstances prevent her from speaking her heart and mind freely to a contemporary she at last can recognize as a sympathetic friend (*E* 459).

As for the novel's marriageable protagonist: Emma herself is, like Jane, a highly intelligent 20-year-old adult rather than an ingenuous recent schoolgirl of 17 like

Harriet. Her natural complexion is rosy with robust health rather than pale like the delicate Jane's; and unlike Jane she's secure, outgoing, and complacent rather than insecure, reserved, and guilt-plagued. These contingent differences might make us expect that Emma would exhibit less visible blushing than Jane rather than more. Nonetheless, in the course of the novel bearing her name Emma blushes about as often as do Jane and Harriet combined. The commonsensical explanation—that because she's the protagonist readers see Emma more often and more deeply than they do the other characters—is true but not sufficient. Emma also blushes as much as she does because she has ample motivation to do so. The novel, as a number of critics have pointed out, is about the mortification of Emma Woodhouse[17]—or, to put it another way, the sometimes painfully self-conscious growth of a sensibility that's quick-witted, good-hearted, and sound-principled but overconfident and often self-deluded.

A few of Emma's blushes rise out of ordinary self-consciousness, for instance when, laughing and blushing, she promises Mr Knightley that she'll use his Christian name at least once: in the parish church at their wedding (*E* 463)—or when, teased by Frank Churchill as they establish amicable mutual understanding towards the end of the novel, she colors with a blend of guilt and amusement at his mocking invocation of the name "Dixon" and then again with embarrassed pleasure when Frank asks if Mr Knightley is well (*E* 477). But before her heart's been pierced and her hand won by Knightley, most of Emma's blushes are the outward and visible signs of character-building. These variations of complexion display her sudden inner enlightenment and enlightenment's attendant consequence, the retrospective awareness of how different she and her actions may have seemed to others than she has hitherto imagined.[18]

As has been the case in some of the passages already quoted, Emma often laughs aloud or silently as she blushes—even at moments of character-changing enlightenment. Having sworn off making matches for Harriet and then caught herself immediately starting to weigh the eligibility of William Coxe, Emma stops to "blush and laugh" at her sudden relapse (*E* 137). The capacity for detachment that allows laughter suggests that the embarrassed confusion attendant on blushing has only a limited power over Emma, an essentially self-confident and resilient person.

---

17 See, for instance, Mark Schorer, "The Humiliation of Emma Woodhouse," in *Jane Austen: A Collection of Critical Essays*, ed. Ian Watt (Englewood Cliffs, NJ: Prentice-Hall, 1963), 98–111.

18 Emma's self-conscious "blush of sensibility" for having to keep Harriet's crush on Knightley a secret, however much he may prefer "the beauty of truth and sincerity in all our dealings with each other" (*E* 446), is a post-engagement blush of delight or of half-amused secrecy. But her earlier blushes are more potentially painful. See, for instance, where after being subjected to Elton's inebriated proposal, a mortified Emma "blushed to think" how much better John Knightley had understood the calculating clergyman's character than she had (*E* 135). Or again when, hearing of the Churchill—Fairfax engagement from Mrs Weston, she asks if the Campbells and Dixons were aware of the young couple's mutual understanding and, thinking of her own misguided and too-vocal suspicions, she cannot "speak the name of Dixon without a little blush" (*E* 399). Or shortly afterward when, alone at Hartfield and meditating on the engagement, she regrets not having been closer to Jane and "blushed for the envious feelings which had certainly been, in some measure, the cause" (*E* 421).

A struggle for this detachment or its appearance is a key feature of her response to Mr Knightley's correction after the Box Hill insult: scolded by her mentor, Emma "recollected, blushed, was sorry, but tried to laugh it off" (*E* 374). Here, the blush and the laugh contradict one another, outward bodily signs of the battle of sensibility Emma's moral intelligence and stubborn self-esteem are waging in her heart and mind. Emma here knows and accepts that Knightley is right; but she remains proud and rational enough to defend herself with two counterattacks, first, "'Nay, how could I help saying what I did?—Nobody could have helped it. It was not so very bad. I dare say she did not understand me,'" and later, "' … you must allow, that what is good and what is ridiculous are most unfortunately blended in her'" (*E* 374–5). When Knightley definitively refutes such self-justifications with his reminder of the inequalities of station that make Emma's wit irresponsible in this case, she can no longer take refuge in rationalization and laughter. The concurrent somatic symptoms of Emma's blush, "her face averted, and her tongue motionless" now straightforwardly proclaim her guilty embarrassment. Nevertheless Knightley, wise but not infallible, misreads her "anger against herself, mortification, and deep concern" (*E* 375–6) as sullen resentment directed at him—and Emma, shamefaced with self-reproach for the wanton cruelty of her insult and with frustration that Knightley has left thinking her impenitent, now gives way to an expression of sensibility extraordinary to her: silent tears.

Darwin studies the blush in *The Expression of the Emotions in Man and Animals* (1872). He had first empirically observed emotions and their somatic expressions many years earlier. Having become interested in human emotions in the 1830s, he had begun in 1839 to keep a notebook recording his firstborn child William's developing expressions and speculating on the thoughts and feelings connected with them. Years later, in 1877, he published these observations in the new psychological journal *Mind* under the title "Biographical Sketch of an Infant" as a sequel to Hippolyte Taine's essay on his own daughter's mental development in her first year-and-a-half. Darwin, like Taine, thus became a pioneer in the new fields of ethology and developmental psychology. It's something of an irony that his trailblazing ideas and observations were already almost forty years old when published. And it is characteristic of Darwin's deliberate way of thinking that a project begun (and in some senses completed) many years before would stay alive in his mind, that he would be so ready to explore related topics, and that an ambitiously wide-ranging explanatory book would eventually result from what had begun almost forty years back as a single observation-centered case study.

Expression of the Emotions proved to be Darwin's first-day bestseller, with 5267 copies sold according to his *Autobiography*. After Darwin's death, his son Francis brought out a second edition (1890), which contained a number of Darwin's accumulated changes and notes. But Paul Ekman, editor of the third edition of *Expression* that appeared in 1998, points out that this book so widely purchased in Darwin's day fell into a 90-year period of obscurity—during the very decades when the social science disciplines Darwin had helped found were taking formal shape.[19] As is often the case with pioneering studies considered retrospectively, certain

---

19 Ekman's assessment appears in his introduction to Charles Darwin, *The Expression of the Emotions in Man and Animals* (New York and Oxford: Oxford University Press, 1998),

aspects of *Expression of the Emotions* can seem methodologically naïve, casually amateur, or simply outdated if viewed from a rigidly professionalized or theoretical perspective that didn't exist in Darwin's day or if placed on a Procrustean bed of presentist norms. Ekman enumerates five chief reasons why *Expression of the Emotions* fell out of favor in the twentieth century. These reasons are all interesting—and one is, in light of Darwin's career as a whole, highly uncharacteristic.

First, the anthropomorphism that we've seen Darwin deploy in other texts as a rhetorical device here is a matter of substance as well as style. Darwin asserts that animals not only display expressions comparable to humans but also experience emotions, a claim that ran counter to the basic premise of behaviorism (*EE* xxix–xxx). Second (and this is the uncharacteristic problem), Darwin's method of gathering second-hand information is flawed—not nearly rigorous enough to satisfy professional standards of evidence as they have evolved in the social sciences. He relied on anecdotal evidence and drew unverifiable conclusions from small and arguably non-representative samples (*EE* xxxi–xxxii). Further, as in his last decades had become increasingly common in his revisions of earlier arguments, Darwin's explanation of the emotions invoked the now-discredited Lamarckian idea that characteristics an individual has acquired over a lifetime can be passed on to the next generation (*EE* xxxii–xxxiii). In the case of blushing, for instance, Darwin claims that the face is the chief site of the blush because "close attention" was directed at the face during many past generations. If the inclusion of Lamarckian explanations undercut Darwin's arguments, his exclusion of commentary on the communicative functions of expression made the book irrelevant to those twentieth-century social scientists whose own studies centered on human expressions as non-verbal forms of communication (*EE* xxxiii–xxxiv). Finally, and most crucial according to Ekman, Darwin's thesis that human expressions of emotion are innate was incompatible with the assumptions of dominant figures and schools of early- to mid-twentieth-century psychology (John Watson and the behaviorists) and anthropology (Margaret Meade and the cultural relativists or social constructionists) who claimed nurture rather than nature, culture rather than heredity, as the origin of human behaviors (*EE* xxxiv–xxxv). At least some of these objections have diminished in recent decades, as scientists have become increasingly inclined to acknowledge the power of nature as well as nurture and as technological and medical advances have made it possible to study the emotions and brain activity in hitherto unimagined ways.

Set in its own time and judged accordingly, *Expression* is a remarkable and highly original work. Resourcefully devising a method of data-gathering to supplement his own direct observation of how feelings are somatically expressed, Darwin resorted to photographs and artworks as both experimental tools and visual supplements in his book. The art historian Phillip Prodger points out that *Expression*, as one of the first scientific books ever published with photographs included, played a major role in introducing photographs as scientific evidence and photography as a research tool.[20]

---

xxix. Subsequent citations to Darwin's text and to Ekman's supplementary materials will refer to this third edition, abbreviated *EE*, and will be parenthetical.

20   Phillip Prodger's essay "Photography and *The Expression of the Emotions*" appears as Appendix III of Ekman's edition, at 399–410.

For physiology, Darwin relied heavily on the experimental research of the French physician Guillaume Duchenne, who demonstrated that the human face contained no muscles specifically devoted to expressing emotions and thus refuted the early nineteenth-century position solidified by Charles Bell that the human face contained particular muscles uniquely designed to express the so-called higher emotions—shame, self-consciousness, spiritual devotion—that God had given only to humans. Darwin also distributed a questionnaire of "Queries about Expressions" to various of his personal correspondents, including several "missionaries or protectors of the aborigines" (*EE* 24) and attempted, by sending copies to be distributed through the Smithsonian Institution, to widen the reach of his net in the New World. Darwin's list of 16 questions can, to a twenty-first-century reader, seem naïve, subjective, Eurocentric, or witness-leading. For example, number 11 reads, "Is extreme fear expressed in the same general matter as with Europeans?" (*EE* 23). Darwin's comment at the questionnaire's conclusion that "Observations on natives who have had little communication with Europeans would be of course the most valuable, though those made on any natives would be of much interest to me" (*EE* 23) has proven an easy target for post-colonialist indignation, and many of the reported anecdotes garnered from those who replied to his questionnaire have the unfortunate air of seeming to derive from privileged Europeans looking down on what they deem a primitive, if intriguingly exotic, otherworld. But despite such infelicities the overall effect of *Expression of the Emotions* is progressive rather than patronizing. Darwin's exposure of the race- and culture-transcending ways human bodies and faces express human feelings asserts the common brotherhood (and sisterhood) of humanity. The non-contingent expression of emotions offers evidence that human races descended from a single ancestor and, further, that there is no unbridgeable gulf between humans and other animals. So beyond presenting all humans as related, Darwin's understanding of the expression of emotions empirically argues for the kinship of all living things.

The second of Darwin's 16 survey questions has to do with blushing. He asks his field observers, "Does shame excite a blush when the colour of the skin allows it to be visible? And especially how low down the body does the blush extend?" (*EE* 22). The physical response and its putative emotional causes—self-attention, shame, shyness, and modesty—fill an entire chapter of the book, the last before Darwin's summarizing conclusion. Blushing occupies this important penultimate position because, Darwin claims in his chapter's first sentence, "Blushing is the most peculiar and the most human of all expressions" (*EE* 310). His reasons for seeing the blush this way lie in its potential emotional triggers and its somatic causes rather than its visible effects, for Darwin distinguishes between the engorged reddening or darkening of blushing and that of flushing, the latter being for him a manifestation of increased cardiac activity due to exertion, anger, or other causes. According to Darwin, blushing has to do with the vascular and nervous systems rather than with the heart:

> The reddening of the face from a blush is due to the relaxation of the muscular coats of the small arteries, by which the capillaries become filled with blood; and this depends on the proper vaso-motor centre being affected. No doubt if there be at the same time much mental agitation, the general circulation will be affected; but it is not due to the action of

the heart that the network of minute vessels covering the face becomes under a sense of shame gorged with blood. (*EE* 310)

Following the lead of Dr Thomas Burgess in *The Physiology or Mechanism of Blushing* (1839), Darwin claims that blushing, unlike other somatic responses, can't be caused by physical means. Unlike Burgess, however, Darwin does not go on to ascribe the phenomenon to divine design. Darwin sees thought and feeling as natural phenomena interacting naturally to provoke a bodily response: "It is the mind which must be affected. Blushing is not only involuntary; but the wish to restrain it, by leading to self-attention, actually increases the tendency" (*EE* 310). Drawing variously on data derived from anecdotes and observations, Darwin goes on to say that young people blush more than old people do, although children don't blush in infancy—that women blush more often than men do—and that the tendency to blush is inherited, so that there are entire families of individual blushers. He remarks that in most cases the face, ears, and neck are the only parts that redden but that some people blush farther down. He reports that all races blush, though the response is less visible in darker complexions (the universality of the blush implicitly supports his argument for the common descent of all races) and that certain characteristic gestures, such as averting or casting down the eyes, are associated with blushing. He says that mental powers are generally confused when one blushes—and that the emotions inducing a blush are shyness, shame, and modesty, with the common element among the three feelings being self-attention. Darwin concludes that the cause of a blush is "a sensitive regard for the opinion, more particularly for the depreciation of others, primarily in relation to our personal appearance, especially our faces; and secondarily, through the force of association and habit, in relation to the opinion of others on our conduct'" (*EE* 334). The stimuli Darwin sees as indispensable for blushing—self-consciousness and the related awareness that others may be perceiving and judging us—had previously been understood as distinctively human attributes bound up with the moral sense since the Genesis account of post-lapsarian Eve and Adam. What Darwin does is remove divine intervention from what, for him, can be explained naturally.

Darwin's tentative explanation of the blush continues:

The hypothesis which appears to me the most probable, though it may at first seem rash, is that attention closely directed to any part of the body tends to interfere with the ordinary and tonic contraction of the small arteries of that part. These vessels, in consequence, become at such times more or less relaxed, and are instantly filled with arterial blood. This tendency will have been much strengthened, if frequent attention has been paid during many generations to the same part, owing to nerve-force readily flowing along accustomed channels, and by the power of inheritance. Whenever we believe that others are depreciating or even considering our personal appearance, our attention is vividly directed to the outer and visible parts of our bodies; and of all such parts we are most sensitive about our faces, as no doubt has been the case during many past generations. Therefore, assuming for the moment that the capillary vessels can be acted on by close attention, those of the face will have become eminently susceptible. Through the force of association, the same effects will tend to follow whenever we think that others are considering or censuring our actions or character. (*EE* 336)

Darwin goes on to cite many other ways that the human body's muscles, organs, and secretions can be affected physically when mental attention is directed to a particular part. The immediate practical effect is to show that blushing differs more in degree than in kind from other complex interactions of feeling, thought, and physical response. Less directly, the small, ephemeral variation called blushing, if understood in Darwin's terms, breaks down barriers between different human races and cultures, much as the other emotional responses Darwin has anatomized and explained bridge the gulf between humans and other animals—or, more precisely, demonstrate that the gulf was a mirage to begin with. Whether Darwin's brave new sense of the emotions and their expression diminishes humanity or exalts the rest of the animal world depends on the perspective of the beholder.

Like Darwin, contemporary medical science views blushing as an involuntary, innate, human response to a social situation most often involving unwanted attention, a response manifested psychologically by a feeling of shame or shyness.[21] Physiologically, blushing entails a temporary increase in the blood volume of the vessels in the skin of the face—and sometimes more extensively in the head and neck. The specific vessels that appear to be most important in the blushing response are not the "small arteries" Darwin identified but instead the subcutaneous venous plexuses of the face, veins lying just below the dermis. During the blushing response, the venous plexuses increase in diameter and thus temporarily become able to hold a larger quantity of blood. This phenomenon, which Darwin correctly recognized as the mechanism of blushing but which still lacks a precise neurophysiological explanation, is referred to as vasodilation. It also remains unclear exactly how or why emotion causes vasodilation, although by definition blushing is a response to a feeling of being embarrassed. The origin of blushing and the adaptive purpose it served or serves, if any, remain matters of speculation. In some ways, we actually know less about blushing than Darwin claimed; for the phenomenon is far more complicated than he, given the information and scientific tools available in his time, could have imagined.

There does, however, appear to be some scientific support for one explanation of the vasodilation of blushing. The venous plexuses beneath the dermis of the face, unlike any other veins, have beta-adrenergic receptors on their vascular cell surfaces. These receptors react to the presence of adrenaline (also known as epinephrine) by relaxing the smooth muscle in the vessel walls, which in turn widens the veins and

---

21 I am grateful to Stephen Y. Wilkerson, MD, PhD and to Richard C. Cooper, MD for medical perspectives on contemporary understandings of the neurophysiology associated with blushing. For discussion of blushing's psychological causes and attendant effects, see C. Castelfranchi and I. Poggi, "Blushing as Discourse: Was Darwin Wrong?", in *Shyness and Embarrassment: Perspectives from Social Psychology*, ed. W. R. Crozier (Cambridge: Cambridge University Press, 1990), 230–54; Michael Lewis, "Self-conscious emotions: Embarrassment, pride, shame, and guilt," in *Handbook of Emotions*, eds Michael Lewis and J. M. Haviland (New York: Guilford Publications, 1993), 353–64; Dachwe Keltner and B. Buswell, "Evidence for the Distinctness of Embarrassment, Shame, and Guilt: A Study of Recalled Antecedents and Facial Expressions of Emotion," *Cognition and Emotion*, X (1996), 155–72. Additional citations of research on blushing appear in Ekman's "Notes to the Commentaries," C66–C75, *EE* 455–6.

thereby increases the volume of blood they can hold. It seems clear that adrenaline causes this vasodilation. Adrenaline release is a characteristic of the activation of the sympathetic portion of the autonomic nervous system (as opposed to the parasympathetic system, which is activated by acetylcholine and generally has an opposite effect). Exactly why the sympathetic portion of the autonomic nervous system responds to embarrassment in this way is not clear. But though it plays a part in the blushing process, beta-adrenergic response to adrenaline does not appear to be a sufficient explanation, because experiments have shown that blood flow to the embarrassed or self-conscious person's face is still increased even when the beta-adrenergic receptors are completely blocked. Thus some other as-yet-unknown mechanism or mechanisms of vasodilation must also be involved. Nor do we know precisely how important the beta-adrenergic receptor response is in terms of the blushing phenomenon as a whole. Why facial vasodilation is a response to feeling embarrassed also remains an enigma.

Juxtaposing Austen's fictive representations with Darwin's scientific discussion and comparing both of them to contemporary medical science's limited understanding of the phenomenon of blushing shows several noteworthy things—and not principally about blushing itself. It is striking how closely Austen's presentation of blushing, its motivation, and its attendant effects corresponds to Darwin's description and hypothesizing. Austen's blushing characters proleptically display the physical and psychological traits Darwin, writing decades later, associates with a blush. The emotional situations precipitating blushes in Austen novels are, without exception, squarely within the parameters laid out in Darwin's model: shyness, shame for oneself or for others, and especially the self-conscious awareness (whether true or imagined) that one is or has been watched or judged by others brings heightened color, on Austen's pages, to cheeks that are more often than not young, female, and unmarried. Despite the remarkable similarities, Austen's representations of blushing have aged better than Darwin's account has. Her blushers can invariably convince the twenty-first-century reader, while Darwin's second-hand anecdotes and some of the conclusions he draws from them can raise objections. This contrast rises partly out of readers' different levels of expectations for novelistic fiction (meant to reflect plausibly) and for scientific discourse (meant not only to reflect plausibly, but also to explain precisely). Paradoxically, Austen's prose seems more convincing precisely because she explains so much less than Darwin does. Austen masterfully situates the blushes she describes in both social and moral contexts, but then only says what she sees. Accounting for the physiology or the evolution of this somatic expression of emotion is not one of her goals. Some twenty-first-century readers may find that what Darwin, crucially concerned with those physiological and evolutionary matters outside Austen's purview, reports is undercut rhetorically (especially by diction that now may seem uncongenial) and methodologically (particularly by reliance on selective, unconfirmable reports and by methods of data-gathering that, with the advance of the natural and social sciences, inevitably appear inadequate to contemporary specialists in the very fields of inquiry Darwin was helping to establish). But the main difference is that in the case of blushing Austen is content to remain locally empirical. Thus her implicit understandings can attain an elegance unavailable to Darwin, who gathers data much more widely and in consequence less adequately. Though precociously correct on a number of large and small aspects of blushing, he hypothesizes more ambitiously than the facts as contemporary neuroscience and psychology now understand them seem to warrant. Even so, it is remarkable that so much of what he observed about the blush remains pertinent more than a century later.

If he falls short in the still-unaccomplished task of explaining and accounting for the phenomenon of human blushing, Darwin links small observed details and large theorized effects more successfully in the last sentences of his previously discussed monograph on orchids. There, his cumulative observation of the different orchid species' contrivances for pollination by insects culminates in a bold generalizing assertion of the benign effects of intercrossing, a theme played out, in many varied forms, throughout the family *Orchidaceae*. Because of the evident scarcity of orchid pollen, the complexity of the botanical taxonomies, and the intricacy of the symbiotic relationships with insects that effect fertilization when self-pollination could be an incomparably simpler and more straightforward arrangement, Darwin reasons that there must be something beneficial about orchids' intercrossing. More broadly, he argues, what holds true for orchids might well have validity in the cases of other plants and animals:

> Nature thus tells us, in the most emphatic manner, that she abhors perpetual self-fertilisation. This conclusion seems to be of high importance, and perhaps justifies the lengthy details given in this volume. For may we not further infer as probable, in accordance with the belief of the vast majority of the breeders of our domestic productions, that marriage between near relations is likewise in some way injurious,—that some unknown great good is derived from the union of individuals which have been kept distinct for many generations? (*FO* 359–60)

The "unknown great good" of genetic outcrossing would not be widely known until some decades after Darwin's death, though the Moravian monk Gregor Mendel had already conducted and published the results of his experiments in breeding peas—and Darwin's interests in this passage slide from botany to animal husbandry to English marriage, particularly his social and personal concerns about how the marriage of first cousins might affect the health of their children.

Viewed from a Darwinian vantage point, *Persuasion* can be seen as (though not reduced to) a comparably close study of a blighted and then blooming heroine who rejects a cousin's proposal and marries outside her circle and her class, with Jane Austen coming to Darwin's conclusion about the healthy benefits of outcrossing. *Persuasion* is a novel displaying different kinds of variation that we have been considering, variations both minute and sweeping, momentary and millennial. Looked at one way, *Persuasion* is about the variable complexion of one human face: the narrative attentively chronicles faded, haggard Anne Elliot's second spring of youth and beauty. But variation on a larger, longer scale also figures implicitly in the novel. A short but pivotal episode takes place on the fossil-rich, eroding, sedimentary south English seacoast that eloquently testifies both to the uniformitarian workings of geology and to the evolutionary pattern of development and extinction evident in the zoological record as read over time.

Persuasion is a novel with four principal settings, two rural, one urban, and one neither: Kellynch, Uppercross, Bath, and Lyme Regis. The first three are necessary in ways familiar to Austen's readers: Kellynch as the native country-house habitat of the heroine, Uppercross as the alternate country-house microcosm to which she's temporarily transplanted, Bath the spa city where she and the other leisured ladies and gentlemen can, figuratively speaking, cross-pollinate. Lyme Regis, destination of a short pleasure excursion shared by a number of the young marriageable characters, is the *Persuasion* variant on the Sotherton visit in *Mansfield Park* or the Box Hill picnic in *Emma*. Crucial as the Box Hill and Sotherton excursions are to their respective narratives, the visit to Lyme is indispensable to *Persuasion* in an even more complex way. Lyme's geographical situation is part, but only part, of the reason why. A coastal town at the western edge of Dorset 17 miles from Uppercross, Lyme Regis is the seaside resort closest to the Musgroves' part of Somersetshire. Captain Wentworth's friends Harville and Benwick currently lodge there, though Austen could have located them on any stretch of the southern seacoast—just as she could have situated the Elliot and Musgrove families in many other neighborhoods or counties. But convenience, seaside location, and friends in fairly easy reach are not the only reasons, and perhaps not even the main ones, for Jane Austen to select it as the Uppercross party's destination, A careful look shows that Lyme, much more than a happily located seaport, has rich personal, historical, natural, and cultural associations that allow it to serve Austen's purposes in various ways.[22]

The town of Lyme lies at the mouth of the River Lym. It was part of the manor of Glastonbury Abbey until 1284, when Edward I acquired it, enfranchised it, and conferred on it the liberties of a haven and a borough. Edward used Lyme in his wars against the French, thus initiating the port town's longstanding historical association with naval matters. The appended title "Regis" recognizes this royal connection. Lyme Regis has a harbor thanks to the Cobb, a curving 870-foot jetty and promenade. Reputed to be the only structure of its kind in England, the Cobb seems to have been built in medieval times, with rows of tree trunks driven as pilings into the sea floor, with stones and cobbles filling the gaps. The name "Cobb" may refer to these stones or may derive from "coble," a flat-bottomed skiff. Whatever the etymology, the structure is breathtaking in its way—capable of evoking descriptions such as that of the narrator in John Fowles's *The French Lieutenant's Woman*: "quite simply the most beautiful sea rampart on the south coast of England … a superb fragment of folk art. Primitive yet complex, elephantine but delicate; as full of subtle curves and volumes as a Henry Moore or a Michelangelo, and pure, clean, salt, a paragon of mass."[23]

---

22 For the history of Lyme, see John Fowles, *A Short History of Lyme Regis* (Boston: Little, Brown, and Co., 1969) and Maggie Lane, *Jane Austen's England* (London: Robert Hale, 1982). Jane Austen's associations with Lyme are also treated in Fanny Caroline Lefroy, "Hunting for Snarkes at Lyme Regis," *Temple Bar* LVII (1879), 391–7; Francis Turner Palgrave, "Miss Austen and Lyme," *The Grove* I (1894), 390–94; and Claire Tomalin, *Jane Austen: A Life* (New York: Knopf, 1997), 175–8.

23 John Fowles, *The French Lieutenant's Woman* (Boston: Little, Brown, and Co., 1969), 9–10.

Boats sailed from Lyme's harbor to meet the Spanish Armada. In 1685, the Duke of Monmouth landed on the beach west of the town to launch his rebellion against James II. Afterward Lyme Regis ceased to be of historical significance. Its commercial importance faded too, for ships had become too large for the limited space of the artificial harbor. Like many southern ports, Lyme became a base for smugglers and fishermen alike before the fashion for seaside resorts began in the eighteenth century. By 1775, sea-bathers drawn by the mild, sunny South Coast summers and autumns had begun to visit the town, first from Bath, connected to it by a direct coach route. Bespeaking its spa status, Lyme boasted a bathing machine, invented by Ralph Allen and sent down from Bath. But Lyme never became a trendy seaside resort, as did such south coast towns as Weymouth with its royal patronage (Austen readers of course remember it as the site of Jane Fairfax's sailing mishap) and Dawlish (where Robert Ferrars fancies building a *cottage ornée*).

In Austen's day, then, Lyme Regis enjoyed a seasonal flutter as a minor coastal resort, offered a congenial spot for stranded naval men to perch in peacetime or when they were otherwise between ships, and sustained the expected maritime assortment of boatbuilders, fisherfolk, wreckers, and smugglers—*Persuasion*'s boatmen and workmen gathered at the Cobb to help or hope to see a "dead young lady" and treated to the spectacle of not one unconscious Musgrove female but two, Louisa with her concussion and Mary in her hysterical swoon. By the time the Musgrove—Elliot—Wentworth party visited Lyme in November 1814, it had also attained a reputation as a treasure trove of fossils on account of several spectacular finds in the strata of its continually eroding sedimentary seacliffs. Lyme's reputation as a sort of Jurassic Park in stone remains to this day. The center of a fossil-rich coastline extending from Exmouth to Bournemouth, Lyme has recently been designated a UN World Heritage Site. A few miles west of Lyme Regis lies Beer Head, the vanishing point after which the south coast's white or whitish chalk, limestone, and shale cliffs change to red Devon sandstone. Dominating Lyme Bay just a bit east of Lyme Regis is the 617-foot hill called Gold Cap, the highest point on the south coast. All around the bay the Blue Lias, soft layers of limestone and shale falling away into the sea, furnish abundant paleontological evidence of now-extinct life forms. Due to the softness of the stone, the fossils are prone to degrade on being extracted unless treated with resins or other preservatives, so some of the most famous early discoveries from Jane Austen's day did not remain intact.

During the first half of the nineteenth century, the most eminent English geologists and paleontologists were engaged in literally and metaphorically groundbreaking work that often centered on Lyme's strata and the fossils embedded there. Among these naturalists were Oxford University's William Buckland, who named the first dinosaur (the *Megalosaurus*), the Rev. William Conybeare, whose parish for some years was nearby Axminster and who predicted and described the plesiosaurs, the collector of splendidly complete (if sometimes spurious) plesiosaur and ichthyosaur skeletons Thomas Hawkins, and Darwin's eventual anti-evolutionary adversary the anatomist Richard Owen, instrumental in the foundation of the Natural History Museum in London. But the most famous geological finds at Lyme fell to a working-class girl, Mary Anning (1799–1847), who was later famed as "the fossil woman," praised as "the greatest fossilist the world ever knew," and commemorated by a stained glass window placed in Lyme's church of St Michael the Archangel by the local vicar and the Geological Society of London.[24] Mary was taught to hunt for fossils by her father, a cabinet-maker called Richard Anning, who died in 1810, leaving a wife and two young children in poverty. With her mother and her brother Joseph, Mary Anning combed the local cliffs for fossils that could be sold as curiosities. Although there is evidence that gentleman collectors had been aware of the presence of "crocodiles" being found by fossil-hunters such as the Annings since at least 1810, Mary's celebrity hinges on a somewhat oversimplified story that she discovered the first complete skeleton of an ichthyosaurus, as the so-called "crocodile" was officially named in 1817. The facts of this discovery are more complex than is the myth. Joseph Anning apparently located the ichthyosaurus specimen in 1811 at Black Ven, a 150-foot hill east of Lyme and next to the fossiliferous shale and limestone of Church Cliffs; and Mary found the remainder of the skeleton in 1812. Described in Sir Everard Home's "Some account of the fossil remains of an animal," an illustrated article appearing in the 1814 volume of the *Philosophical Transactions of the Royal Society*, this find was the first to come to the attention of learned circles. Over the next decades at Lyme fossil-hunting was a flourishing pastime dominated by such local collectors as the Annings, who had to sell their specimens for a living, and the prosperous Philpott sisters, whose specimens now are housed in the Oxford University Museum and in Lyme Regis's Philpott Museum. The most distinguished English geologists would sometimes join the self-taught Mary Anning in hunting fossils and reported her finds (without crediting the finder) in naturalist circles. In 1823 Mary Anning discovered a specimen recognized by Conybeare as the first virtually complete remains of a plesiosaurus and purchased by the Duke of Buckingham. In 1828 she found the first fossil of a British flying reptile, described as *Pterodactylus macronyx* by Buckland, who stressed its bizarre nature as "a monster resembling nothing that has ever been seen or heard-of upon earth, excepting the dragons of romance and heraldry" (qtd in Torrens, 266). In 1829 Mary Anning discovered *Squaloraja*, a fossil fish seen as transitional between sharks and rays. In 1830 she found *Plesiosaurus macrocephalus*, named by Buckland in 1836 and described by Richard Owen in 1840. Her growing celebrity and expertise at mining the fossil-rich seascape brought crowds of curious amateurs as well as the big guns of the Geological Society to Lyme.

Fossil-hunting or even mere seaside exploring around Lyme was, and still is, a rather risky business. Fossils are best sought at low spring tides when the sea-covered strata are most extensively exposed, especially after storms when the rock layers are likeliest to be scoured of seaweed and freshly eroded. Footing can be precarious at the tideline, and turning tides can pose dangers. Richard Owen recorded a near misadventure he, Conybeare, Buckland, and Anning shared at Lyme in 1839: "Next day we had a geological excursion with Mary Anning, and had like to have been swamped by the tide. We were cut off from rounding a point, and had to scramble over the cliffs" (McGowan, 164). Even above the tideline the soft

---

24 Mary Anning's life and accomplishments are chronicled in Christopher McGowan, *The Dragon Seekers* (Cambridge, MA: Perseus Publishing, 2003) and Hugh Torrens, "Mary Anning (1799–1847) of Lyme: 'The greatest fossilist the world ever knew,'" *British Journal for the History of Science* XXVIII (1995), 257–84.

sedimentary cliffs are prone to crumble—sometimes spectacularly—when saturated by groundwater. The Bucklands, visiting Lyme to geologize over the Christmas holidays a few months after the narrow escape Owen chronicled, were on site to witness the great landslide west of Lyme Regis in 1839. This dramatic subsidence opened a vast chasm about three-quarters of a mile long and hundreds of feet deep, sent 50 acres of the Undercliff sliding into the sea, and created a temporary barrier reef of slippage in Pinhay Bay. It might seem that exploring such shaky ground would in Regency times not be thought suitable for genteel young ladies, but the *Persuasion* narrator's nostalgic and detailed evocation of Lyme's environs strongly suggests that the consistently empirical Jane Austen was no stranger to the charms of Charmouth, the Undercliff, and Pinhay.

At any rate, we know that the Austens visited Lyme. After the Rev. George Austen relinquished his Hampshire livings and his Steventon parsonage to his eldest son James and retired with his wife and daughters to Bath in 1800, the Austens vacationed at a number of seaside resorts in Devon and Dorset, Lyme among them; and they may also have been at nearby Charmouth in the summer of 1803 (Tomalin, 175). We know that they visited Lyme in November, for Jane's letter of October 7 to 9, 1809 to Cassandra compares a fire at Southampton to a notable Lyme Regis conflagration of November 5, 1803: "The Flames were considerable, they seemed about as near to us as those at Lyme, & to reach higher" (*JAL* 143–4). The Austens were at Lyme once again for several weeks in the summer of 1804. They shared lodgings with Jane's favorite brother Henry and his wife Eliza, though the Henry Austens and Cassandra continued on to Weymouth, just then also being favored by the Royal Family's presence. This division of the party gave Jane occasion to send a letter dated September 14 detailing her circumstances at Lyme. If only this letter were redolent with unironized essences of the sublime and picturesque, prominent in the *Persuasion* narrator's suggestively personal effusions about the sea and landscape at Lyme but unusual elsewhere in Austenworld! But it isn't. Instead, the letter offers an unremittingly prosaic account of Lyme doings to Cassandra. It announces that Jane and her parents have been to a ball and states that she's walked on the Cobb with a new female acquaintance, bathed in the sea, and caught a "little fever and indisposition." It waspishly reports and reacts to family news from their Aunt Leigh Perrot's letter, provides wry descriptions of the lodgings and the domestic help— "The servants behave very well & make no difficulties, tho' nothing certainly can exceed the inconvenience of the Offices, except the general Dirtiness of the House & furniture, & all it's Inhabitants" (*JAL* 93)—and mocks Jane's performance of domestic duties in the absence of responsible, competent Cassandra: "I detect dirt in the Water-decanter as fast as I can, and give the Cook physic, which she throws off her Stomach" (*JAL* 93). Pale prophecies of *Persuasion* are perhaps discernible in Aunt Leigh Perrot's deplorable inability to distinguish a frigate from a sloop and in the account of a "new, odd looking Man who had been eyeing me for some time, & at last without any introduction asked me if I meant to dance again" (*JAL* 94). Could this interested male gaze, even if it issues from a face far from possessing the handsomeness of the "Elliot countenance," have provided the germ for Mr Elliot's admiring glances, first fixed on Anne by the sea at Lyme and then in the hotel corridor? Austen imagines her real-life mystery man "to belong to the Hon[ble].

Barnwalls, who are the son & son's wife of an Irish Viscount—bold, queerlooking people, just fit to be Quality at Lyme" (*JAL* 94). The Irish peerage and the watering-place snobbery detectable here might make *Persuasion* readers think of the Elliots' cousin Viscountess Dalrymple and her daughter, second- or third-class celebrities sufficient to impress Sir Walter and Elizabeth and to cut a swathe among the birds of passage at Bath.

According to family tradition Jane may have met a man much more congenial than the supposed Barnwall during this visit to Lyme Regis. A story Cassandra passed on in later years to her niece Caroline mentioned Jane's forming a friendship that showed signs of becoming a romantic attachment at one of the Devonshire resorts they visited. There was talk of meeting again the following summer; but instead of a happy reunion, a report of the young man's death ended the story before it had properly started. One might wonder whether faint, lingering sadness over such a curtailed romance could explain some of *Persuasion*'s famed "autumnal" melancholy, could have suggested Captain Benwick's loss of his young love Fanny Harville, and could account for why the narrator suggests that Lyme must not just be "visited" but "visited again" for its worth to be understood.

Jane Austen, destined never to return to Lyme in life, revisited it in art with an intensity that has inspired many other pilgrims. Alfred Lord Tennyson visited Lyme primarily for its Austen sites rather than its historical resonances, maritime climate, or sublime views. According to his son Hallam's memoir, Tennyson walked nine miles from Bridport to Lyme on August 23, 1867—"led on to Lyme by the description of the place in Miss Austen's *Persuasion*." Arriving, Tennyson called on his friend Palgrave, and "refusing all refreshment, he said at once, 'Now take me to the Cobb, and show me the steps from which Louisa Musgrove fell.' Palgrave and he then walked to the Undercliff."[25]

Charles Darwin's son Francis similarly became interested in the geography of Lyme Regis on account of *Persuasion* and commemorates his visit there in an essay collection titled *Rustic Sounds*. The younger Darwin, his eye conditioned by Austen's Lyme chapters, notices the steep hill sloping down into the village with the hotels at the bottom, thinks it impossible to say at which the Musgrove party put up, but hypothesizes, "I am inclined to believe it was that on the west side." He supposes that the house in which the Austens are likely to have lodged is probably Captain Harville's. His most compelling interest, however, is in answering the question of precisely where Louisa's accident occurred. Here are Francis Darwin's words on the matter:

> There are three separate flights of steps on the Cobb, and the local photographer, in the interests of trade, had to fix on one of them as the scene of the jump. I cannot believe that he is right. These steps are too high and too threatening for a girl of that period to choose with such a purpose, even for Louisa, whose determination of character we know to have been one of her charms. Then again, this particular flight is not (so far as I could make out) in the New Cobb, which is where the accident is described as occurring. It is true that at first sight it hardly looks dangerous enough to bring about the sight which

---

25   Hallam Lord Tennyson, *Alfred Lord Tennyson: A Memoir by His Son* (London: Macmillan, 1897), II, 47.

delighted the fishermen of Lyme, namely, a "dead young lady," or rather two, for the sensitive Mary contributed to the situation by fainting. I am, however, confirmed in my belief by what happened to myself, when I went to view the classic spot. I quite suddenly and inexplicably fell down. The same thing happened to a friend on the same spot, and we concluded that in the surprisingly slippery character of the surface lies the explanation of the accident. It had never seemed comprehensible that an active and capable man should miss so easy a catch as that provided by Louisa. But if Captain Wentworth slipped and fell as she jumped, she would have come down with him.[26]

A few small inaccuracies or imprecisions aside, the blend of empirical observation and literary hypothesizing evident in Francis Darwin's pilgrimage and his analysis alike testifies eloquently to how real the presence of Austen's Lyme has become to her readers.

Back to firmer footing now, and a close look at *Persuasion*'s account of Lyme Regis. The excursion from Uppercross lies at the exact center of the novel, in the last two chapters, XI and XII, of the first volume. Anne's feelings about her relationship with Wentworth frame the section. Thanks to the sequence of events, those feelings change radically from an anxiety to avoid crossing paths with him at Kellynch Hall (so painfully associated with their former attachment and breakup) and to keep him and Lady Russell apart to a comfortable and gratified awareness that he values her friendship and defers to her judgment. The changes in both Wentworth's attitude and Anne's perception of it rise out of several causes associated with the visit to Lyme.

Notes of intemperance surround the excursion from its very inception. "The young people were all wild to see Lyme," says the narrator. "The first heedless scheme had been to go in the morning and return at night" (*P* 94). The enthusiasm for accompanying Wentworth back to the town where his naval friends the Harvilles are lodged begins with Louisa, "the most eager of the eager," but spreads to the whole younger generation at Uppercross: Charles, Mary, Anne, Henrietta, and Louisa are all to go.

When the party arrives at the resort "too late in the year for any amusement or variety" in its public life (*P* 95), what's left are the charms of nature and of private society. The narrator's description of the environment displays a fervor for Lyme's sublime natural features comparable to the Uppercross party's purported wildness to see them:

> ... a very strange stranger it must be, who does not see charms in the immediate environs of Lyme, to make him wish to know it better. The scenes in its neighbourhood, Charmouth, with its high grounds and extensive sweeps of country, and still more its sweet retired bay, backed by dark cliffs, where fragments of low rock among the sands make it the happiest spot for watching the flow of the tide, for sitting in unwearied contemplation;—the woody varieties of the cheerful village of Up Lyme, and, above, all, Pinny, with its green chasms between romantic rocks, where the scattered forest trees and orchards of luxuriant growth declare that many a generation must have passed away since the first partial falling of the cliff prepared the ground for such a state, where a scene so wonderful and lovely is exhibited, as may more than equal any of the resembling scenes of the far-famed Isle

---

26 Francis Darwin, *Rustic Sounds* (Freeport, NY: Books for Libraries, 1969, repr.), 76–7.

of Wight: these places must be visited, and visited again, to make the worth of Lyme understood. (*P* 95–6)

Readers would have to look to the literary likes of Thomas Hardy for so loving an appreciation of south-coast nature rather than culture—and certainly Austen the novelist, who generally like Mary Crawford seems to find nature more worth noticing when it's the backdrop for human nature, seldom if ever displays quite so antisocial an aesthetic.

Who of the Uppercross party is most worthy of savoring these sublime and beautiful views? Anne, presumably—but we don't find out, for the group is soon at the shore where, after "lingering only, as all must linger and gaze on a first return to the sea, who ever deserve to look on it at all," (*P* 95) they turn their steps to the Harvilles' small house near the foot of an old pier. The chapter's recurrent motif of revisiting here modulates out of the melancholy key associated with it at the start of the chapter, when Anne so feared encountering Wentworth at Kellynch, and becomes a more optimistic, almost Wordsworthian way of seeing that allows place to serve as a sustaining palimpsest of past and present. Similarly, the motif of parted lovers here takes a new form with the entry of Captain Benwick, still mourning the loss of Fanny Harville yet seen by Anne as "younger in feeling, if not in fact" than herself: "he will rally again, and be happy with another" (*P* 97). The unvoiced implication that Anne won't rally is shortly to be challenged.

Next to enter the scene are the amiable Harvilles, the wife "a degree less polished than her husband," though both have "the same good feelings" (*P* 97). From the Harvilles' example Anne finds that, despite Lady Russell's opinion, a marriage need not involve social equals to be a good one. When the Uppercross party is invited to the Harvilles' modest dwelling, Anne discerns both an unpretentious ease and a domesticity unlike anything she's known at Kellynch. The "degree of hospitality so uncommon, so unlike the usual style of give-and-take invitations, and dinners of formality and display" and the "ingenious contrivances and nice arrangements" Captain Harville has fashioned to "turn the actual space to the best possible account" (*P* 98) give Anne a rosy picture indeed of married life in naval circles. "'These would have been all my friends,' was her thought" (*P* 98). That thought is voiced in exaggerated form by Louisa, her companion on the walk back to the hotel, who "burst forth into raptures of admiration and delight on the character of the navy— their friendliness, their brotherliness, their openness, their uprightness; protesting that she was convinced of sailors having more worth and warmth than any other set of men in England; that they only knew how to live, and they only deserved to be respected and loved" (*P* 99). Anne might not have Louisa's tendency to declare her sentiments in sweeping superlatives and absolutes, but she does share the sentiments themselves. Thrown into contact with Captain Wentworth on his turf (or should we say "quarterdeck"?) rather than her father's, Anne now thinks herself growing accustomed to being in Wentworth's company without confusion. But her evening's spent mostly with Captain Benwick, and principally devoted to discussing the Romantic poetry of Scott and Byron that they both admire, and for some of the same reasons. Benwick shewed himself so intimately acquainted with all the tenderest songs of the one poet, and all the impassioned descriptions of hopeless agony of the other; he repeated, with such tremulous feeling, the various lines which imaged a broken heart, or a mind destroyed by wretchedness, and looked so entirely as if he meant to be understood, that she ventured to hope he did not always read only poetry ... (*P* 100)

As was the case on listening to Louisa shortly before, Anne finds herself hearing her own feelings expressed in an untempered form. Her corrective prescription of morally edifying prose may be apt, but she ends the chapter fearing "that, like many other great moralists and preachers, she had been eloquent on a point in which her own conduct would ill bear examination" (*P* 101). That Anne can sympathetically recognize her own melancholy failing in Benwick and then be amused at the likeness and at the gap between her advice and her own practice yet again shows that, despite the hypothetical charms of might-have-been, she is closer than before to abandoning the backward glance.

Chapter XII brings enough incident to put an end to introspection. An early morning walk by the breezy seaside—assisted, perhaps, by the correspondent breeze stirred up in her heart and by her memory of the night before—has Anne "looking remarkably well; her very regular, very pretty features, having the bloom and freshness of youth restored by the fine wind which had been blowing on her complexion, and by the animation of eye which it had also produced" (*P* 104). This re-Anne-imation so ideally suited to psycho-physiological explanation by Darwin attracts a look of "earnest admiration" from the passing gentleman who later turns out to be Mr Elliot. His attraction spurs Captain Wentworth, just ahead partnering Louisa, to look back and, in his turn, to appreciate what he sees with his own somatic expression of emotions, though it may be that his weathered maritime complexion doesn't change color as readily as Anne's does. "He gave her a momentary glance,—a glance of brightness, which seemed to say, 'That man is struck with you,—and even I, at this moment, see something like Anne Elliot again'" (*P* 104). The unknown gentleman has a second run-in with Anne as they nearly collide in the hallway of the inn, and this time it is further evident that he has exceedingly good manners and an agreeable person, enough to make Anne feel "that she should like to know who he was" (*P* 105). She learns directly, for the gentleman's curricle is departing and a waiter's at hand to say to whom the equipage belongs: "'Mr Elliot; a gentleman of large fortune ... in his way to Bath and London'" (*P* 105). This information, Mary's snobbishly fussy reaction to it, and Anne's "secret gratification to herself have seen her cousin" (*P* 106) lay the groundwork for one of the subsequent misconceptions that will teasingly delay the novel's romantic denouement: Wentworth's belief that Anne reciprocates Mr Elliot's regard. But her enhanced appreciation of Wentworth himself is the next thing the morning's events promote, for with the arrival of Captain Benwick, still "a young mourner," Captain Harville is impelled to describe how attentive Wentworth had been to the freshly bereaved Benwick: on the Laconia's arrival at Plymouth, Wentworth "wrote up for leave of absence, but without waiting the return, travelled night and day till he got to Portsmouth, rowed off to the Grappler that instant, and never left the poor fellow for a week; that's what he did, and nobody else could have saved poor James. You may think, Miss Elliot, whether he is dear to us!" (*P* 108).

Directly afterward, Anne sees Wentworth's grace under pressure at first hand and he sees hers, as what Maggie Lane has termed "the most dramatic incident in the whole of Jane Austen's writing outside her childhood burlesques" (105) unfolds. The party is making a farewell visit to the Cobb, too windy up top for the ladies to find agreeable. All pass quietly and carefully down the steep steps that may or may not have been the stair that locals call "Granny's Teeth": all except Louisa.

> She must be jumped down them by Captain Wentworth. In all their walks, he had had to jump her from the stiles; the sensation was delightful to her. The hardness of the pavement for her feet, made him less willing upon the present occasion; he did it, however; she was safely down, and instantly, to shew her enjoyment, ran up the steps to be jumped down again. He advised her against it, thought the jar too great; but no, he reasoned and talked in vain; she smiled and said "I am determined I will:" he put out his hands; she was too precipitate by half a second, she fell on the pavement on the Lower Cobb, and was taken up lifeless! (*P* 109)

The horror of that moment takes diverse forms: Mary's scream and swoon into Charles's arms, Henrietta's faint, intercepted by Benwick and Anne, Wentworth's despairing "'Is there no one to help me?'" as he supports the unconscious Louisa. Anne, the first to regain practical sense, instructs Benwick "'Go to him, go to him ... Rub her hands, rub her temples; here are salts,—take them, take them.'" When these preliminary measures have no effect, Wentworth's reaction is bitter emotional agony, capped and curtailed by sound practical sense from Anne:

> "Oh God! Her father and mother!"
> "A surgeon!" said Anne.
> He caught the word; it seemed to rouse him at once, and saying only "True, true, a surgeon this instant," was darting away, when Anne eagerly suggested,
> "Captain Benwick, would not it be better for Captain Benwick? He knows where a surgeon is to be found."
> Everyone capable of thinking felt the advantage of the idea. (*P* 110)

The "completely rational" members of the party left behind are Wentworth, Charles Musgrove, and Anne. Of the three, she's the one who takes charge: "Anne, attending with all the strength and zeal, and thought, which instinct supplied, to Henrietta, still tried, at intervals, to suggest comfort to the others, tried to quiet Mary, to animate Charles, to assuage the feelings of Captain Wentworth. Both seemed to look to her for directions" (*P* 111). "Strength, zeal, and thought": three virtues Wentworth, disappointed back in the day when his young fiancée yielded to Lady Russell's persuasion, would not in times since have ascribed to Anne.

The Harvilles, alerted to the emergency by seeing Captain Benwick rushing past their house, arrive on the scene and add to the party of the sensible and useful. A look between husband and wife determines what's to be done—Louisa must be moved into their own house and tended by Mrs Harville, herself an experienced nurse, and her competent nursery maid. The rest of the chapter displays Wentworth and Anne as a capable couple like the Harvilles, briskly settling things between themselves, though not without the intrusion of powerful, unrelated feelings. Wentworth says,

> "If one stays to assist Mrs Harville, I think it need be only one.—Mrs Charles Musgrove will, of course, wish to get back to her children; but, if Anne will stay, no one so proper, so capable as Anne!"
>
> She paused a moment to recover from the emotion of hearing herself so spoken of. (*P* 114)

Anne must recover from two things: the compliment—a mode of address largely unfamiliar to her—and the first-name intimacy into which Wentworth, in the warmth of the moment, has relapsed. She rightly senses that he has forgiven her in his heart. "'You will stay, I am sure; you will stay and nurse her;' cried he, turning to her and speaking with a glow, and yet a gentleness, which seemed almost restoring the past.—She colored deeply." (*P* 114)

In the hands of a less resourceful and more conventional spinner of romances, this emotionally expressive moment, a textbook Darwinian pas de deux of fervent flushing and conscious blushing, would be a rapprochement. But Austen has another full volume of frustrations to lay before her star-crossed lovers, and some of these now intervene. Mary's ill-judging, aggrieved sense of consequence makes her clamor to stay behind with Charles and instead have Anne accompany Henrietta home to Uppercross in Wentworth's carriage. Wentworth's "evident surprise and vexation, at the substitution of one sister for the other" (*P* 115) mortifies Anne, who thinks he values her "only as she could be useful to Louisa," believes he suspects her of trying to evade attending Louisa, and assumes that his bitter laments of regret bespeak a lover's regard for the comatose girl (*P* 116). But their last moment together, as he prepares to return Henrietta to her parents, restores the mutual respect and like-mindedness that had earlier united them and that characterizes the Harvilles' interaction.

> "I have been considering what we had best do. She must not appear at first. She could not stand it. I have been thinking whether you had not better remain in the carriage with her, while I go in and break it to Mr and Mrs Musgrove. Do you think this a good plan?"
>
> She did: he was satisfied, and said no more. But the remembrance of the appeal remained a pleasure to her—as a proof of friendship, and of deference for her judgment, a great pleasure; and when it became a sort of parting proof, its value did not lessen. (*P* 117)

So why Lyme Regis? As the empirical Austen depicts it in *Persuasion*, the town of Lyme is as different from a workaday seaport such as Portsmouth in *Mansfield Park* as it is from a new-built holiday town such as her imaginary Sanditon. Despite locals' curiosity about the better-born who are passing through, Austen's out-of-season Lyme lacks the class-consciousness of Bath or of the tenant villages surrounding estates like Kellynch or even Uppercross. It is a setting suited to the unpretentious amiability of Wentworth's fellow officers, a place where Anne can escape from the hierarchies that constrain her inland, whether she's at home or away—where the idea of romance across classes can be entertained. If Anne can see Wentworth at his best among his peers, the friends who would have been hers had she married him, he can see her at her best in the emergency that calls forth her nerve, zeal, and thought—qualities damped down or repressed in her daily round of country life as visiting spinster sister or younger daughter.

Lyme Regis as rendered by Austen offers a remarkable fit between place and feeling, nature and human nature, geology and sociology. Lyme's vistas inspire the transports of sensibility just as its bracing air invigorates the body; but nowhere else in the Austen canon have the rewards of balance been so concisely demonstrated and the perils of imbalance so dramatically and literally punished as on the Cobb. The sea breezes Anne enjoys there bring some color back to a complexion faded by eight years of lonely, cloistered penance, the consequence of yielding to a perspective too heavy on Lady Russell's sense. In contrast, the stone steps offer headstrong Louisa Musgrove a temptation, a fall, and an ensuing concussion, unconsciousness from a blow to the head being an ironically suitable fate for her excessive sensibility and resistance to persuasion. Louisa, knocked unconscious by her willful and passionate lover's leap, may be Austen's posterchild of senselessness. Leave it to Anne to chart a fair course between the extremes of sense and sensibility. Accustomed to moral discipline, she recovers animal vitality at Lyme. Its sublimity is the background to her reanimated beauty. Its eroding cliffs, packed with the remnants of long-extinct species, point her seaward. Lyme prepares Anne eventually to turn her back on those dying dinosaurs among whom she's lived, the landed Elliots, and to cast her lot with the ascendant meritocracy of the British navy, the captains whose ships rule the waves where plesiosaurs and ichthyosaurs once swam.

England's south-eastern landscape of sedimentary coast and chalky downland—the region containing Lyme Regis with its Cobb and fossiliferous cliffs, Southampton and the lesser naval ports from which Captain Wentworth might sail and where Anne Elliot Wentworth perhaps might lodge on those sad occasions when she, like other naval wives, faced a period of separation from her seagoing husband—also contains Chawton and Winchester, the Hampshire sites of Jane Austen's final residences, and Darwin's Kentish home in the village of Downe. This region offers common ground for both Austen's and Darwin's respective final books: the 12-chapter fragment now called *Sanditon* on which Austen was working until her terminal illness in 1817, and Darwin's *The Formation of Vegetable Mould, through the Action of Worms, with Observations on Their Habits* (1881). Austen's incipient novel seems to be setting out to offer a case study of the shortsighted human hubris that in the years between her birth and Darwin's death marked and marred the natural English landscape in unprecedented, accelerating ways that still continue. Darwin, gazing over a longer vista in time, shows nature's corrective. In different ways and on different scales, these two texts chronicle the ecological dance of damage and recovery that involves unformitarianism, variation, and the incremental power of small acts to achieve vast consequences.

At the end of *Persuasion* Austen's heroine cast her lot with up-and-coming seafarers rather than stagnant or degenerating hereditary landowners, but in contrast *Sanditon* seems to be taking shape as a denunciation of the enterprising (here, not naval officers but land developers), with the vanishing rural status quo glowing in a particularly attractive light because it's about to vanish.[27] When an extract from the literary fragment first was published in James Austen-Leigh's 1871 *Memoir* of his aunt, it might have struck the preservationist-minded people who two decades later would found the British National Trust as prime evidence for the necessity of their cause. The new and "improved" shape of Sanditon is a product of design rather than evolution. Formerly an unpretentious coastal fishing village, the community is being rapidly transformed by its principal landowners, Mr Parker and Lady Denham, into a seaside spa: "the favourite—for a young & rising Bathing-place, certainly the favourite spot of all that are to be found along the coast of Sussex" (*MW* 368). In short, just the sort of watering-place prosperous nineteenth-century invalids of Darwin's sort might frequent. Sanditon enjoys "some natural advantages in its position," as Austen's narrator puts it (*MW* 371). Parker the developer is more enthusiastic:

> "Nature had marked it out—had spoken in most intelligible Characters—The finest, purest Sea Breeze on the Coast—acknowledged to be so—Excellent Bathing—fine hard Sand—Deep Water 10 yards from the Shore—no Mud—no Weeds—no slimey rocks—Never was there a place more palpably designed by Nature for the resort of the Invalid—the very spot which Thousands seemed in need of." (*MW* 369)

Only a few years earlier, Sanditon might have been a smaller, even more modest counterpart to Lyme Regis. Its inland hillsides, in past generations covered with native vegetation that might well include wild native orchids of the sort Darwin would later collect one county eastward, will now sprout *cottages ornées* and detached or semi-detached villas, seasonal nests to shelter an invasive variety of the human species: the valetudinarian on holiday. From the aesthete's, the ecologist's, or the traditionalist's vantage point, what a change for the worse!

But to despair would be to take the short view. Villas, however well constructed and whether detached or semi-detached, cannot hold perpetual sway over the English landscape—a palpable point proven by the Roman remains serendipitously discovered in a ploughed field at Abinger Hall, the Surrey estate of Thomas Farrer, Darwin's friend and fellow botanizer and future father-in-law of the youngest Darwin son Horace. At Farrer's invitation, a fascinated Darwin watched the excavation of Roman masonry and tessellated floors that had been with the passage of centuries buried five feet deep by the rich black soil of wormcasts. According to Darwin's calculations, wormcasts had covered the subsiding pavements at a rate of one inch

---

27 For various perspectives on where *Sanditon* might be headed and how important it might have turned out to be if finished, see Brian Southam, *Jane Austen's Manuscripts* (New York: Oxford University Press, 1964), 102; Alistair Duckworth, *The Improvement of the Estate* (Baltimore, MD: Johns Hopkins University Press, 1971), 210; Marilyn Butler, *Jane Austen and the War of Ideas* (London and New York: Oxford University Press, 1975), 286; Brian Southam, "*Sanditon*: The Seventh Novel," in *Jane Austen's Achievement*, ed. Juliet McMaster (New York: Barnes and Noble, 1976), 1–26; and John Halperin, *The Life of Jane Austen* (Baltimore, MD: Johns Hopkins University Press, 1984), 326–35. "Sanditon and speculation," the final chapter of Peter Knox-Shaw's *Jane Austen and the Enlightenment*, offers a particularly strong reading of the fragment in its historical, cultural, and intellectual contexts.

in 12 years. *Sic transit gloria aedificatoris*, as the Roman villa-builder might have put it could he have returned from his own burial site and joined Darwin and Farrer during the archaeological dig.

Like others of his long-considered projects, Darwin's study of worms and their work had begun 40 years earlier, with an episode uncannily proleptic of the later experience at Abinger. On an 1837 visit to Maer Hall in Staffordshire, Darwin was fascinated when Josiah Wedgwood, the uncle who would soon become his father-in-law, pointed out how after only a few years a still-intact layer of cinders and marl that had been spread on the surface of his meadowlands now lay several inches under the turf, buried by the continual action of worms bringing fine earth from below the marl-cinder stratum to the surface in the form of their castings. This observation resulted in an 1837 paper presented to the Geological Society of London. But Darwin, a landowning empiricist, was not through with worms when he finished the paper. Over the years, Darwin took a keen interest in the work of earthworms and enlisted his children and other collaborators in observing how these "archaeologists in reverse," in Janet Browne's phrase (*CDPP* 447), were covering the turf of various British locations with their loamy excretions, in the process burying stones, sinking ancient monuments, and transforming the landscape. He again published short pieces on worms in 1844 and 1869. By the late 1870s worms and their habits seemed an ideal book-length project for an elderly country invalid rooted in his local surroundings. In the year of the Abinger excavations, Darwin and his research assistant Francis devised a series of behavioral experiments that gauged earthworms' responses to a rather whimsical-sounding range of stimuli—tobacco smoke, heat radiating from a poker, light, the tones of Francis's bassoon or Emma's piano—and tested worms' resourcefulness at determining the best means of drawing cabbage leaves, pine needles, or angular paper shapes into their holes. The patiently accrued result of his decades-long observations and data-gathering combined with the more recent experiments to furnish materials for *The Formation of Vegetable Mould*, a reader-friendly masterpiece of minute observation and momentous conclusion-drawing. Darwin had learned how earthworms choose to drag leaves into their burrows but also had discerned their cumulative role in undermining and burying the pillars of Stonehenge and other such human edifices. "Worms have played a more important part in the history of the world than most persons would at first suppose,"[28] he dryly begins the conclusion to his book—and in the chapters leading up to this remark his meticulous explanation of the particular ways they do so perfectly illustrates how the empirical naturalist whose already sharp eyes were opened to the possibilities of going past observation to explanation by the world-ranging voyage of the *Beagle* had brought his talent to fruition deep-rooted in locality.

Like Jane Austen, Darwin had his beginnings in a country neighborhood, and like her he found the same sort of place both a congenial home and a fertile field for

---

28 Charles Darwin, *The Works of Charles Darwin*, Vol. XXVIII, eds Paul H. Barrett and R. B. Freeman, *The Formation of Vegetable Mould, through the Action of Worms* (New York: New York University Press, 1989), 136. Barrett and Freeman reprint the first edition of 1881. Subsequent citation will refer to this edition, abbreviated *FVM*, and will appear parenthetically.

study. A clear, trained, and honest eye like Austen's or Darwin's sees that what can be unearthed in such a locality, however apparently insignificant, is connected to the momentous. What more comprehensible instance of uniformitarianism in action than earthworms on the Down House lawn? What better evidence that if in the short term bustling humans encrust the natural world with mushrooming Sanditons, the natural agents of change will, given time, nullify their ephemeral efforts? There's something both grand and humbling in this awareness, beautifully voiced in the worm book's concluding sentences, with cadences that echo and vary the ending of *Origin of Species*:

> When we behold a wide, turf-covered expanse, we should remember that its smoothness, on which so much of its beauty depends, is mainly due to all the inequalities having been slowly leveled by worms. It is a marvelous relfection [*sic*] that the whole of the superficial mould over any such expanse has passed, and will again pass, every few years through the bodies of worms. The plough is one of the most ancient and valuable of man's inventions; but long before he existed the land was in fact regularly ploughed, and still continues to be thus ploughed by earth-worms. It may be doubted whether there are many other animals which have played so important a part in the history of the world, as have these lowly organized creatures. (*FVM* 139)

A worm's apotheosis. An empiricist's monument and *memento mori*.

Select Bibliography

Primary Works

Austen, Jane. *Emma*, ed. R. W. Chapman. London and New York: Oxford University Press, 1933; repr. 1971.
_____. *Jane Austen's Letters*, ed. Deirdre Le Faye. London and New York: Oxford University Press, 1995.
_____. *Mansfield Park*, ed. R. W. Chapman. London and New York: Oxford University Press, 1934; repr. 1970.
_____. *Minor Works*, ed. R. W. Chapman. London and New York: Oxford University Press, 1959; repr. and rev. by Brian C. Southam, 1972.
_____. *Northanger Abbey and Persuasion*, ed. R. W. Chapman. London and New York: Oxford University Press. 1933; repr. 1972.
_____. *Pride and Prejudice*, ed. R. W. Chapman. London and New York: Oxford University Press, 1932; repr. 1971.
_____. *Sense and Sensibility*, ed. R. W. Chapman. London and New York: Oxford University Press, 1933; repr. 1971.
Darwin, Charles. *The Autobiography of Charles Darwin 1809–1882*, ed. Nora Barlow. New York and London: Norton, 1958.
_____. *The Collected Papers of Charles Darwin*, ed. Paul H. Barrett. Chicago, IL: University of Chicago Press, 1977.
_____. *The Correspondence of Charles Darwin*, eds Frederick H. Burkhardt, Sidney Smith, Duncan M. Porter, *et al.* Cambridge: Cambridge University Press, 1985–.
_____. "Darwin's Ornithological Notes," ed. Nora Barlow. *Bulletin of the British Museum (Natural History). Historical Series* II (1963), 201–78.
_____. *The Expression of the Emotions in Man and Animals*, with an introduction, afterword and commentaries by Paul Ekman. New York and Oxford: Oxford University Press, 1998.
_____. *Fertilization of Orchids by Insects*. Stanfordville, NY: Earl M. Coleman, 1979.
_____. *On the Origin of Species: A Facsimile of the First Edition of 1859*, with an introduction by Ernst Mayr. Cambridge, MA: Harvard University Press, 1964.
_____. *The Variation of Animals and Plants under Domestication*, ed. Harriet Ritvo. Baltimore, MD: Johns Hopkins University Press, 1998.
_____. *The Works of Charles Darwin*, eds Paul H. Barrett and R. B. Freeman. Vols XXI–XXII: *The Descent of Man*. New York: New York University Press, 1989.
_____. *The Works of Charles Darwin*, eds Paul H. Barrett and R. B. Freeman. Vol. XXV: *The Effects of Cross and Self-Fertilization in the Vegetable Kingdom*. New York: New York University Press, 1989.

_____. *The Works of Charles Darwin*, eds Paul H. Barrett and R. B. Freeman. Vol. XXIX: *Erasmus Darwin by Ernst Krause with a Preliminary Notice by Charles Darwin*. New York: New York University Press, 1989.

_____. *The Works of Charles Darwin*, eds Paul H. Barrett and R. B. Freeman. Vol. XXVIII: *The Formation of Vegetable Mould, through the Action of Worms*. New York: New York University Press, 1989.

_____. *The Works of Charles Darwin*, eds Paul H. Barrett and R. B. Freeman. Vol. VIII: *The Geology of the Voyage of HMS* Beagle*: Vol I—The Structure and Distribution of Coral Reefs*. New York: New York University Press, 1987.

_____. *The Works of Charles Darwin*, eds Paul H. Barrett and R. B. Freeman. Vol. IX: *The Geology of the Voyage of HMS* Beagle*: Vol. III—Geological Observations on South America*. New York: New York University Press, 1986.

_____. *The Works of Charles Darwin*, eds Paul H. Barrett and R. B. Freeman. Vols II–III: *Journal of Researches*. New York: New York University Press, 1987.

Secondary Works

Allen, David Elliston. *The Naturalist in Britain: A Social History*. London: Allen Lane, 1976.

Austen, Caroline. *Reminiscence of Caroline Austen*, ed. Deirdre Le Faye. N.P.; Jane Austen Society, 1986.

Austen-Leigh, James. *A Memoir of Jane Austen*, ed. R. W. Chapman. Oxford: Clarendon Press, 1926.

Barash, David P., and Nanelle R. Barash. *Madame Bovary's Ovaries: A Darwinian Look at Literature*. New York: Delacorte Press, 2005.

Barber, Bernard. *Science and the Social Order*. Glencoe, IL: Free Press, 1952.

Beer, Gillian. *Darwin's Plots: Evolutionary Narrative in Darwin, George Eliot, and Nineteenth-Century Fiction*. London and Boston: Routledge & Kegan Paul, 1983.

Blake, William. *Complete Poems and Prose*, ed. David V. Erdmann. Berkeley, CA and Los Angeles: University of California Press, 1982.

Brown, Julia Prewitt. *Jane Austen's Novels: Social Change and Literary Form*. Cambridge, MA: Harvard University Press, 1979.

Browne, Janet. *Charles Darwin: Voyaging*. Princeton, NJ: Princeton University Press, 1995.

_____. *Charles Darwin: The Power of Place*. Princeton, NJ: Princeton University Press, 2002.

Butler, Marilyn. *Jane Austen and the War of Ideas*. London and New York: Oxford University Press, 1975.

Byron, George Gordon, Lord. *Don Juan*, ed. Jerome J. McGann. Oxford: Clarendon Press, 1986.

Campbell, John A. "Charles Darwin: Rhetorician of Science," in *The Rhetoric of the Human Sciences*, ed. John S. Nelson *et al*. Madison, WI: Wisconsin University Press, 1989, pp. 69–86.

_____. "The Invisible Rhetorician: Charles Darwin's 'Third Party' Strategy," *Rhetorica*, VII (1989), 70–74.

_____. "Scientific Revolution and the Grammar of Culture: The Case of Darwin's Origin," *Quarterly Journal of Speech* LXXII, 4 (1986), 351–76.

Castelfranchi, C., and I. Poggi. "Blushing as Discourse: Was Darwin Wrong?," in *Shyness and Embarrassment: Perspectives from Social Psychology*, ed. W. R. Crozier. Cambridge: Cambridge University Press, 1990, pp. 230–54.

Chancellor, John. *Charles Darwin*. London: Weidenfeld & Nicolson, 1913.

Coleridge, Samuel Taylor. *Aids to Reflection*, Vol. IX of *The Collected Works of Samuel Taylor Coleridge*, ed. John Beer. Princeton, NJ: Princeton University Press, 1993.

Darwin, Francis (ed.). *Life and Letters of Charles Darwin, Including an Autobiographical Chapter*. London: John Murray, 1888.

_____. *More Letters of Charles Darwin*, co-edited with A. C. Seward. New York: Appleton and Co., 1903.

_____. *Rustic Sounds*. Freeport, NY: Books for Libraries, 1969, repr.

Dawkins, Richard. *The Selfish Gene*. New York: Oxford University Press, 1989.

Dear, Peter (ed.). *The Literary Structure of Scientific Argument: Historical Studies*. Philadelphia, PA: University of Pennsylvania Press, 1991.

Desmond, Adrian, and James Moore. *Darwin*. New York: Warner Books, 1991.

Drake, Stillman. *Galileo Studies*. Ann Arbor, MI: University of Michigan Press, 1970.

Duckworth, Alistair. *The Improvement of the Estate*. Baltimore, MD: Johns Hopkins University Press, 1971.

Dunn, Judy, and Robert Plomin. *Separate Lives: Why Siblings Are So Different*. New York: Basic Books, 1990.

Emsley, Sarah. *Jane Austen's Philosophy of the Virtues*. New York: Palgrave Macmillan, 2005.

Ferguson, Moira. "Mansfield Park: Slavery, Colonialism, and Gender," *Oxford Literary Review* XIII (1991), 118–39.

Fowles, John. *The French Lieutenant's Woman*. Boston: Little, Brown, and Co., 1969.

_____. *A Short History of Lyme Regis*. Boston: Little, Brown, and Co., 1969.

Gottschall, Jonathan, and David Sloan Wilson (eds). *The Literary Animal*. Evanston, IL: Northwestern University Press, 2005.

Grant, Peter and Rosemary. "The Calmodular pathway and evolution of elongated beak morphology in Darwin's finches," *Nature* CDXLII (August 2006), 563–7.

_____. *Ecology and Evolution of Darwin's Finches*. Princeton, NJ: Princeton University Press, 1986; repr. 1999.

_____. *Evolutionary Dynamics of a Natural Population: The Large Cactus Finch of the Galapagos*. Chicago, IL: University of Chicago Press, 1989.

_____. "Phenotypic and genetic effects of hybridization in Darwin's finches," *Evolution* XVIII (1994), 297–316.

_____. "Predicting microevolutionary responses to directional selection on heritable variation," *Evolution* XLIX (1995), 241–51.

Greenacre, Phyllis. *The Quest for the Father: A Study of the Darwin—Butler Controversy, As a Contribution to the Understanding of the Creative Individual.* New York: International Universities, 1963.

Greenhill, William Alexander. "Medicina," in William Smith, *A Dictionary of Greek and Roman Antiquities.* London: John Murray, 1875, pp. 745–7.

Halperin, John. *The Life of Jane Austen.* Baltimore, MD: Johns Hopkins University Press, 1984.

Herschel, John. *A Preliminary Discourse on the Study of Natural Philosophy.* London: Longman and John Taylor, 1830.

Hutton, James. *James Hutton in the Field and the Study.* Delmar, NY: Scholars Facsimiles and Reprints, 1997.

Huxley, Julian, and H. B. D. Kettlewell. *Charles Darwin and His World.* New York: Viking, 1965.

Huxley, Thomas Henry. "The Connection of the Biological Sciences with Medicine," *Nature: A Weekly Illustrated Journal of Science* DCXV (1881), 342–46.

Inchbald, Elizabeth. *The British Theatre, or a Collection of Plays Which Are Acted at the Theatres Royal, Drury-Lane, Covent Garden, and Haymarket.* London: Longman, Hurst, Rees, and Orme, 1808.

Jacobus, Mary. *Tradition and Experiment in Wordsworth's Lyrical Ballads (1798).* Oxford: Clarendon Press, 1976.

Jamoussi, Zouheir. *Primogeniture and Entail in England: A Survey of Their History and Representation in Literature.* N.P., Centre de Publication Universitaire, 1999.

Johnson, Claudia L. *Jane Austen: Women, Politics, and the Novel.* Chicago, IL: University of Chicago Press, 1988.

Keltner, Dachwe, and B. Buswell. "Evidence for the Distinctness of Embarrassment, Shame, and Guilt: A Study of Recalled Antecedents and Facial Expressions of Emotion," *Cognition and Emotion* X (1996), 155–72.

Knox-Shaw, Peter. *Jane Austen and the Enlightenment.* Cambridge: Cambridge University Press, 2004.

Konisberg, Ira. *Narrative Technique in the English Novel: Defoe to Austen.* Hamden, CT: Archon Books, 1985.

Landau, Misia. *Narratives of Human Evolution.* New Haven, CT: Yale University Press, 1991.

Lane, Maggie. *Jane Austen's England.* London: Robert Hale, 1982.

Le Faye, Deirdre, *et al. Jane Austen, A Family Record.* Cambridge: Cambridge University Press, 2004.

Lefroy, Fanny Caroline. "Hunting for Snarkes at Lyme Regis," *Temple Bar* LVII (1879), 391–7.

Levine, George. *Darwin Loves You: Natural Selection and the Re-enchantment of the World.* Princeton, NJ: Princeton University Press, 2006.

Lewis, Michael. "Self-conscious emotions: Embarrassment, pride, shame, and guilt," in Michael Lewis and J. M. Haviland (eds), *Handbook of Emotions.* New York: Guilford Publications, 1993, pp. 353–64.

Loehlin, John C. *Genes and Environment in Personality Development.* Newbury Park, CA: Sage Publications, 1992.

MacIntyre, Alasdair. *After Virtue: A Study in Moral Theory*. Notre Dame, IN: University of Notre Dame Press, 1984.
Macpherson, Sandra. "Rent to Own; or, What's Entailed in *Pride and Prejudice*," *Representations* LXXXII (Spring 2003), 1–23.
McGowan, Christopher. *The Dragon Seekers*. Cambridge, MA: Perseus Publishing, 2003.
Merton, Robert K. *Science, Technology, and Society in Seventeenth-Century England*. New York: Howard Fertig, 1938; repr. 1970.
———, and Elinor Barber. *The Travels and Adventures of Serendipity: A Study in Sociological Semantics and the Sociology of Science*. Princeton, NJ and Oxford: Princeton University Press, 2004.
Mill, James. *The History of British India*. London: Baldwin, Cradock, and Joy, 1817.
Miller, Jonathan, and Borin Van Loon. *Darwin for Beginners*. New York: Pantheon, 1982.
Neill, Edward. *The Politics of Jane Austen*. New York: Macmillan, 1999.
Oehlschlaeger, Fritz. *Love and Good Reasons*. Durham, NC: Duke University Press, 2003.
O'Farrell, Mary Ann. *Telling Complexions: The Nineteenth-Century English Novel and the Blush*. Durham, NC and London: Duke University Press, 1997.
Palgrave, Francis Turner. "Miss Austen and Lyme," *The Grove* I (1894), 390–94.
Plasa, Carl. *Textual Politics from Slavery to Postcolonialism: Race and Identification*. New York: St Martin's Press, 2000.
Plomin, Robert, *et al*. "Parent-Offspring and Sibling Adoption Analyses of Parental Ratings of Temperament in Infancy and Childhood," *Journal of Personality* LIX (1991), 705–32.
———, and Denise Daniels. "Why Are Children in the Same Family So Different from One Another?," *Behavioral and Brain Sciences* X (1987), 1–60.
Poovey, Mary. *The Proper Lady and the Woman Writer*. Chicago, IL and London: University of Chicago Press, 1984.
Prodger, Phillip. "Photography and *The Expression of the Emotions*," in *The Expression of the Emotions in Man and Animals*, with an introduction, afterword and commentaries by Paul Ekman. New York and Oxford: Oxford University Press, 1998.
Rossdale, P. S. A. "What Caused the Quarrel Between Mr. Collins and Mr. Bennet? Observations on the Entail of Longbourn," *Notes and Queries* XXVII (1980), 503–4.
Said, Edward W. *Culture and Imperialism*. New York: Alfred A. Knopf, 1993.
Scarr, Sandra, and Susan Grajek. "Similarities and Differences among Siblings," in *Sibling Relationships: Their Nature and Nurture Across the Lifespan*, ed. Michael E. Lamb and Brian Sutton-Smith. Hillsdale, NJ: Lawrence Erlbaum, 1982, pp. 357–81.
Schorer, Mark. "The Humiliation of Emma Woodhouse," in *Jane Austen: A Collection of Critical Essays*, ed. Ian Watt. Englewood Cliffs, NJ: Prentice-Hall, 1963.
Scott, Sir Walter. *Journal of Sir Walter Scott*, ed. W. K. Anderson. Oxford: Clarendon Press, 1972.

Seeber, Barbara K. *General Consent in Jane Austen: A Study in Dialogism.* Montreal: McGill-Queen's, 2000.

Smith, Adam. "History of the Ancient Logics and Metaphysics," in *Essays on Philosophical Subjects*, ed. W. P. D. Wightman and J. C. Bryce. Oxford: Clarendon, 1980.

Smith, Johanna M. "'My only sister now': Incest in *Mansfield Park*," *Studies in the Novel* XIX.1 (Spring 1987), 1–15.

Southam, Brian. *Jane Austen's Manuscripts.* New York: Oxford, 1964.

———. "*Sanditon*: The Seventh Novel," in *Jane Austen's Achievement*, ed. Juliet McMaster. New York: Barnes and Noble, 1976, pp. 1–26.

———. "The Silence of the Bertrams: Slavery and the Chronology of Mansfield Park," *TLS* (17 February 1995), 13–14.

Staves, Susan. *Married Women's Separate Property in England, 1660–1833.* London and Cambridge, MA: Harvard, 1990.

Stewart, Maaja A. *Domestic Realities and Imperial Fictions: Jane Austen's Novels in Eighteenth-Century Contexts.* Athens, GA: University of Georgia Press, 1993.

Stott, Rebecca. *Darwin and the Barnacle.* London: Faber and Faber, 2003.

Sulloway, Frank J. "The *Beagle* Collections of Darwin's Finches (*Geospizinae*)," *Bulletin of the British Museum of Natural History (Zoology)*, XLIII (1982), 49–94.

———. *Born to Rebel: Birth Order, Family Dynamics, and Creative Lives.* New York: Pantheon, 1996.

———. "Darwin and His Finches: The Evolution of a Legend," *Journal of the History of Biology* XV (1982), 1–53.

———. "Darwin's Conversion: The *Beagle* Voyage and Its Aftermath," *Journal of the History of Biology* XV (1982), 325–96.

Tennyson, Hallam, Lord. *Alfred Lord Tennyson: A Memoir by His Son.* London: Macmillan, 1897.

Thompson F. M. L. *English Landed Society in the Nineteenth Century.* London, Routledge & Kegan Paul, 1963.

Todd, Janet (ed.). *Jane Austen: New Perspectives.* New York: Holmes and Meier, 1983.

Tomalin, Claire. *Jane Austen: A Life.* New York: Knopf, 1997.

Torrens, Hugh. "Mary Anning (1799–1847) of Lyme: 'the greatest fossilist the world ever knew,'" *British Journal for the History of Science* XXVIII (1995), 257–84.

Tuite, Clara. "Domestic Retrenchment and Imperial Expansion: The Property Plots of Mansfield Park," in *The Postcolonial Jane Austen*, eds You-me Park and Rajeswari Sunder Rajan. New York: Routledge, 2000, pp. 93–115.

———. *Romantic Austen: Sexual Politics and the Literary Canon.* London: Cambridge University Press, 2002.

Waldron, Mary. *Jane Austen and the Fiction of Her Time.* London: Cambridge University Press, 1999.

Walpole, Horace. *Horace Walpole's Correspondence*, ed. W. S. Lewis. New Haven, CT: Yale University Press, 1960.

Watson, James. *The Indelible Stamp: The Evolution of an Idea.* Philadelphia, PA: Running Press, 2005.

Watt, Ian. *The Rise of the Novel: Studies in Defoe, Richardson, and Fielding.* Berkeley, CA and Los Angeles: University of California Press, 1957.

Weiner, Jonathan. *The Beak of the Finch: A Story of Evolution in Our Time.* New York: Knopf, 1994.

Whewell, William. *Selected Writings on the History of Science*, ed. Yehuda Elkana. Chicago, IL: University of Chicago Press, 1984.

White, Laura Moneyham. "Jane Austen and the Marriage Plot: Questions of Persistence," *Jane Austen and Discourses of Feminism*, ed. Devoney Looser. New York: St Martin's Press, 1995, pp. 71–86.

Williams, Raymond. *The Country and the City.* New York: Oxford University Press, 1973.

_____. *The English Novel from Dickens to Lawrence.* New York: Oxford University Press, 1970.

Wilson, Edward O. *From So Simple a Beginning: The Four Great Books of Darwin.* New York: Norton, 2006.

_____. *Sociobiology: The New Synthesis.* Cambridge, MA and London: Belknap Press of Harvard University Press, 1975.

Wiltshire, John. "Decolonising Mansfield Park," *Essays in Criticism* LIII.4 (October 2003), 303–22.

_____. *Jane Austen and the Body.* Cambridge: Cambridge University Press, 1992.

Wollstonecraft, Mary. *A Vindication of the Rights of Men with A Vindication of the Rights of Woman and Hints*, Cambridge Texts in the History of Political Thought ed. Sylvana Tomaselli. Cambridge: Cambridge University Press, 1995.

Index

Because brief and comparative discussion of Austen's novels and characters pervade the chapters of this book, the following index does not contain all references to individual texts or characters. Novels' citations refer to passages in which discussion centers on an individual text. The same is true for Austen's characters. References to them are not indexed with separate entries but are mentioned within the listings of the novels in which they appear.

Allen, David Elliston 184
Anning, Mary 171–2
Anthropomorphism 143, 163
Arran, Isle of 22–3, 31
Artificial selection 135–6
    and domestic pigeons 137–42
    breeders' tastes and 140–42
Associational psychology 148
Attachments in Austen's novels 104–109
Austen, Anna 17–18
Austen, Caroline 101, 184
Austen, Cassandra 15, 50–51, 53, 148, 172–3
    engagement to Tom Fowle 103
Austen, Cassandra Leigh (Mrs.) 52
Austen, Charles 50–51
Austen, Edward 50–51,
    and Chawton's disentailment 101
Austen, Eliza 50
Austen, Francis 50–51
Austen, George 50–51
Austen, Rev. George 52, 98
Austen, Henry, 18, 50–51
Austen, James 18, 50–51
Austen, Jane "3 or 4 Families in a Country Village" 1, 17–18, 21
    amid her siblings 50–51
    and minutae 16
    as uniformitarian novelist 148–50
    correspondence with James Stanier Clarke 19–21
    defense of novels 21–2
    education of 52
    letter on mutability 148
    possible romantic attachment formed at Lyme 173
    principles of thinking and writing 15–22
    proposal from Harris Bigg Wither 103
    writes to Cassandra from Lyme Regis 172–3
Austen, Jane, Works:
    The Beautifull Cassandra 152
    Emma 183
        as "knowable community" 30–45
        blushing in 158–62
            Harriet Smith 159
            Jane Fairfax 159–60
            Emma Woodhouse 160–62
        concluding marriages in 118–19
        dedication to the Prince Regent 19–20
        Emma as imaginist 39–41
        Harriet Smith as empirical observer 36, 38–9
        Knightley brothers' personality development 70–71
        Miss Bates as "mere empiricist" 36–38
        Mrs. Elton's tiresome loquacity 35–6
        sketching Harriet's portrait 41–5
        Woodhouse sisters 80–81
    Love and Freindship 152–3
    Mansfield Park 183
        concluding marriages in 113–14
        Sir Thomas Bertram as possible slave-owner 56–8

Ward sisters' divergent personalities
and marriages 71–4
Northanger Abbey 30, 183
Catherine Morland blushing in
157–8
concluding marriages in 112–13
defense of novels 21–2
Morland family 64–6
Persuasion 30, 183
concluding marriages in 119–20
Elliot sisters 80–81
Lyme Regis's significance in 174–9
Musgrove family 66–7
Pride and Prejudice 29–30, 183
Bennet sisters 81–6
Chapman's chronology of 149
concluding marriages in 117–18
Mr. Collins's proposal to Elizabeth
93–5
primogeniture and 100–101
Sanditon 179–80
Sense and Sensibility 29, 183
blushing in 155–6
concluding marriages in 114–17
Dashwood sisters 76–80
Jenkins sisters 75–6
Steele sisters 75–6
Austen–Leigh, James Edward 18–19, 31,
180, 184

Barash, David P. and Nanelle R. 184
Bacon, Francis 6, 13
Barber, Bernard 5, 184
Barber, Elinor 4–5
Barlow, Nora 11–12, 24, 96, 130, 183
Barnacles 26–9, 45
Beagle voyage 13, 23
father opposed Darwin embarking on 54
geological observations on 147–8
Bees 143–4
Behaviorism 163
Bell, Charles 164
Blake, William 22, 184
Blushing 151–68, 178
Austen's blushing heroines 156–62
comparison of Austen and Darwin on
blushing 167–8
contemporary medical understanding of
166–7

Darwin's study of 162–7
etymology of word 151–2
figurative and hypothetical blushes
154–5
in *Sense and Sensibility* 155–6
physiology of 164–7
Blyth, Edward 139
Boccacio 8
Bovary, Emma 32
Brown, Julia Prewitt 87, 184
Browne, Janet 54, 56, 143, 181, 184
Buckland, William 170, 172
Burgess, Thomas 165
Buswell, B. 166
Butler, Marilyn 180, 184
Byron, George Gordon, Lord 16, 150–51,
176, 184

Campbell, John A. 184
Cape Verde Islands 23
Castelfranchi, C. 166, 185
Catastrophism 133–4, 146–8
and Noah's flood 146–7
Catskill wolves 84
Chancellor, John 54, 185
Chambers, Robert 11, 29
Chapman, R. W. 149
Childbirth 104
Clarke, James Stanier 19–21
Cobb, the 169, 172–4
in *Persuasion* 177–8
Coleridge, Samuel Taylor 6, 10, 185
Conybeare, William 170, 172
Cooper, Richard C. 166
Coral reefs 15, 147–8
Cuvier, Georges 146

Daniels, Denise 48, 186
Daphne Major 25–6, 31, 146
Darwin, Caroline 53, 55–6
Darwin, Charles amid his siblings 53–6
anxiety about consanguineous marriages
127–9
as writer 14
breeding pigeons 137–42
children who died young 130
geological observations and theories
146–8
illness or weakness in family 130

Index

in search of a wife 89–93
loss of imaginative and aesthetic
    pleasures 14
orchid observations 142–6
proposal to Emma Wedgwood 95–8
relations with father 53–4
relations with mother 54–5
religious doubts 131
self-assessment 12–15
study of blushing 162–8
use of photographs 163
Darwin, Charles, Works:
Autobiography 10–15, 183
    tribute to Emma, 131
"Biographical Sketch of an Infant" 162
Coral Reefs 147–8, 183
Cross and Self-Fertilization 128, 183
Descent of Man 100–102, 183
    marriage in 125–8
Erasmus Darwin 11–12, 184
Expression of the Emotions 162–8, 183
Formation of Vegetable Mould through the Action of Worms 179–82, 184
Geological Observations on South America 147–8, 184
Journal of Researches 184
Orchids 14, 142–6, 183
    advantages of intercrossing detailed in 143
Origin of Species 14, 45, 182–3
    Catskill wolves in 84
    CD's instructions to Emma for publication 27, 131–2
    concluding paragraph 47
    genesis of 29
    inbreeding and outcrossing in 128, 143
    "Ornithological Notes," 183
Structure and Distribution of Coral Reefs 184
Variation 16, 135–42, 183
Volcanic Islands 147–8, 184
Darwin, Emily Catherine 53, 55
Darwin, Emma Wedgwood 11, 27, 54
    CD's decision to propose to 90–91, 95–8
    CD's appreciation of 130–31
    religious faith of 131
Darwin, Erasmus (CD's grandfather) 10–12, 28, 53–4

and *Loves of the Plants* 28, 143
Darwin, Erasmus Alvey 53, 55–6
Darwin, Francis 27, 144, 181
    pilgrimage to Lyme Regis 173–4, 185
Darwin, George 128
Darwin, Henrietta 138
Darwin, Horace 181
Darwin, Marianne 53, 55
Darwin, Robert Waring 10–12, 53–4, 56, 91
    grief over wife's death 55
Darwin, Susan 53, 55
Darwin, Susanna Wedgwood 10, 53, 55
Darwin, William 162
Dawkins, Richard 78, 185
Dear, Peter 185
Defoe, Daniel 8
Descartes 8
Design 144–5, 163–5
Desmond, Adrian 27, 185
Disruptive selection 49–50
Drake, Stillman 50, 185
Duchenne, Guillaume 164
Duckworth, Alistair 180, 185
Dunn, Judy 48, 185

Ekman, Paul 162–63, 166, 183
Eliot, George 31, 34, 149
Empiricism 2–4, 12, 23
    in *Emma* 32–5
Entailment 99
    and Austen family 101
Emsley, Sarah 149, 185

Farrer, Thomas 180
Ferguson, Moira 57, 185
Feuillide, comtesse de *See* Austen, Eliza
Fielding, Henry 8
Finches 23–6, 146
Firstborn siblings in Austen novels 68–9
Flaubert, Gustave 32
Forbes, Edward 28
Fossils 147
    discovered at Lyme Regis 170–72
Fowle, Thomas Craven 51, 103
Fowles, John, 169–70, 185
Fox, William Darwin 45, 137–8, 140

Galápagos Islands 23–6, 146
Galileo 50

Galton, Francis 10, 128–9
Gardners Chronicle 142
Gattaca 129
Geology 13
    of Lyme Regis 170–72
    variation in 146–8
Gérard, Frédéric 28
Gould, John 25
Gottschall, Jonathan 185
Grajek, Susan 48
Grant, Peter and Rosemary 25–6, 146, 185
Grant, Robert 28
Gray, Asa 144
Greenacre, Phyllis 54, 186
Greenhill, William Alexander 186

Halperin, John 180, 186
Hamilton, William D. 78
Hardy, Thomas 175
Henslow, John Stevens 12–13
Herschel, John 3–4, 186
Hobbes, Thomas 152
Home, Sir Everard 171
Homology 145
Hooker, J.D. 27, 142
Horner, Leonard 90
Horner sisters ("the Horneritas") 90
Horwood, John 143
Hutton, James 22–3, 146–7, 186
Huxley, Aldous 129
Huxley, Julian 54, 186
Huxley, T.H. 3–4, 7, 28, 186

Ichthyosaurus 171
Inbreeding 127–30, 168
Inchbald, Elizabeth 91–2, 186

Jacobus, Mary 35, 186
James, Henry 149
Jamoussi, Zouheir 99, 186
Johnson, Claudia L. 87, 112, 115, 186

Keltner, Dachwe 166, 186
Kettlewell, H.B.D. 54
"knowable communities," 9, 22–45
    barnacles 26–29
    Daphne Major finches 25–6
    Highbury as 30–45
    Galápagos Islands 23–6

Hutton and the Isle of Arran 22–3
Knox-Shaw, Peter 148–9, 180, 186
Konisberg, Ira 9, 186

Lamarck, Jean Baptiste 11, 163
Landau, Misia 186
Lane, Maggie 169, 177, 186
Le Faye, Deirdre 1, 15, 186
Lefroy, Fanny Caroline 169, 186
Lefroy, Tom 148
Levine, George 186
Lewis, Michael 166, 186
Lloyd, Martha 16
Locke, John 8
Loehlin, John C. 48, 186
Lubbock, Sir John 128
Lyell, Charles 13
Lyme Regis 169–79
    Austen visit to 172–3
    fossil hunters in 170–72
    history of 169–70
    landslide of 1839 172
    role in *Persuasion* 174–9

MacIntyre, Alasdair 187
Macpherson, Sandra 99, 187
Marriage 87–132
    and Darwin's "This is the Question 91–3
    and eugenics 129–30
    as sexual selection 102
    money and 98–101
    Charles and Emma Darwin's 124–5, 130–32
    consanguineous 128–9
    in Austen's novels 109–124
        mid–novel marriages 110–12
        marriages concluding *Northanger Abbey* 112–13
        Mansfield Park 113–14
        Sense and Sensibility 114–17
        Pride and Prejudice 117–18
        Emma 118–19
        Persuasion 119–20
        married couples, 121–4
    in Darwin's *Descent of Man* 125–8
McGowan, Christopher 171, 187
Meade, Margaret 163
Mendel, Gregor 10, 127, 168

Merton, Robert K. 4–5, 187
Mill, James 3–4, 187
Miller, Jonathan 53–4, 187
Mockingbirds 24
Money and marriage 101
    Austen family finances 98
    Darwin family finances 98
    dowries in Austen's novels 99
Moore, Alexander 143
Moore, James 27, 185
Multi–sibling families Austens 50–53, 102–103
    Darwins 53–4, 102
    Morlands 64–6
    Musgroves 66–7
    Wedgwoods 54

Natural selection 47, 136
    and Galápagos finches 23–5
    and orchids 144–5
    primogeniture at odds with 100
Naturalist 2, 6–7
Neill, Edward 115–16, 187
Neville, Lady Dorothy 143
Novel(ists) 2, 8–10, 21–2

Oehlschlaeger, Fritz 70, 80, 187
O'Farrell, Mary Ann 153, 187
Only children in Austen's novels 61
Orchids 142–6, 168
Owen, Fanny 89, 94
Owen, Richard 171–2

Palgrave, Francis Turner 169, 187
Photographs, Darwin's use of 163
Pigeons 16, 137–42
    breeders 139–42
    common descent from *columba livia* 141
Plasa, Carl 187
Plomin, Robert 48, 187
Poggi, I. 166, 185
Primogeniture 69–71, 100
    and male characters in Austen novels 100–102
    in *Descent of Man* 100–101
Poovey, Mary 116, 187
Prodger, Phillip 163, 187

Realism 8, 34
Rhea darwinii 135
Richardson, Samuel 8
Romance 8–9, 21
Rossdale, P.S.A. 99, 187
Rutherfurd, Edward-*Sarum* 149

Said, Edward W. 57, 187
Scarr, Sandra 48, 187
Schorer, Mark 161, 187
Scientist 2, 6–7, 12
Scott, Sir Walter 19, 176, 187
Sedgwick, Adam 13
*See*ber, Barbara K. 113, 116, 188
" Selfish gene" 78
Sensibility 152–3, 161
Serendipity 2, 4–5, 23
Sexual selection 126–8
    marriage as 102
Shaftesbury, Lord 152
Sibling personality development in Austen's novels 58–86
    in dysfunctional families 67–8
    in the Austen family 50–53
    in the Darwin family 53–6
    of brothers in Austen novels 69–71
    of firstborns in Austen novels 68–9
    of sisters in Austen novels 74–85
    Sulloway's theory of 47–50
Sisters in Austen novels 74–85
    Bennet sisters 81–5
    Dashwood sisters 76–81
    Elliot sisters 77
    Jenkins sisters 75–6
    Steele sisters 75–6
Slavery, and *Mansfield Park* 56–8
    Darwin's comparison of marriage to 96–7
Smith, Adam 150–51, 188
Smith, Johanna M. 113, 188
Southam, Brian 57, 180, 188
Southey, Robert 35
Spencer, Herbert 136
Spiranthes autumnalis 144
Staves, Susan 99, 188
Stewart, Maaja A. 57, 188
Stott, Rebecca 27, 188
Sulloway, Frank J. 24, 47–51, 53, 61, 68, 76, 80, 188

Darwinian theory of sibling
    differentiation 46–50
sibling theory applied to Austen's novels
    58–86
"survival of the fittest" 136

Taine, Hippolyte 162
Tegetmeier, William 140
Tennyson, Alfred, Lord 173
Tennyson, Hallam, Lord 173, 188
Thompson, F.M.L. 72, 188
Todd, Janet 188
Tomalin, Claire 98, 169, 188
Torrens, Hugh 171, 188
Tortoises 24
Tuite, Clara 57, 112, 188
Turnbull, George 143
Two–parent families in Austen novels 64–7

Uniformitarianism 133–4, 146–8
    and Austen's novels 148–50
Ussher, Bishop James 146

Van Loon, Boren 53–4
Variation 23–4, 133–82

biological 134
in Austen's character types 134
in *Persuasion* 168–9, 174–80
meanings of the word 134
Vonnegut, Kurt 23

Waldron, Mary 112, 188
Wallace, Alfred Russel 7, 29
Walpole, Horace 2, 4–7, 188
Watson, James 188
Watt, Ian 8–9, 189
Wedgwood, Emma *see* Darwin, Emma
    Wedgwood
Wedgwood, Josiah 10, 53–4, 181
Weiner, Jonathan 25–6, 189
Wells, H. G. *The Time Machine* 149
Whewell, William 6–7, 189
White, Laura Mooneyham 115, 189
Wilkerson, Stephen Y. 166
Williams, Raymond 9, 189
Wilson, Edward O. 78, 189
Wiltshire, John 57, 153, 189
Wither, Harris Bigg 103
Wollstonecraft, Mary 78, 189
Wordsworth, William 35